Strategy
and
Policy Formation:

a multifunctional orientation

Strategy
and
Policy Formation:
a multifunctional
orientation

Robert C. Shirley
state university of new york, albany
Michael H. Peters
Adel I. El-Ansary
louisiana state university

A Wiley/Hamilton Publication
JOHN WILEY & SONS, INC.
Santa Barbara • New York • London • Sydney • Toronto

Library of Congress Cataloging in Publication Data:
Shirley, Robert C.
    Strategy and policy formation.

    "A Wiley/Hamilton publication."
    Includes bibliographies and index.
    1. Decision-making.   2. Industrial management.
I. Peters, Michael H., joint author.   II. el-Ansary,
Adel I., joint author.   III. Title.
HD69.D4S45   658.4'03   75-25814
ISBN 0-471-78643-8

Contents

1 STRATEGY AND POLICY: a framework for analysis 3

Case Studies and Computer Simulations 4

    The Analysis of Cases 4
    Use of This Text in Case Analysis 5

An Overview of the Framework 6

Stage 1: Classification of Case Data 6

    Environmental Dimension 8
    Strategic Dimension 8
    Program Dimension 9
    Structural Dimension 9
    Behavioral Dimension 10
    Additional Remarks 11

Stage 2: Analysis of Case Data 11

    The Class 1 and Class 2 Decision Variables 13
    The Class 3 and Class 4 Decision Variables 15
    Additional Remarks 16

Stage 3: Identification of Problems and/or Issues 17

Stage 4: Formulation of Recommendations 18

Summary 19

READING: Powell, Reed M., *"The Multidimensional Field of Management"* 21

2 STRATEGIC DECISIONS: the impact of environmental forces 27

The Concept of Strategy 27

v

The Strategic Decisions 28
Determinants of Strategy 30
The Relationship of Strategy Formulation to
Implementation 31
The Strategy Formulation Process 31
Environmental Forces 31
Economic Forces 31
Social Forces.. 34
Technological Forces 35
Political/Legal Forces 36
Environmental Research: Its Role and Forms 37
Summary 39
READING: Mintzberg, Henry, *"Strategy Making in
Three Modes"* 40

3 STRATEGY FORMULATION: relating environmental forces to internal capabilities and values 59

The Assessment of Capabilities 59
The Capability or Resource Audit 59
Human Resources... 60
Financial Resources 60
Physical Resources and Production 60
Marketing.. 60
Research and Development.. 60
Organizational 60
Present Strategic Posture 61
Environmental Research Capabilities 61
Establishing a Competitive Advantage.................................... 61
The Concept of Synergy... 62
The Influence of Personal Values on Strategy 64
Culturally Derived Values 65
Organizationally Derived Values... 67
Cases of Conflicting Values 67
The Resolution of Conflicting Values 69
Summary 70
READING: Buchele, Robert B., *"How to Evaluate a Firm"* 72

4 MARKETING: the interdependent nature of decision making 95

Marketing Decision Variables 96

Product Research and Development 97
Marketing Research and Information Systems 102
Distribution Channel Structure 104
Price 105
Discounts: Type and Structure 106
Promotion 107
Credit 109
Packaging 110
Physical Distribution and Inventory Levels 110
Functionally Independent Marketing Variables 114
Summary 115
READING: Adler, Lee, *"A New Orientation for Plotting
Marketing Strategy"* 116

5 PRODUCTION/OPERATIONS: a multifunctional view 137

Types of Production/Operations Systems 139
Production/Operations Decision Variables 140
Plant Location and Capacity 140
Facilities Layout 144
Process Planning and Job Design 147
Planning of Aggregate Output 150
Raw Materials and Work-in-Process Inventory
Levels 151
Functionally Independent Production/Operations
Decision Variables 152
Summary 153
READING: Skinner, Wickham, *"Manufacturing—Missing Link
in Corporate Strategy"* 154

6 FINANCIAL ANALYSIS: process and techniques 171

Finance Decision Variables 172
Level of Working Capital 172
Level of Dividend Payment 174
Functionally Independent Finance Variables 177
Financial Analysis in Business Policy Cases 177
Analysis of the Situation 177
Basic Financial Statements 178
Evidence of Financial Objectives 178
Evidence of External Effectiveness 178

Profitability Indicators 178
Liquidity Indicators 181
Leverage Indicators 181
Overall Ability to Obtain Funds 181
Evidence of Internal Efficiency.. 182
Further Analysis of Financial Indicators 182
Diagnosis of Problems 195
Development of Plans of Action 196
Break-Even Analysis.. 198
Summary 203

7 ORGANIZATIONAL STRUCTURE: a general management perspective 207

Forces Affecting the Evolution of
Organizational Structure.. 208
Time 208
Size of the Organization 208
Product/Market Complexity 209
Growth Rate of the Industry... 209
Alternative Structural Forms 210
The "Small" Structure 210
The Functional Structure 211
The Divisional Structure 212
Product Departmentation 214
Territorial Divisionalization 215
Basic Advantages 215
Project Management 215
The Matrix Organization 219
Summary 222
READING: Lorsch, Jay W. and Lawrence, Paul R.,
"Organizing for Product Innovation" 223

8 ORGANIZATIONAL CHANGE: an integrated approach 243

The Concept of Organizational Change.................................... 243
The Organizational Change Process 245
Forces Toward Change.. 245
Perception of Forces.. 245
Development of Change Goals... 247
Determination of Change Targets 249
Organization for Implementation 249

Determination of Change Tactics and Channels
of Influence 249
Results of Change and Intervening Variables 251
Additional Remarks 251

Resistance to Change 252

Openness to Change 252
Method of Implementation of Change 253
Other Factors Affecting Acceptance of Change 255

Summary 257

INDEX **259**

About the Authors

ROBERT C. SHIRLEY received his Ph.D. in Policy and Environment from Northwestern University. Presently he is Assistant to the President and Associate Professor, Business Administration, SUNY, Albany. He has also been on the faculty at Louisiana State University. Articles by Dr. Shirley have appeared in the *Academy of Management Journal, Journal of General Management, MSU Business Topics,* and other journals. He is a Vice President of the Southwest Division, Academy of Management and an active member in other professional groups. His current research interests are goal formation processes and long-range planning in higher education.

MICHAEL H. PETERS received both his D.B.A. and M.B.A. in Production Management from Indiana University. He also holds a B.M.E. from General Motors Institute. At present, he is an Associate Professor at Louisiana State University and has had many years of industrial experience, including private consulting work with Exxon Corporation and the Louisiana Board of Education. Articles by Dr. Peters have appeared in such publications as *Current Concepts in Management,* edited by O. Jeff Harris, and in *Proceedings of the American Institute for Decision Sciences Fourth Annual Meeting,* and he is coeditor of the *Proceedings of the Fifteenth Annual Meeting of the Academy of Management, Southwest Division.* Dr. Peters is a member of numerous professional and honorary associations.

ADEL I. EL-ANSARY, Associate Professor of Marketing at Louisiana State University, is a native of the Arab Republic of Egypt. He received his B.Com. from Cairo University in Egypt and his M.B.A. and Ph.D. in Marketing from Ohio State University. Dr. El-Ansary served as a research assistant and consultant at the National Institute for Management Development (NIMD), Cairo, Egypt, before commencing his graduate study as a Fulbright Scholar. He also served as a research assistant and associate during his graduate study at Ohio State. His articles have appeared in the *Journal of Marketing, Journal of the Academy of Marketing Science, Journal of Marketing Research,* and *Journal of Retailing.* He serves on the Board of Editors and Reviewers of the first two. Dr. El-Ansary is an active member of the American Marketing Association, Southern Marketing Association, Academy of Marketing Science, and Beta Gamma Sigma. He is also a member of the National Advisory Council to the United Small Business Administration. His research and teaching interests are in the areas of distribution channels, international marketing, social marketing, and corporate strategy and business policy.

Preface

In recent years, new developments in the fields of strategy, policy, and general management have brought about more meaningful approaches to managing a total enterprise. The "general management perspective" is now recognized as being quite different from a functional or elemental perspective on organizational problems. This is because the unit of analysis that is of concern to a general manager is the *total* organization, rather than any specialized part of it. The general manager is confronted with problems and issues that transcend functional area boundaries and cannot be neatly categorized as, for example, purely marketing or financial in nature. This multifunctional nature of the general manager's job derives from his two major tasks: (1) definition of the relationship between the total organization and its environment (external-oriented), and (2) coordination and control of total organizational activities to effectuate a defined strategy (internal-oriented). It is obvious that a specialist or elemental view of an enterprise is inappropriate to those two basic tasks.

This book presents a general management, or holistic, view of organizational decision-making that covers both strategy formulation and functional area interrelationships. It is intended for use in policy courses that utilize either case analysis or computer simulation exercises as primary learning tools. It begins by developing a framework that identifies the major parts of the organization, and the nature of their "linkages," through various decision processes. The remainder of the book elaborates on the major elements of that framework. Chapters 2 and 3 cover the subject of corporate strategy in some detail. Chapters 4, 5, and 6 focus on marketing, production, and finance, respectively, with emphasis on the *interactions* that occur between the functional areas for decision-making purposes. Chapter 7 discusses the alternative forms of organizational structure available to a firm, and pays particular attention to the interrelation of strategy and structure. Since students are always faced with the problem of developing recommendations and providing for their implementation, Chapter 8 discusses the subject of organizational change at some length. Finally, readings are included after certain chapters to add depth to the discussion of particular issues. Such readings have been chosen on the basis of quality, unconstrained by any artificial criteria such as date and/or source of publication.

This book does *not* provide students with all the material needed to fully address and resolve the numerous issues related to strategy and policy formation. No single volume can accomplish that end, because the very nature of policy courses presumes—and indeed usually demands—that students complete prerequisites in management, organizational behavior, marketing, finance, economics, accounting, production/operations, and quantitative methods. Consequently, this book aims at the development of a structure for analysis—a means by which students can approach the complex and multidimensional field of policy. This analytical structure should facilitate the resolution of problems from a general manager's perspective and prevent the student from becoming hopelessly enmeshed in the vast number of details usually found in policy cases. The authors have frequently found it necessary to deal with some issues in a rather broad fashion in order to develop a comprehensive scheme. However, the approach taken is consistent with the assumption that students in a policy course have completed a set of prerequisites similar to those mentioned above.

Many individuals have contributed to the development of this book. The authors extend special thanks to Raymond V. Kinnunen, now Assistant Professor at Northeastern University in Boston, for his contributions toward development of the overall framework and for material on the subject of strategy and organizational structure. Several reviewers have made invaluable comments: Charles Wetmore, California State University at Fresno; Geoffrey King, California State University at Fullerton; Charles Gudger, Oregon State University; Earl Goddard, Oregon State University; and Elliott Carlisle, University of Massachusetts. With their help, many improvements were made in the original draft of the manuscript. Mrs. Gloria Armstead and Ms. Liz Anderson, both of Louisiana State University, deserve special gratitude for their excellent and tireless typing of the manuscript. Finally, the authors are, of course, indebted to their wives, who exhibited the patience and offered the encouragement necessary for the completion of this book. It is dedicated to them.

Robert C. Shirley

Michael H. Peters

Adel I. El-Ansary

Strategy
and
Policy Formation:

a multifunctional
orientation

1

Strategy and Policy:
a framework for analysis

Strategy and Policy:

a framework for analysis

In the past few years, the field of corporate strategy and policy has received increasing attention. Many undergraduate and graduate business curricula now include a required integrative course in policy.[1] These courses focus on the application of broad, diverse skills to the solution of complex business problems that transcend traditional functional area boundaries. Because of this, most students must complete courses in marketing, finance, accounting, economics, quantitative methods, production/operations, organization behavior, and general management before they can enter a policy course. This allows the course to focus on problems and issues that are *multifunctional* in nature—those problems and issues that cannot be neatly categorized as, for example, purely financial or purely marketing in nature. Emphasis is placed on viewing the firm as a complex system and on seeing the relations between the various functional areas from the perspective of a general manager. Consequently, the nature of policy courses requires an integrative view of the various academic disciplines involved. Otherwise, the unique purposes and attributes of policy courses would be lost, and discussions would revert to purely financial, marketing, production, or organizational behavior problems.

The field of strategy and policy represents the study of top or general management decision making. Consequently, analysis must focus on the organization as a complete entity, rather than on a specific area or department. The emphasis on functional area interrelationships and the integration of all organizational activities in a policy course is derived from the two basic tasks that face all general managers: they must understand the interplay between the organization and its environment (external-oriented) and must integrate and direct the efforts of the total organization toward reaching predetermined objectives (internal-

---

[1] The American Assembly of Collegiate Schools of Business requires that undergraduate curricula include "a study of administrative processes under conditions of uncertainty, including integrating analysis and policy determination at the overall management level." Although the phraseology of this requirement may change, all indications are that the substance will remain the same for the foreseeable future.

oriented).[2] It is obvious that a specialist or elemental view of an organization is inappropriate to these two general tasks. This text focuses on the analytical constructs and methods that are useful for solving the multifunctional problems encountered in policy courses.

CASE STUDIES AND COMPUTER SIMULATIONS

Varied approaches to learning have been used to accomplish the integrative purpose of a policy course: computer simulation "games," case analyses, various experiential exercises, and more traditional lecture/discussion sessions. These approaches all have one thing in common when used in a policy course: they are directed toward solving problems and resolving issues from a general management perspective since, by definition, such a perspective *must* be multifunctional and integrative in nature. Case analysis is the most widely used vehicle for instilling this perspective in students and for developing a capacity for solving complex problems, although the other techniques mentioned (especially computer simulation exercises) have become increasingly popular in recent years. This book has been designed to assist students who are engaged in either case analysis or computer simulation exercises. For purposes of convenience, the word "cases" is used throughout the text, although the material should be of equal benefit to students using computer simulation as their primary learning tool.

The Analysis of Cases

The use of cases exposes the student to the real experiences of existing companies. This provides the opportunity to assess the past failures and successes of well-known firms in order to evaluate *why* certain actions or decisions were desirable, and why others were not. Case analysis is frequently criticized because complete information is not usually available to students—especially where company names are disguised and students cannot do outside research on the firm in question. But, when well-written cases that include most of the information relevant to understanding the total firm situation from a general management perspective are available, this ceases to be true. In addition, much important out-of-class research *can* be done on the industry or industries in which a particular firm operates. Besides, no one, not even the chief executive who actually experienced the events described in a case, ever has as much information as would be desirable in resolving matters of strategy and policy.

---

[2] As used here, the term "general manager" refers not only to the president or chief executive officer of an organization, but also to those individuals charged with the overall management and direction of the major units of a firm. Such units may be either subsidiaries or major product divisions of the larger organization. Thus, a "general manager" is one who manages and coordinates a variety of production, marketing, and financial activities in pursuit of the overall objectives of the unit or larger organization.

Thus, cases, as well as many simulation exercises, are realistic in the sense that some desirable information may be missing. This is characteristic of top-management decision making; consequently, the student is also exposed to some of the frustration and chagrin that is frequently experienced in the "real world." It is important that the student (1) recognize and delineate what desirable information is missing from a case, and treat this as a constraint on, or a limitation of, the analysis and (2) be willing to "stick his or her neck out" under conditions of uncertainty in order to make a decision—not hastily, but after a thorough and informed analysis.

Use of This Text in Case Analysis

This text has been designed as a comprehensive guide to the analysis of corporate strategy and policy. Specifically, it provides an approach to analysis and decision making that emphasizes functional interrelationships and focuses on the kinds of functional area analyses that should be performed from a general management perspective. Because of this, the book may be used in conjunction with traditional casebooks on policy or computer-simulation materials. Its analytical framework provides a foundation that will help the student to make the transition from a somewhat elemental view of an organization to a total systems or top-management approach.

The rest of this chapter takes the first step toward developing an analytical framework by constructing its "skeleton." Subsequent chapters "put the meat on the bones" by discussing functional area interrelationships in more detail. In this way, the material focuses on integrative, multifunctional approaches to analysis and a systemic perspective, rather than an elemental one, is stressed throughout.

There are no quick and easy formulae available for the solution of policy issues. A good deal of considered judgment is required to isolate complex problems and to develop workable recommendations for future action. Thus, although the analytical framework and integrative material in this book will help the student to structure and focus his or her efforts, it can provide no ready answers to many questions and issues encountered in policy cases and in computer simulations. Similarly, the student should recognize that there is very rarely only *one* desirable answer to questions of strategy and policy. The ability to reason through the limited information available, and to support one's conclusions with facts and/or logic, must be the primary criteria for evaluating work of this kind. Therefore, one should not be dismayed to learn that he or she has developed an analysis that is quite different from that of fellow students. Frequently the unique and creative solution is the most desirable one, but *only* if it can be supported with hard facts (where available), incisive logical reasoning, and the proper assessment of the implications of recommended courses of action. With this in mind, the student should be prepared to stretch and exercise imagination and analytical ability—not in the sense of "wild" or "far-out" conclusions under the guise of creativity, but by thorough and careful analysis of the information presented in order to develop sound, supportable conclusions.

AN OVERVIEW OF THE FRAMEWORK

Figure 1-1 presents an overview of the integrative framework for the analysis of strategy and policy cases. Stage 1 of the framework requires that all relevant case information be sifted and sorted along the five basic dimensions of any organization: environmental, strategic, program, structural, and behavioral. These basic organizational dimensions are explained more fully below. They represent a comprehensive set of categories for classifying all of the relevant information to be found in any case.

Stage 2 is where the process of *analysis* of the data really begins. Note that, in each area, analysis is conducted from the integrative total systems perspective of general or top management—as opposed to the more elemental perspective of a vice president of marketing, for example. Just how this may be accomplished is, of course, the basic subject matter of this book.

Stage 3 involves the identification of the problems and/or decision issues facing the firm. The analysis conducted in Stage 2 should indicate the major areas in which the firm is experiencing difficulties or facing unresolved issues. If difficulties exist, Stage 3 will require a decision as to *why* the difficulties are occurring. Where there are unresolved issues, the student will have to pinpoint the *specific* issues that must be resolved in order to ensure the future viability of the firm.

Finally, Stage 4 requires the student to either eliminate the problems or resolve the issues with appropriate recommendations.

This brief overview provides a basic background for a more detailed discussion of each major stage of the process.

STAGE 1: CLASSIFICATION OF CASE DATA

Because of the multifunctional nature of policy study, cases used in this course are necessarily very complex. They generally are somewhat longer than cases to which students have been exposed in such functional area courses as marketing and include descriptions of all the facets of a firm's operations, making it necessary to have some mechanism for *organizing* the case information. Without some attempt at organization before beginning the actual analysis, the student will likely become lost in a maze of seemingly unrelated incidents, issues, and problems. The following paragraphs delineate the elements of a comprehensive scheme which may be used to sift, sort, and classify all case data. It should be noted that not all of the types of information discussed below will be present in every case. Our task at this point, however, is to develop a comprehensive framework that will serve for all policy cases. As discussed earlier, five basic categories of information may be found in any case. These categories correspond to the basic dimensions or parts of any organization. Each dimension is discussed separately below. As the student reads through the case, he or she should attempt to classify all relevant information into one or more of these five categories.

Stage 1
Classification of Case Information

Organizational Dimensions

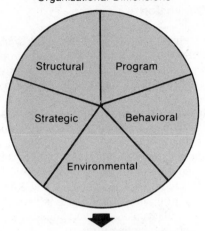

Stage 2
Analysis of Case Information

General Management Perspective

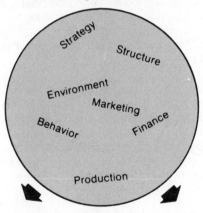

Stage 3
Identification of Problems and/or Issues

What are the underlying causes of observed difficulties?

What major issues must be resolved to ensure future viability?

Stage 4
Formulation of Recommendations

Elimination of problems

Resolution of issues

FIGURE 1-1: An integrative framework for the analysis of strategy and policy cases.

Environmental Dimension

First, every organization has an *environmental dimension* within which it operates. The particular external conditions faced by any firm always may be further classified into one of four major (although obviously interrelated) sectors of the environment. Each of these sectors is outlined as follows:

1. *Economic sector*—includes phenomena such as the nature of competition, structure of the industry, competitors' strengths and weaknesses, market trends, demand for products, money markets, capital markets, general economic conditions, lines of credit available to the firm, and other information which is economic in nature *and* external to the firm.
2. *Social sector*—includes larger societal values, ethical customs, consumer behavior, minority group influences, various demographic data of concern to the firm, the general issue of social responsibility, and similar phenomena.
3. *Technological sector*—includes information about technological developments in the industry or elsewhere that have an impact on new product development, improvement of production processes, and the like.
4. *Political/legal sector*—includes information related to legislation, regulatory agencies, court decisions, executive acts, foreign policy, tariffs, policies of other countries toward foreign investment, and similar matters which either may present new opportunities to the firm or act as constraints on its operations.

Taken together, these four sectors comprise the total set of environmental conditions faced by any firm. The dynamic nature of their influence on strategy formation and on internal operations is discussed more fully in Chapters 2 and 3. However, it should be noted that the various types of environmental forces present a firm with *both* opportunities and constraints. The basic task of top management is to develop an overall strategy for the firm that fully exploits available opportunities, subject to the constraints placed on it by the environment and by internal capabilities and resources.

Strategic Dimension

The *strategic dimension* of the firm refers to its basic product/market scope and objectives, both present and projected. Stated simply, every firm has a basic strategic posture which requires determination of, or decisions about, the following:

1. *Customer targets*—the market segment(s) of concern to the firm.
2. *Product mix*—the products to be produced and distributed to the market segments defined.
3. *Geographic limits of the market(s) to be served*—the boundaries of principal concern to the firm.

4. *Competitive emphasis*—some distinctive competence of the firm that gives it an edge over competitors.
5. *Objectives*—targets and performance criteria for the firm as a whole with regard to profitability, growth, market share, and survival.

Regardless of whether management has formulated a specific and *explicit* strategy, the student usually can infer the firm's present product/market scope, although future strategy may or may not be as evident. If it is not clear-cut, this would be dealt with in the subsequent stages of analysis and problem identification, to be discussed later. Similarly, specific objectives (for example, profitability, growth, market share, survival) for a given firm being studied may or may not be evident. The student should attempt to develop as much information about present and future strategy as possible at this stage, to be utilized in subsequent analyses of issues and problems. Chapters 2 and 3 discuss the concept and process of strategy formulation in detail in order to aid the student in his or her analysis.

Program Dimension

The *program dimension* of an organization comprises the plans developed by a firm to effect its overall strategy. This refers to information about the *technical specifics* of programs, in terms of objectives, processes, and techniques to be utilized in each implementation area to accomplish the firm's objectives. Included here would be the detailed plans for marketing (distribution, sales, promotion, and market research), finance, production, research and development, engineering, purchasing, personnel administration, and other major task areas. The three major programs of any firm are:

1. *Production*—information about plant and equipment, the technology of production, materials utilized, inventory management, scheduling, and similar matters would be classified here.
2. *Marketing*—this would include the structure of distribution channels, promotional programs and technologies, market research, salespeople and their territories, and similar information.
3. *Finance*—information about liquidity, leverage, profitability, and other elements of the firm's overall fiscal situation and methods of financial management would be classified here.

These three areas of analysis are covered in detail (from a general management perspective) in Chapters 4, 5, and 6 respectively.

Structural Dimension

The *structural dimension* of a firm refers to the formal arrangements, both horizontal and vertical, which have been established to coordinate the total activities involved in the implementation of a given strategy. In a sense, this dimension reflects the "anatomy" of a firm through its focus on mechanisms and processes that *link* (again, both vertically and horizontally) the various parts of an organization. For purposes of analysis it is useful to classify the major elements of organizational structure as follows:

1. *Distribution of functions throughout the organization*—includes definition of functions to be performed, groupings of functions, and the vertical and horizontal task relationships among functions.
2. *Vertical and horizontal authority relationships*—who has the authority to do what and in which areas.
3. *Reporting relationships*—definition of superior/subordinate relationships and spans of control.
4. *Communication/decision processes*—the manner in which formal decisions are made and by whom, supporting informational inputs, and the information systems established to provide the inputs to decision makers.
5. *Policies*—the decision rules or guidelines established in finance, marketing, production, personnel, purchasing, research and development, and other areas; these guidelines serve to tie the performance of specific functions to the firm's overall strategy and objectives.
6. *Formal incentive systems*—compensation plan characteristics, fringe benefits, incentive or bonus plans, promotion criteria, and other features of the organization's formal reward system.

Taken together, these structural elements establish the basic conditions under which organizational members perform their various roles. Information about each element should be gleaned from the case data and recorded for reference in accomplishing Stages 2 and 3, discussed below. The major focus for analysis of structure from a general management perspective is discussed in Chapter 7.

Behavioral Dimension

Finally, the *behavioral dimension* comprises various considerations related to human behavior in organizations. For the purpose of sorting and classifying case information, it is useful to subdivide this dimension as follows:

1. *The individual*—all relevant information related to individual beliefs, values, and attitudes should be recorded here, as well as overt behavior which appears to be dysfunctional; also includes considerations of abilities, satisfaction, personalities, and other behavioral phenomena of an individualistic nature.
2. *Interpersonal relationships*—whereas the preceding focus was on the individual, the appropriate information in this category relates to the interactions between two persons in accomplishing tasks. Any evidence of difficulties in personal interactions not of a group nature should be noted here (for example, constant friction between the heads of production and marketing).

3. *Group behavior*—all information related to the work group as a unit of analysis should be recorded here—presence or absence of group cohesiveness; informal group goals, leaders, and members; influence of the group over individuals; group norms; processes utilized by the group to maintain itself; and other behavioral phenomena which are of a group nature.
4. *Intergroup behavior*—whereas the preceding focus was on the single work group, the appropriate information in this category relates to the interactions of two or more work groups in accomplishing tasks. Any evidence of difficulties in group interactions that are not purely individualistic or interpersonal in nature should be noted here (for example, constant friction between all personnel in marketing and all personnel in production as a result of differing goal and value orientations across these two groupings).

The major focus for analysis of behavior from a general management perspective is discussed in Chapters 7 and 8.

Additional Remarks

The five basic dimensions and their components provide a comprehensive set of reference points for the student. Sorting and classifying information into the categories presented is the first step in "getting a handle" on a particular firm's characteristics and overall situation, both externally and internally. Figure 1-2 summarizes these categories. Once this step is completed, some order has been introduced into the process of analysis, and the student can proceed to Stage 2, discussed below. As a final note, it should be emphasized that the student is assumed to have completed the various functional area course requirements before embarking on a course in policy. Such a background should permit the student to distinguish between relevant and irrelevant information in this first stage of the process.

STAGE 2: ANALYSIS OF CASE DATA

Once the student has completed the "sifting and sorting" just described, he is ready to begin Stage 2 of the process. This is where analysis really begins, since Stage 1 has provided only the framework within which analysis may proceed. As depicted in Figure 1-1, the analysis is prepared from a "general management perspective" and focuses on the five major dimensions previously discussed (see Figure 1-2). The "program dimension" in Stage 2 has been subdivided into production, marketing, and finance to emphasize the importance of analysis in these three program areas. The remainder of the book provides much material to help the student in the analysis of all the areas shown. The material is *integrative* in nature, in keeping with the purposes of a policy course and the multifunctional nature of the general manager's job. For example, Chapter 4 focuses primarily on those marketing decision variables that are

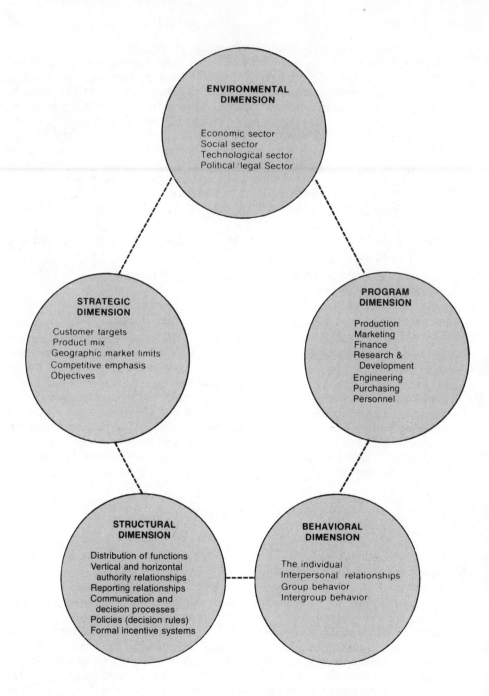

FIGURE 1-2: The five major dimensions and their components.

concerned with inputs received from such other functional areas as production and research and development. This approach should prevent the student from becoming hopelessly enmeshed in the innumerable marketing details that may be appropriate for consideration in a marketing problems course but not in a policy course. Furthermore, focusing on multifunctional decision variables necessarily means that they are the decisions of concern to the general manager who, by definition, is concerned with *coordinating* the numerous and diverse activities of a firm.

As stated before, the analytical emphasis in this text is on decision making. More specifically, the focus is on those decisions with which general or top management is most concerned, regardless of who actually has the responsibility for the decisions. Figure 1-3 has been prepared to lend some clarity to what this "general management perspective" entails. That figure distinguishes between four major classes of organizational decision variables: strategic (C_1), multifunctional coordinative (C_2), functionally dependent (C_3), and functionally independent (C_4). The types of decisions included in each class as well as the interrelationships of the four classes are discussed below.

The Class 1 and Class 2 Decision Variables

The C_1 (strategic) decision class includes decisions on the major strategic variables identified earlier in this chapter. Decisions concerning these variables define the basic relationship between the firm and its environment. Furthermore, once these decisions are made, they provide inputs to the decision-making process in the form of constraints on C_2 variables. This second class has been labeled "multifunctional coordinative decisions" because, like the C_1 variables, they are total-firm oriented and usually are finally made by top or general management. In relation to the C_1 (strategic) decisions, the C_2 decisions are *implemental* in nature and provide the basic set of major policies or conditions to guide lower-level organizational decisions and activities. Decisions here include the basic organizational structure (for example, definition of functions and their interrelationships, authority relationships, basic information flow processes to provide data for decision making); the allocation of resources (both for operating and capital budgets) to various divisions, departments, projects, or for other uses; manpower development programs, compensation plans, fringe benefit programs; financing policy, including sources of funds and desired capital structure; overall pricing policies; and basic operating objectives for various units of the firm.

The latter two C_2 decision variables deserve further elaboration. Overall pricing policy does *not* refer to specific decisions about the prices of individual items produced by a particular firm. Rather, it includes the basic policies developed by general or top management that guide the more specific marketing decisions on exact prices and discounts. Broad policies are necessary to ensure that specific product prices are consistent with overall firm objectives and resources. For example, Gulf Oil Corporation once had a company policy that banned participation in local gasoline "price wars"—a decision which obviously

Decision Variables
Class 1
Strategic decisions

Objectives	Customer mix
Product mix	Competitive emphasis
Geographic limits of market	

Class 2
Multifunctional coordinative decisions

Organizational structure, including information flows
Resource allocation (operating and capital budgets)
Manpower development and compensation policies
Financing policy
Functional area objectives
Pricing policy

Class 3
Functionally dependent decisions
PROGRAM AREAS

PRODUCTION	MARKETING	FINANCE
Examples:	Examples:	Examples:
Plant capacity	Distribution channels	Dividend policy
Production schedules	Prices and discounts	Working capital needs

Class 4
Functionally independent decisions

PRODUCTION	MARKETING	FINANCE
Examples:	Examples:	Examples:
Quality control techniques	Advertising media	Accounting procedures
Equipment maintenance schedules	Sales territories and routes	Cost analysis techniques

FIGURE 1-3: Classes of organizational decision variables.

had ramifications for the total firm and not just for its marketing activities. Another basic pricing policy decision (in this case, designed to achieve a basic competitive advantage) may be seen in A&P's 1972 decision to initiate its WEO (Where Economy Originates) program. This *resulted* in significant price reductions on many food and beverage items in the supermarket—quite different from the subsequent decision as to how much to reduce the price of, perhaps, a particular brand of lima beans.

Basic operating objectives for the various units of the firm necessarily must be derived from and be consistent with the overall objectives of the firm. Thus, if a firm's return on investment (ROI) objective is 13%, the particular sales volume objective for the marketing group must make a 13% ROI possible. Similarly, the firm's strategy with regard to product quality (an element of the product mix decision) must be translated into specific quality control objectives for the production area, such as "a 95% probability that no more than .001% of the units produced are defective." Regardless of whether these area or departmental objectives are determined unilaterally by top management or formulated through a consultative, mutual influence process with departmental heads, they represent the "link" between strategy formulation and implementation. Subsequent, lower-order decisions on methods to *implement* the area objectives then may be made by the functional areas affected. For example, quality control sampling techniques and inspection procedures can be decided upon by lower-level personnel charged with that responsibility.

To summarize, the C_2 multifunctional coordinative decisions link the overall strategy of a firm to actual operational activities. They provide, in conjunction with the strategic decisions, a basic set of constraints for production, marketing, finance, research and development, and the other basic task areas. The work in all the task areas *must* reflect and be consistent with the basic C_1 and C_2 decisions, or else the firm is headed toward a path of suboptimization and faulty implementation of overall strategy.

The Class 3 and Class 4 Decision Variables

Two basic types of organizational decisions depicted in Figure 1-3 remain to be discussed. Decisions included in the C_3 and C_4 classes actually operationalize a firm's strategy (C_1) and major coordinative policies (C_2). That is, given the C_1 and C_2 decisions already made, various task areas (especially production, marketing, and finance) are provided with the necessary guidance for what work has to be done and under what basic conditions or constraints. Deciding *how* to do the work and how to coordinate, when necessary, with other task areas, however, are generally the responsibilities of the respective heads of the various task areas. Much of the work to be done or decisions to be made in each area require little, if any, consultation with other functional areas. On the other hand, much of the work to be done or decisions to be made affects, or is affected by, the work or decisions of other areas. This basic distinction provides the criterion for developing the final two classes of organizational decisions.

Class 3 decisions are those generally associated *primarily* with one particular functional area, but their outcomes depend heavily on inputs from the other areas. For example, a major production decision variable is that of plant capacity; however, this decision depends heavily on, among other things, long-range sales forecasts and the structure of distribution channels (marketing inputs), forecasted developments in production technology (a research and development input), and the firm's cost of capital (a finance input), as well as on such production inputs as operating costs.

Finally, the Class 4 decisions, termed "functionally independent," are those that can be made by a particular task area in a virtually autonomous fashion, given the C_1 and C_2 constraints. In the marketing sphere, for example, decisions on advertising media and formats to be utilized, sales territories and routes, and similar matters require virtually no interaction with other task areas. The same is true of such production area decisions as purchasing requirements, quality control techniques, and scheduling of equipment maintenance. These C_4 decisions receive virtually no attention (only a detailed listing in appropriate chapters) in this book.

Additional Remarks

Several clarifications are in order at this point. The C_1 decision variables establish the strategic posture of the firm at any point in time. That is to say, decisions on these variables establish the relationship between the firm as a whole and its environment, by specifying the types of products and markets, the basis on which the firm will compete, and the criteria by which success will be measured. Once decisions are made here, a set of coordinative policies must be developed (the C_2 decisions) to provide guidance and direction to task performance and interactions *throughout* the enterprise. The C_3 (functionally dependent) variables represent decisions of a third order that are implemental in nature and are generally the responsibility of a particular functional area. The fact that the C_3 decisions are highly dependent on other functional area inputs, however, means that, regardless of the locus of decision-making authority, they are worthy of inclusion in the "general management perspective." This is because general managers, by definition, are concerned with the overall coordination of activities which interrelate in a cross-functional fashion. Finally, it follows that the C_4 (functionally independent) variables are not included in the "general management perspective." As noted above, these types of decisions require little if any consultation across functional areas. Such decision variables in marketing, for example, are very worthy of study in a marketing problems course but not in a policy course.

The Class 1, 2, and 3 variables thus constitute the focus of this book. By definition, then, the material presented in subsequent chapters shows interrelationships of the various functional areas and focuses on decisions of major importance to the firm. It should provide the student with the analytical framework necessary to identify key problems or issues facing the firm, as discussed in Stage 3 below.

It should be recognized that the decision framework presented in Figure 1-3 is *not* intended as an exhaustive list of the various problems and concerns of top management. Rather, the framework delineates those major organizational decisions which define the overall strategy of the firm and the types of lower-order decisions which have to be monitored for purposes of overall integration and coordination of organizational activities. It is thus a device for structuring one's view of the total decision-making system of an organization. General managers obviously have responsibilities and obligations both inside and outside the organization related to public relations, maintenance of ethical standards, and other matters which are not depicted in Figure 1-3. A more exhaustive listing of such responsibilities is presented at the end of the present chapter in the reading entitled "The MultiDimensional Field of Management." The responsibilities referred to in that article should be recognized as having great bearing on decisions which must be made by general managers consistent with the overall framework presented in this chapter.

STAGE 3: IDENTIFICATION OF PROBLEMS AND/OR ISSUES

As shown in Figure 1-1, the analysis conducted in Stage 2 should culminate in the identification of basic problems and/or key decision issues facing the firm. The term "problem" is used here to mean the underlying cause of some observed difficulty within the firm. It must be distinguished from the term "symptom," which is actually synonymous with the difficulty itself. Thus, if an observed difficulty (symptom) within the firm is high employee turnover, one must search for and analyze all relevant information to determine *why* this exists. Similarly, a declining profit margin is never a problem, it is only a symptom of some problem which is causing the reduced margin. The reason for making this distinction between symptoms (difficulties) and problems (causes) is to ensure that the student's point of attack for case solution is poised at the proper level. Unless the underlying cause of the observed difficulty is eliminated, similar types of difficulties may arise again in the future.

In addition to the identification of problems, the student frequently finds that there are key issues facing a firm. What should be the firm's future strategy? What steps must be taken to *prevent* problems from occurring in various aspects of the firm's operations? How could the firm better standardize its production operations without sacrificing the desires of marketing personnel for more flexibility in product design? These and similar issues are not really "problems" in the sense in which we are using the term. Rather, they represent focal points for action that might improve the firm's effectiveness or efficiency in relating to environmental demands even though no real or apparent difficulty in present operations appears to exist.

In arriving at conclusions concerning what problems and/or issues are facing the firm, the student is urged to utilize the framework presented earlier in Stage 1. As should be recalled, that stage involves sorting and classifying all the given information along the various dimensions and their components. The analytical process begun in Stage 2 focuses on those same dimensions from a general management perspective. In effect, the student is trying, throughout Stage 3, to determine what the key problems and/or issues are. The multifunctional nature of the problems and issues in a policy case forces one to abandon any inherent marketing, production, or financial bias, as all matters to be focused on generally will be either Class 1, 2, or 3 in nature.

STAGE 4: FORMULATION OF RECOMMENDATIONS

Once the student is confident that the underlying causes of difficulties and any key decision issues have been pinpointed, he or she is ready to proceed to the recommendations stage. This basically involves the formulation of alternative solutions to the problems identified in Stage 3. It is extremely important for the student to consider more than one possible solution (or set of solutions) to the problems identified. Otherwise, the tendency is to select the first idea which comes to mind, and to ignore the fact that there usually are several feasible points of attack and that one's first idea is not necessarily the best approach. Beyond this admonition, there are four equally important points to bear in mind. The recommendations formulated must:

1. Eliminate all problems identified in Stage 3, as well as resolve all significant issues
2. Be *feasible*
3. Avoid the creation of *new* problems in the process of solving old ones.
4. Be *justified*

The first item needs no elaboration except to say that recommendations must be specific and provide appropriate guides for action. The second point, however, is worth exploring—the recommendations must be feasible in a *financial* sense. Students frequently prepare proposals with only one thought in mind: to eliminate the problems or to resolve the issues. Often, however, the recommendations would require large amounts of funds which the firm may not have available. Also, the firm's debt ratio and other indicators of credit-worthiness may preclude the obtaining of outside funds. Therefore, one must estimate to the extent possible the cost of implementing the proposals; these costs then must be evaluated in light of the firm's financial capabilities.

The recommendations also must be feasible in the *human* sense. This means that not only the necessary quantity and quality of manpower skills must be available but also that any significant resistance to change which may be encountered must be recognized. For example, the recommendation to fire a company president who is a member of the family who owns controlling interest in a firm may make sense based on a rational assessment of company difficulties; however, its feasibility may be seriously questioned. In situations such as this, it is necessary to "back off" from the ideal and treat such a phenomenon as a *constraint* on any proposals which may be developed. The student must understand that the ideal solution may not be feasible in light of the constraints of the situation. Similarly, all recommendations must be congruent with the value systems of key personnel, a subject covered more fully in Chapter 3.

The student's recommendations must minimize the creation of *new* difficulties in the process of solving old ones. Each proposal must be thoroughly examined not only to establish its effectiveness in solving existing problems but also to establish that no long-run dysfunctional consequences may occur. For example, a recommendation to alter the product mix in light of changing market trends may promise to arrest a previous decline in sales. However, it may be that existing distribution channels and sales methods are inadequate to the new requirements. This illustrates the need to thoroughly evaluate all proposals to determine their effects throughout the organization. In this sense, the process of formulating recommendations should be viewed as iterative in nature, as proposals are continually recycled and refined until the most desirable one is found. Once the most desirable recommendation or set of recommendations is finally developed, the student must *justify* the final proposals, the fourth point listed. Why is the proposal better than the other alternatives considered? On what grounds did the student choose one solution over another?

SUMMARY

This chapter has provided the student with a general framework for the analysis of corporate strategy and policy. It has focused on developing the means for directing one's analysis toward those decisions or problems of most concern to general managers. The remaining chapters and readings provide the student with a great deal of detail on functional area interrelationships and on the integrative, multifunctional nature of top management decision making. Chapters 2 and 3 discuss the process of strategy formation and evaluation in depth, including consideration of the external and internal forces (including values) impinging on strategic decisions. Chapters 4, 5, and 6 discuss the major decision variables in marketing, production, and finance, respectively, *with emphasis on functional area interrelationships.* Chapter 7 focuses on the development of organizational structure for the total firm, with emphasis on alternative structural arrangements and their relationship to corporate strategy. Finally, Chapter 8 discusses the subject of organizational change in some depth. It is appropriate to emphasize this subject in a separate chapter, as recommendations for problem solution *always* necessitate change on the part of affected organizational members. Chapter 8 also discusses the overall process of change, various change techniques, and factors commonly associated with resistance to change.

As a final note, it should be emphasized that there is no step-by-step approach which will guide students through the analysis of complex policy cases. However, the framework presented in this chapter should provide some structure for the process. Also, the material presented in subsequent chapters and in the readings will illuminate potential problem areas by emphasizing total-firm oriented decisions and interactions. It also should serve to restrict analysis in a policy case to matters of general management concern, namely, relating the firm to its environment and coordinating the numerous internal activities in the pursuit of overall corporate objectives.

The Multidimensional Field of Management

Reed M. Powell

Management as we know it today is really middle-level and lower-level management oriented. In general, the university textbooks, the MBA programs at the various universities, and the various management development program efforts all deal with a concept of management that applies to these middle and lower levels.

From the time and work of Henri Fayol and Frederick W. Taylor forward, management has been concerned first with principles and later with people, within organizational frameworks. Whether the emphasis has been upon principles or people, both have ultimately been viewed within the parameters of the functions of management. Courses in planning, direction, organizing, staffing, and control have been developed in a wide variety of situations and with diverse emphasis.

Yet this approach to management leaves many chief executive officers cold. This is because it is basically unrelated to his management job and to the types of problems he faces.

Source: Reed M. Powell, "The Multidimensional Field of Management." This previously unpublished paper is printed by permission of the author.

Many of the people in management development have wondered why chief executive officers resist becoming involved. Of course, there are a number of reasons for this. One of them is the fact that their jobs do not center around organizing, planning, staffing, developing, directing, and in general, the management functions.

The concerns of the chief executive officers of America's firms tend to focus upon the following problem areas:

1. How to provide the creative thinking necessary, from the office of the chief executive officer, for the survival of the firm. All through the organization, people are anticipating the reactions and the thinking of those higher up the ladder.

The lowest level manager is anticipating his boss, and so it goes on up through the company. In a very real sense, the entire organization is attempting to anticipate the chief executive officer. From him must come much of the creative thinking relative to the future direction of the firm.

2. Today the chief executive officer must necessarily be concerned with

how to acquire other companies and/or how to keep from being acquired by others, or how to be acquired, if this is important to him.

3. The president and top management of a firm must necessarily be concerned about the relationship between their organization and the federal government. This is one of the great concerns of business today.

4. The upper level executive is involved in determining the international role of his firm and attempting to understand the implications and the consequences of this role or lack of it insofar as his company is concerned.

5. The chief executive officer is very much involved in meeting the problems and challenges of racial, ethnic and religious integration as they affect his firm. Under the new federal statutes, he is required to take affirmative action and whether he likes it or not he is deeply involved in "playing the numbers game."

The extent and the degree to which business firms are being forced to think about these problems at each and every installation in the different parts of the country is amazing when one begins to investigate it.

6. A chief executive officer has a fundamental responsibility for providing experiences for his executives that will keep them alive and help them to maintain the ability to roll with the punch, and to make quick and basic adjustments to new situations and conditions. These are the A,B,Cs of survival in the management of firms today.

7. The top management needs to think about the management of technological growth in an increasing number of firms in different industries. This has become a way of life for most companies today. They are deeply enmeshed in the management of technological growth and change, and in the management of change itself.

8. The chief executive officer is fundamentally concerned with the management *of* profits, rather than the management *for* profit. He still needs to be alert as to whether the firm is making a profit, and if it isn't, he has to do something about it. However, he has an additional problem when the firm is running normally—the management of the profit dollars that have already been earned by the company.

9. Perhaps one of the greatest things that the executive is searching for today is a standard of right and wrong. In a very real sense, top management is faced with a moral crisis in business and they are searching for a philosophy.

They need a philosophy that will help them define for themselves the manner in which they should direct the activities of the firm. As a part of this philosophy, they need to think through the problems of means and ends, and whether or not the ends justify the use of certain means.

10. Every top executive today has the problem of defining the role and place of the firm, not only within the business environment, but also within the overall framework of American

society. This definition of the purpose and role of the firm in our social system is one of the overriding concerns with which the executive must deal.

11. Today the top management of more and more firms feel that they must think about the very survival of the free enterprise system. Therefore, they need to know the symptoms of the weakness of that system and whether or not it is in ill health or fundamentally strong, because companies are increasingly recognizing that the survival of all of them is related to the continuing existence of the system which permits them to function and to thrive.

12. More and more, chief executive officers are sitting in their large suite-type offices, swiveling around in their large chairs, looking out the window and questioning what their personal aims in life are. They are asking: "What are my personal goals and how can I best achieve the sense of fulfillment I desire?" Moreover, they are asking: "What are the goals of the organization?"

Perhaps as never before chief executive officers are thinking about the aims of the organization and how they and other individuals can best fit their goals into the framework of the organization.

2

Strategic Decisions:

the impact of environmental forces

Strategic Decisions:

the impact of environmental forces

Chapter 1 has delineated the elements of a comprehensive scheme for the analysis of corporate strategy and policy cases. This chapter explores the concept of strategy formulation and the numerous variables relevant to that process in more detail and thus focuses on the strategic decision class (C_1) referred to briefly in Chapter 1. It should clarify the somewhat ambiguous notion of strategy and provide an understanding of the numerous factors involved in strategy formulation.

THE CONCEPT OF STRATEGY

Strategy can be defined in many ways. The term, as generally used, refers to the overall purposes, goals, and scope of a firm's operations. There is a tendency to attach identical meanings to the words "strategic" and "important." Just because a decision is important to the success of a firm, however, does not mean that it is necessarily an element of the firm's overall strategy. What is needed is a conceptualization of the strategy phenomenon that will enable one to consistently distinguish strategic decisions from other types, regardless of the particular firm being examined.

What then is a strategic decision? The issue may be clarified by understanding the purpose of strategy—to define the nature of the relationship between a firm and its environment. Given this comprehensive definition, it is possible to identify the five key decisions that comprise the overall strategy of any firm. These decisions are:

1. Customer mix
2. Product mix
3. Geographic limits of the market to be served
4. Competitive emphasis
5. Objectives (performance criteria)

Each of these decisions will be discussed in more detail later. However, it is important to emphasize that these decisions are formulative rather than implemental. They *define* the nature of the firm's relationship to its environment but do not indicate *how* the relationship will be effectuated. They are the "first-order" decisions of any firm, and once clearly delineated, they provide direction to lower-order implemental considerations in production, marketing, finance, research and development, engineering, and other areas. Consequently, very important decisions on channels of distribution, methods of financing, pricing, resource allocation, type of production process, and similar matters are not regarded as a part of a firm's strategy. As discussed below, these and other considerations greatly influence strategy and help determine its nature; however, they are only *inputs* to the definition of strategy through an iterative, analytical process of decision making. Before moving to the subject of strategy determinants, a more detailed look at the strategic decisions themselves is necessary.

The Strategic Decisions

The five basic strategic decision areas are obviously interrelated. For example, a definition of the customer mix (target group[s] of customers) of the firm cannot be accomplished without deciding on the product mix, and vice versa. *Similarly, quantifiable objectives concerning desired profitability, growth, and market share cannot be formulated independently of decisions on the other elements of strategy, simply because what may be a feasible objective in some industries may not be in others.* Note that the term "objectives" is not used here to refer to general, nonoperational types of statements—for example, "maximize profits," "become the leader in the industry." Rather, the term is used to refer to measurable performance criteria which can operationalize subunit or functional area objectives as well as serve as evaluation criteria in assessing the degree of success of a firm's strategy. With the exception of a new firm just beginning operations, it is impossible for the setting of objectives to precede the determination of the product mix and the other elements of strategy indicated above. Established firms are generally constrained by physical, human, and financial resources which limit the setting of feasible objectives independently of their influence. For example, it probably would be unrealistic for a food retailer to establish a profit margin objective of 10 percent on sales when the characteristics of the industry are such as to preclude, at the present time, a margin of much over 2 or 3 percent. On the other hand, in the dynamic electronics industry a much larger margin is generally the case and is essential for continued investment in new product development. Thus we must recognize that the development of corporate strategy is an iterative, interdependent process rather than a sequential one.

In one instance, a particular and unique resource base possessed by a firm (that is, the competitive advantage which is stressed by the firm—perhaps its product design ingenuity) may be the major influence on a decision to enter a new product market, given a reasonable projection of potential volume. Another firm, however, may consider entering a new market because of the over-whelming opportunities that exist in terms of perceived consumer needs, and only later attempt to develop a unique competitive advantage. In the first instance, we see that the determination of competitive advantage was *followed* by a change in the product and customer mixes of the firm, while in the second instance the reverse was true. Consequently, it is impossible to state that the determination of one element of strategy precedes the determination of another. The process is not simple; it is not subject to an explicit sequence of decisions, nor is it susceptible to a generic algorithm. Rather, the decisions are made in a complex and iterative process characterized by much subjective evaluation. In this sense we reason that it is better to approach such a complex and ambiguous problem area with some structure for analysis than with none at all. Recognizing these limitations, this chapter and the following one attempt to provide such a framework for analysis.

A useful starting point in building this overall framework is the identification of the *specific* decisions which must be made with respect to the five major components of strategy. These decisions are listed below in the form of questions which any firm must answer in determining its strategy.

What is our target group(s) of customers? What are their needs and wants? What segmentation criteria appear to be appropriate? What geographic market areas will we cover? What will be our market niche(s)?

What specific products, or services, should we produce? Which products will receive the greatest emphasis? What will be the price/quality relationships of our various lines? What are the basic characteristics of the products? Can the characteristics be differentiated from those of similar products offered by our competitors? What end uses do the products serve? At what point in time should new products be introduced?

What factor(s) will we stress to provide us with a unique competitive advantage? Is it our price? Quality? Service? Design? Differentiated product? Other? What can we do better than our competitors?

What are our basic objectives? What return on investment (ROI) do we seek? What should be our profit margin on sales? What are our growth objectives with regard to total assets, total sales, net worth, or number of employees? What share of the market do we seek and in what time period? What is the minimum return we must achieve to avoid liquidation and/or redeployment of our assets?

As will be seen later, there are many factors to be assessed (both externally and internally) before a firm can ever begin to answer the above questions, or before it can ever finally decide on its basic strategy. Note, however, that answers to these questions define specifically the product mix, customer mix, geographic limits of the market, competitive emphasis, and objectives of the firm. In general, the total set answers the overall question of "what business are we in." The firm then has, in effect, defined the relationship desired between itself and the environment. It then can focus on implementation considerations, which are concerned with *how* to achieve the corporate strategy. Final decisions on financing methods, supplier sources, marketing programs, production processes, organization structure, control systems, and so forth can be effected *only* after decisions are reached on the basic strategy. As will be seen later, such considerations are obviously analyzed before the final strategy is developed to ensure its feasibility. Yet, we should not let this fact distort the basic notion that the implementation of strategy follows its formulation.

Determinants of Strategy

As mentioned above, the process of strategy formulation is extremely complex and iterative in nature, involving consideration of numerous external and internal forces which impinge on the five basic decision areas. The process basically involves a *matching of external opportunities and constraints with internal values and capabilities at an acceptable level of economic and personal risk.*[3] The four major components of the strategy formulation process are readily identifiable: (1) external opportunities, (2) external constraints, (3) internal capabilities, and (4) personal values, including propensity to assume risk. The environment, composed of economic, social, technological, and political/legal sectors, presents various opportunities to the firm. However, the firm's capabilities (human, physical, and financial resources) limit the extent to which it may capitalize on such opportunities, as do environmental constraints (laws, highly effective competitors, and the like). Moreover, the final strategy must be congruent with the value structures of key personnel in order to inspire commitment. Final decisions on the five basic strategic variables result from a dynamic assessment and evaluation of the environment in relation to organizational skills, resources, and values. This "matching process" is discussed in greater detail in Chapter 3.

One important point pertinent to this section is that, with respect to internal influences, strategy is a *multifunctional* phenomenon. This means that decisions on the five basic variables are dependent on inputs from *all* functional areas of the firm. Even though a consumer-need orientation may be of the highest priority in strategy formation, decisions on customer and product mixes are *not* marketing decision variables. The fact that decisions on these variables establish direction, constraints, and operating modes for *all* functional areas necessitates their finally being made by the top or general management of the firm.

---

[3] The inspiration for this concise description of the process is derived from Christensen, Andrews, and Bower's discussion of the concept of corporate strategy. See Christensen et al., *Business Policy: Text and Cases* (Homewood, Ill.: Richard D. Irwin, 1973), pp. 107–11.

The Relationship of Strategy Formulation to Implementation

It was noted earlier that the formulation of strategy should be distinguished from its implementation. Figure 2-1 has been prepared to further clarify this distinction. The left-hand side of the figure depicts the basic ingredients of strategic planning. The complex and iterative process of assessing environmental factors in relation to internal capabilities and values culminates in decisions on the five basic strategic variables. Once decisions are made concerning overall strategy, detailed implementation plans then can be developed for the various functional areas of operation, as shown on the right side of Figure 2-1. Consequently, "strategic planning" may be thought of as the basic, analytical process of strategy formulation. On the other hand, "implementation planning" is the basic process of developing internal plans for operationalizing a given strategy. The feedback loop emphasizes the need to continually assess implementation plans and performance results in order to determine any needed changes in strategy. It should be emphasized that environmental forces also must be continually monitored in order to anticipate needed shifts in strategy. This point is elaborated more fully later.

THE STRATEGY FORMULATION PROCESS

As discussed earlier, strategy is a function of four major types of variables: external opportunities, external constraints, internal capabilities, and personal values. The remainder of this chapter will explore more fully the influence of external opportunities and external constraints on strategy. Chapter 3 will then consider the dynamic process of relating these environmental forces to internal capabilities and values of the firm.

Environmental Forces

When analyzing the environment within which a given firm operates, it is useful to think in terms of four distinct (although obviously interrelated) types of environmental forces: economic, technological, social, and political/legal. All four present both opportunities and constraints to a firm, as discussed below.

Economic forces. As noted in Chapter 1, economic forces in a given firm's environment include nature and types of competition, structure and characteristics of the industry, overall market trends for present and potential products or services, lines of credit available, tax credits, supplier characteristics, stockholder characteristics and investment motivation, and similar phenomena. General economic conditions also are important to specific firms, including growth of gross national product, disposable personal income, money markets, capital markets, and other phenomena more of a macro nature. Detailed analysis by a given firm tends to concentrate on the more micro forces, however, because

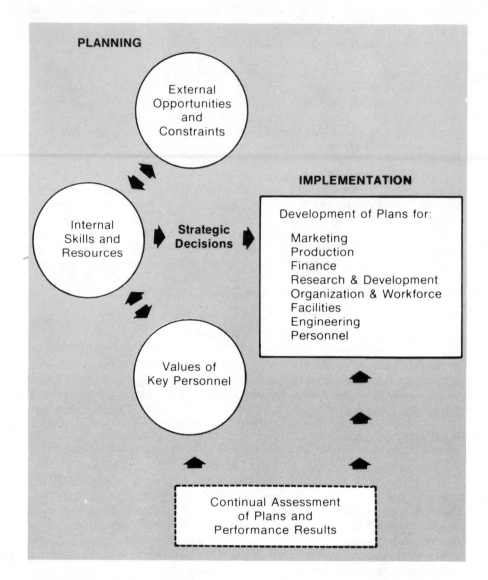

FIGURE 2-1: The process of strategy formulation and implementation.

they tend to exert the greatest *direct* influence on desirable product and customer mix and overall strategy.

With respect to analysis of competitor strengths and weaknesses, it becomes mandatory for the firm to assess the overall strategies of competitors, emphasizing the determination of the competitive advantages sought by those firms so that its own distinctive competence is not diluted. It also is very important to assess how competitors may react *in advance* of major strategy changes. This is particularly true if the industry is characterized by large firms, each having a relatively substantial share of the market. With respect to analysis of other industry characteristics, Seymour Tilles has identified five key areas for assessment:

1. The effect of cyclical swings in the relationship between supply and demand for the industry as a whole.
2. The effect of dynamic technology on product evolution.
3. The effect of widening geographic horizons.
4. The effect of economies of scale and learning.
5. The effect of integration, both forward and backward.[4]

Each of these five areas represents a key focal point for assessing the firm's capabilities in relation to industry structure and competitive requirements.

Insofar as the analysis of overall market trends for present and potential products or services is concerned, one is usually provided a good deal of "demand" information in a policy case. A note of caution is appropriate here, however, as the tendency is to assume that a given firm should attempt to exploit the area of greatest volume potential in the market. This ignores the fact that a given firm may not have the resources necessary to meet larger and stronger competitors "head-on" in the market place. Witness American Motors' classic decision to concentrate on the small car segment of the automobile market in the mid-1950s, while the "Big 3" concentrated on appealing to the faster-growing large automobile segment. American Motors, realizing it could not hope to match strengths with the larger firms, developed its own competitive advantage and was very successful. As a more recent example, International Multifoods entered the cheese market in 1971 through acquisition. Rather than attempting to compete directly with Kraft and Borden, however, the firm chose to concentrate on the relatively uncrowded specialty snack segment of the market. The strategy to date has had positive results. On the other hand, many firms have fallen prey to the lure of high potential markets without sufficient recognition of the strengths of competitors. For example, during the past few years Bell and Howell Co., a highly successful pioneer in home movie equipment, attempted to move into such growth fields as printing, aerospace equipment, and copiers, and soon found itself up against the likes of Kodak and Xerox. The result has been rapidly declining earnings per share in the late 1960s and a subsequent trimming of many product lines.

Closely associated with this point is the fact that it well may be more feasible, and more profitable, to capture a larger share of a declining market than to pursue what inevitably may be only a very small share of an expanding market because of the larger number of competitors involved. This only accentuates

---

[4] Seymour Tilles, "Making Strategy Explicit," in *Business Strategy*, edited by H. Igor Ansoff (Middlesex, England: Penguin Books, 1969), p. 191.

the need for assessment of opportunities *not* in an idealistic vacuum but in relation to what the firm is capable of accomplishing. A good example of this is the product-mix and customer-mix strategy of Fisher-Price Toys, Inc. in 1973. While Mattel, Ideal Toy Corporation, and other firms in the industry have expanded their strategy to include toys, games, and hobbies for all ages, Fisher-Price has concentrated on toys for the preschool child which, during 1973, made up only about 10 percent of the total toy market. A quality product is stressed and promotional efforts are aimed at young mothers. As a result, Fisher-Price has now become the number one growth company in the industry. Because the United States birthrate has slowed considerably, one could argue that Fisher-Price is concentrating on a declining market. Yet, the company's success has resulted from its strong reputation as *the* producer of preschool toys. It has clearly exploited a specialized market niche.

In general, the student's prior coursework in economics, marketing, finance, and statistics should have provided the basic tools for assessing the significance of external economic forces. Social, technological, and political/legal forces can be equally important, however, and are discussed below.

Social forces. Perhaps the most important contemporary social influence on the process of strategy formation is the doctrine of social responsibility, which emphasizes the consideration of social criteria along with the more familiar economic criteria in the development of corporate strategy. Many scholars, most notably Milton Friedman, argue vigorously that business has no social obligation whatsoever other than to make as much money for their stockholders as possible.[5] This implies that business has no obligation other than conformity to law and ethical custom, and that the impetus for social action programs must emanate from the governmental sector of the economy in a democratic society. On the other hand, advocates of the doctrine basically espouse the notion that technological progress in the pursuit of profit has had dysfunctional consequences for the ecological "quality of life," not to mention other aspects of social welfare which have suffered from an overemphasis on profits—equality of hiring and promotional opportunity, product quality, fair pricing, and the like.

Regardless of one's particular *philosophy* concerning the social obligations of business, the practical implications of the social responsibility doctrine cannot be ignored.

Carl A. Gerstacker, chairman of Dow Chemical Co., wastes no time on flowery phrases about "social responsibility" and "commitment to a cause" when telling why his company has undertaken costly antipollution and product safety programs. Rather, he states baldly: "Our motive is profit."

With just that in mind, Dow is putting into effect a program that it calls "product stewardship," under which it assumes total responsibility for how its products affect people. Indeed, more and more industrial companies are looking

---

[5] Milton Friedman, *Capitalism and Freedom* (Chicago: The University of Chicago Press, 1962), p. 133.

beyond their immediate commercial customers and into the marketplace to make sure that their products will not have an adverse effect on the environment or the end-user. Dow, for its part, thinks it has come up with an effective marketing tool as well: It will offer a virtual guarantee of harmlessness. "If we do a better job of product stewardship than our competitors," Gerstacker says, "we believe it will be recognized in the marketplace."[6]

The following indicates that the "product stewardship" program at Dow Chemical is not mere window dressing:

A number of important findings have come out of the program already. One product, an organic arsenical, was thought by the company to have considerable potential as an ingredient in paint for the bottoms of ships, since it would bleed slowly out of the paint and retard the growth of barnacles and other organisms. Doubts about the product's effect on the marine environment over a long period, however, and the need for additional costly research led to a "kill" decision—despite an urgent need by customers for such a product.[7]

Organized movements are underway for "social accounting" and "social auditing" of business firms. In marketing, the "consumerism" and "societal marketing" emphases are exerting influence in both academic and industry circles. In general, the increased attention being given to the subject of "business and society," whatever the particular variation, has resulted in a great deal of publicity and public debate. Even if one's basic philosophy precludes the use of other than economic criteria in strategic decision making, top management must recognize and adjust for the societal value shift that the doctrine implies. The particular impact of the doctrine will vary for each firm, depending on the desires of stockholders, values and attitudes of top management, the firm's location and community influence, its "pollution propensity," and other matters.

Technological forces. The third major type of environmental force which must be reckoned with is the phenomenon of technological developments outside the firm. The firm constantly must be aware of new discoveries, both in its own industry and in others, that may impinge upon its future viability. Technological developments are important for the firm in two major areas: product development and process improvement. As an example of the importance of continued assessment insofar as product development is concerned, one only has to consider the hundreds of products that either have become technologically obsolete or have lost consumer utility in the past few years. In addition, product improvement is frequently contingent upon the incorporation of new ·

---

[6] "Dow's Big Push for Product Safety," *Business Week*, 21 April 1973, p. 82.

[7] Ibid.

components or other features made possible by expanding technology. For example, Magnavox's failure to anticipate the need to develop color televisions with solid state circuitry left it at a distinct competitive disadvantage in the early 1970s vis à vis Zenith, RCA, and Motorola. As a result, the company lost several major distribution outlets, such as Marshall Field, the Chicago department store chain, and suffered a loss of momentum with others.

In general, the more stable the outlook for a product or industry, the less the need to actively search the technological environment, and vice versa. Certainly, an active, product-oriented research and development group is *relatively* more important in the electronics industry than in steel. It is also important to note that technological developments may present either opportunities or constraints to a firm. If a firm is active either in its own research and development and/or in obtaining intelligence about developments in other organizations, the chances are much greater that new technologies will present opportunities rather than constraints. This is because of the importance of *timing* in capitalizing on new developments, as is well-illustrated by the Magnavox example.

Political/legal forces. External forces in this category include legislation, executive acts, court opinions, regulatory agencies, foreign policy developments, fiscal policy, monetary policy, and other political/legal phenomena that impinge on the firm's operations. Obviously, some pieces of legislation, such as the Robinson-Patman Act, affect all firms, while others may involve only specific industries or product areas. By the same token, the role and authority of regulatory agencies may be either universal or industry- or product-specific.

As in the other major types of external forces, it is important to realize that political/legal phenomena present *both* opportunities and constraints to a firm with regard to strategy determination. Although the tendency is to classify or view such phenomena as the regulatory power of the Federal Trade Commission or the Food and Drug Administration as constraints, at the same time these political/legal forces can operate to present significant opportunities for some firms. Consider the profitable opportunities now existing for efficient manufacturers of antipollution equipment who service the various industries now subject to legal constraints on product or process characteristics. In this case, the same legal phenomenon—antipollution laws and control standards—has created an opportunity for some firms and a constraint for others. Also, consider the impact of foreign policy developments on strategy formulation. Multinational firms have alternately prospered or suffered, depending on government decisions concerning tax treatment, accounting practices, antitrust provisions, and other matters. Thus it is now necessary, in the case of multinationals, to extend one's political/legal analysis to the policies and decisions of foreign governments as significant factors in shaping strategy.

The four major types of external forces include various phenomena that provide both opportunities *and* constraints to a given firm, depending on the particular force being considered, the present strategy of the firm, the efforts made by the firm to influence its environment, and the particular capabilities (or lack thereof) possessed by a firm to respond to environmental shifts. The next section discusses the basic role of externally oriented research by a firm, as well as the various forms that such research may assume.

Environmental Research: Its Role and Forms

As implied above, whether a particular environmental force constitutes an opportunity or a constraint depends in many cases on the firm itself, particularly the adequacy of its externally oriented research efforts. Many critics of external research have argued that the typical state of uncertainty associated with most environmental variables—namely, the inability to accurately forecast future values of the variables—works against even attempting to do so. There is a basic contradiction in this argument, precisely because the role of environmental research is to provide the firm with a larger degree of *control* over the uncertain environmental forces.

To illustrate the preceding point, it is useful to visualize for any given environmental variable a continuum such as the one shown in Figure 2-2. Obviously,

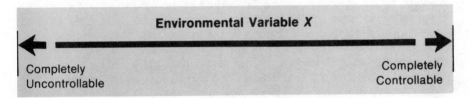

FIGURE 2-2: "Control" continuum for environmental variables.

very few environmental variables are ever completely controllable by the firm. Where a firm has a long-term contract for supplying a consumer—for example, Whirlpool's agreement for many years with Sears—it may be construed as having gained almost complete control (although perhaps only temporarily) over the important external variable of consumer demand. Quite obviously, however, an overwhelming majority of all businesses are faced with environmental forces which are at, or very near, the uncontrollable end of the continuum. The essential point is that the more information a firm gains about an environmental variable, the greater the degree of "control" the firm has over that same variable. Thus, even though a firm very rarely achieves a large degree of control over, say, consumer demand (as in the captive outlet case referred to above or in a monopoly situation), in effect it is able to influence the future state or value of the variable by forecasting. The increased information about a given force enables the firm to more accurately predict the effect of that force on strategy and operations, providing advance opportunity to adjust for such effects. In this sense, the firm obtains a measure of control over the environment and over changes in the environment by having already activated response mechanisms to cope with such changes.

Based on the preceding discussion, it follows that firms may be readily distinguished on the basis of their attempts to influence and control environmental forces. On the one hand, there are very "active" firms which seek—through economic forecasting, market research, lobbying or other means—to influence the environment and to control, to the extent possible, their own destiny. On the other hand, many "passive" firms merely respond to shifts in the environment as they occur, with little if any attempt to predict or plan strategy adjustments *in advance* of the changes. Such firms frequently find themselves fighting fires and engaged in "crisis management," because of their failure to formulate future-oriented strategy on a rational, although always imperfect and incomplete, base. As an example, consider the case of American Brands, for years the number one company in cigarette sales. Failing to actively monitor changing market trends, American was slow to respond to the "filter revolution" within the industry. Consequently, American Brands now ranks fourth in the industry in cigarette sales, behind Reynolds, Philip Morris, and Brown & Williamson.

There are several forms of environmental research. Perhaps the most familiar type is frequently referred to as *market research*. This is generally restricted, however, to the economic and social sectors of the environment, focusing on customer needs, demand trends, competitor strengths and weaknesses, industry characteristics, demographic aspects of the market, and similar factors which impinge rather directly on both present and future sales. A second form of environmental research tends to "fill out" the firm's assessment of the economic sector—namely *economic forecasting*. This usually focuses on the macro variables affecting the firm's success (for example, gross national product, disposable personal income, inventory accumulation in the economy), as well as on the firm's capital and money markets. Very large firms may have completely separate groups to perform the market research and economic forecasting functions.

A third form of environmental research is known as *research and development*. Although this function is frequently internal-oriented and concerned with product and/or process innovation, its successful accomplishment requires continuing surveillance of the technological sector of the firm's environment. Finally, to cover the remaining sector of the environment, *political/legal research* constitutes the fourth form of external research. This is generally performed by legal departments, or by a retained attorney, and, in the case of large firms, also by lobbyists who attempt not only to influence the legislative process but also to discern important political and legal developments in advance of their formal announcement.

In many firms, a general coordinative and/or technical staff exists to assume responsibility for overall environmental assessment. Most commonly known as *long-range planning* groups, they perform two major functions: (1) overall coordination of the various forms of environmental research (usually participating in one or more forms of the research themselves) and (2) relating externally identified opportunities and constraints to corporate goals and capabilities for the purpose of recommending strategic realignments to top management.

Although the exact nature of, and organization for, environmental research varies from firm to firm, it is useful to think in terms of the basic forms of environmental research noted above. Very large and profitable firms may have separate groups of people, one group for each of the major forms. On the other hand, very small firms may have only one group, or perhaps only one person, charged with "scanning" the total environment. Of course the "passive" type of firm discussed earlier may perform no environmental research at all, under the erroneous assumption that the firm is a closed system.

It should be emphasized that the ultimate goal of *all* the forms of environmental research is the identification and analysis of opportunities and constraints which are operative in the firm's environment. As noted earlier, however, this is only the first step in the process of strategy formation. Once the opportunities and constraints are identified, they must be related in some systematic fashion to the firm's internal capabilities and resources. Unless this analytical process occurs, the firm can never rationally assess the strategic implications of environmental forces. This "matching" of external opportunities and constraints with internal capabilities and resources is the subject of the next chapter.

The reading immediately following the present chapter focuses on the process of strategy formation in more detail, with emphasis on the varying approaches utilized by different firms.

SUMMARY

The first part of this chapter discussed the general concept of corporate strategy. It identified five key decision areas as strategic issues: customer mix, product mix, geographic limits of the market to be served, competitive emphasis, and objectives. The chapter discussed the interrelationship of these five decision areas, as well as the major inputs to such decisions. Environmental inputs were emphasized with several examples given to illustrate how organizations have responded to various economic, social, technological, and political/legal forces. The last part of the chapter concentrated on the various types of environmental research that are conducted by firms in order to maintain effective strategies in the face of changing conditions.

Strategy-Making in Three Modes

Henry Mintzberg

How do organizations make important decisions and link them together to form strategies? So far, we have little systematic evidence about this important process, known in business as *strategy-making* and in government as *policy-making*. The literature of management and public administration is, however, replete with general views on the subject. These fall into three distinct groupings or "modes." In the *entrepreneurial* mode, found in the writings of some of the classical economists and of many contemporary management writers, one strong leader takes bold, risky actions on behalf of his organization. Conversely, in the *adaptive* mode, described by a number of students of business and governmental decision-making, the organization adapts in small, disjointed steps to a difficult environment. Finally, the proponents of management science and policy science describe the *planning* mode, in which formal analysis is used to plan explicit, integrated strategies for the future.

Source: Henry Mintzberg, "Strategy-Making in Three Modes." © 1973 by The Regents of the University of California. Reprinted from *California Management Review*, Vol. XVI, No. 2, pp. 44–53, by permission of The Regents.

I shall begin by describing each mode as its proponents do, in simple terms and distinct from the other two. Considered in this way, each may appear to be a naive reflection of the complex reality of strategy-making. But taken as a set of three, as I shall do in subsequent sections, to be combined and alternated by managers acting under different conditions, these modes constitute a realistic and useful description of the strategy-making process. To illustrate this point, I shall cite studies of the strategy-making behaviors of a number of very different kinds of organizations—hotels, hospitals, car dealerships, modeling agencies, airports, radio stations, and so on. Finally, I shall discuss some important implications for strategic planning.

THE ENTREPRENEURIAL MODE

The entrepreneur was first discussed by early economists as that individual who founded enterprises. His roles were essentially those of innovation, of dealing with uncertainty, and of brokerage. The entrepreneur found capital which he brought together with marketing opportunity to form, in the words of Joseph Schumpeter, the well-known Harvard economist, "new combinations."

In a recent book called *The Organization Makers,* Orvis Collins and David Moore present a fascinating picture of those independent entrepreneurs, based on a study of 150 of them. The authors trace the lives of these men from childhood, through formal and informal education, to the steps they took to create their enterprises. Data from psychological tests reinforce their analysis. What emerges are pictures of tough, pragmatic men driven from early childhood by a powerful need for achievement and independence. At some point in his life, each entrepreneur faced disruption ("role deterioration"), and it was here that he set out on his own:

> What sets them apart is that during this time of role deterioration they interwove their dilemmas into the projection of a business. In moments of crisis, they did not seek a situation of security. They went on into deeper insecurity. . . .[1]

A number of management writers view the entrepreneurial mode of strategy-making not only in terms of creating new firms but in terms of the running of ongoing enterprises. Typical of these is Peter Drucker, who writes in a recent article:

> Central to business enterprise is . . . the entrepreneurial act, an act

of economic risk-taking. And business enterprise is an entrepreneurial institution. . . . Entrepreneurship is thus central to function, work and performance of the executive in business.[2]

What are the chief characteristics of the entrepreneurial mode of strategy-making as described by economists and management writers? We can delineate four:

1. *In the entrepreneurial mode, strategy-making is dominated by the active search for new opportunities.* The entrepreneurial organization focuses on opportunities; problems are secondary. Drucker writes: "Entrepreneurship requires that the few available good people be deployed on opportunities rather than frittered away on 'solving problems'."[3] Furthermore, the orientation is always active rather than passive. Robert McNamara, when he was Secretary of Defense, stressed the active role for the government administrator:

> I think that the role of public manager is very similar to the role of a private manager; in each case he has the option of following one of two major alternative courses of action. He can either act as a judge or a leader. In the former case, he sits and waits until subordinates bring to him problems for solution, or alternatives for choice. In the latter case, he immerses

---

[1] O. Collins and D. G. Moore, *The Organization Makers* (New York: Appleton, Century, Crofts, 1970), p. 134.

[2] P. F. Drucker, "Entrepreneurship in the Business Enterprise," *Journal of Business Policy* (1:1, 1970), p. 10.

[3] Ibid., p. 10.

himself in the operations of the business or the governmental activity . . .

I have always believed in and endeavored to follow the active leadership role as opposed to the passive judicial role.[4]

2. *In the entrepreneurial organization, power is centralized in the hands of the chief executive.* Collins and Moore write of the founder-entrepreneur: "The entrepreneurial personality . . . is characterized by an unwillingness to 'submit' to authority, an inability to work with it, and a consequent need to escape from it."[5] In the entrepreneurial mode, power rests with one man capable of committing the organization to bold courses of action. He rules by fiat, relying on personal power and sometimes on charisma. Consider this description of an Egyptian firm:

The great majority of Egyptian-owned private establishments . . . are organized closer to the pattern of the Abboud enterprises. Here the manager is a dominant individual who extends his personal control over all phases of the business. There is no charted plan of organization, no formalized procedure for selection and development of managerial personnel, no publicized system of wage and salary classifications.

. . . authority is associated exclusively with an individual . . .

Abboud is the kind of person most people have in mind when they discuss the successful Egyptian entrepreneur.[6]

But while there may be "no charted plan of organization," typically one finds instead that strategy is guided by the entrepreneur's own vision of direction for his organization—his personalized plan of attack. Drucker writes:

Every one of the great business builders we know of—from the Medici and the founders of the Bank of England down to IBM's Thomas Watson in our days—had a definite idea, indeed a clear "theory of the business" which informed his actions and decisions.[7]

3. *Strategy-making in the entrepreneurial mode is characterized by dramatic leaps forward in the face of uncertainty.* Strategy moves forward in the entrepreneurial organization by the taking of large, bold decisions. The chief executive seeks out and thrives in conditions of uncertainty, where his organization can make dramatic gains.. The entrepreneurial mode is probably most alive in the popular business magazines such as *Fortune* and *Forbes* which each month devote a number of articles to

---

[4] Quoted in C. J. Hitch, *Decision-making for Defense* (Berkeley: University of California Press, 1967).

[5] Collins and Moore, op. cit., p. 45.

[6] F. Harbison and C. A. Myers, *Management in the Industrial World* (New York: McGraw-Hill, 1959), pp. 40–41.

[7] Drucker, op. cit., p. 5.

the bold actions of manager-entrepreneurs. The theme that runs through these articles is what has been referred to as the "bold stroke," the courageous move that succeeds against all the odds and all the advice.

4. *Growth is the dominant goal of the entrepreneurial organization.* According to psychologist David McClelland, the entrepreneur is motivated above all by his need for achievement. Since his organization's goals are simply the extension of his own, we can conclude that the dominant goal of the organization operating in the entrepreneurial mode is growth, the most tangible manifestation of achievement. *Fortune* magazine came to this conclusion in a 1956 article about the Young Presidents' Organization entitled "The Entrepreneurial Ego":

> Most of the young presidents have the urge to build rather than manipulate. "Expansion is a sort of disease with us," says one president. "Let's face it," says another. "We're empire builders. The tremendous compulsion and obsession is not to make money, but to build an empire." The opportunity to keep on pushing ahead is, indeed, the principal advantage offered by the entrepreneurial life.[8]

In summary, we can conclude that the organization operating in the entrepreneurial mode suggests by its

actions that the environment is malleable, a force to be confronted and controlled.

THE ADAPTIVE MODE

The view of strategy-making as an adaptive process has gained considerable popularity since the publication of two complementary books in 1963. Charles Lindblom and David Braybrooke wrote *A Strategy of Decision* about policy-making in the public sector, while Richard Cyert and James March published *A Behavioral Theory of the Firm* based on empirical studies of decision-making.

Lindblom first called this approach "the science of 'muddling through'," later "disjointed incrementalism."[9] The term "adaptive" is chosen here for its simplicity. As described by Lindblom, the adaptive policy-maker accepts as given a powerful status quo and the lack of clear objectives. His decisions are basically remedial in nature, and he proceeds in small steps, never moving too far from the given status quo. In this way, the policy-maker comes to terms with his complex environment.

Cyert and March's strategy-maker, although working in the business firm,

---

[8] S. Klaw, "The Entrepreneurial Ego," *Fortune* (August 1956), p. 143.

[9] See C. E. Lindblom, "The Science of 'Muddling Through' " *Public Administration Review* (19, 1959), pp. 79–88; C. E. Lindblom and David Braybrooke, *A Strategy of Decision* (New York: Free Press, 1963); C. E. Lindblom, *The Intelligence of Democracy* (New York: Free Press, 1965); and C. E. Lindblom, *The Policy-making Process* (Englewood Cliffs, N.J.: Prentice-Hall, 1968).

operates in much the same fashion. Again, his world is complex and he must find the means to cope with it. Cyert and March suggest that he does so in a number of ways. He consciously seeks to avoid uncertainty, sometimes solving pressing problems instead of developing long-run strategies, other times "negotiating" with the environment (for example, establishing cartels). Furthermore, because the organization is controlled by a coalition of disparate interests, the strategy-maker must make his decisions so as to reduce conflicts. He does this by attending to conflicting goals sequentially, ignoring the inconsistencies:

> Just as the political organization is likely to resolve conflicting pressures to "go left" and "go right" by first doing one and then the other, the business firm is likely to resolve conflicting pressures to "smooth production" and "satisfy customers" by first doing one and then the other.[10]

Four major characteristics distinguish the adaptive mode of strategy-making:

1. *Clear goals do not exist in the adaptive organization; strategy-making reflects a division of power among members of a complex coalition.* The adaptive organization is caught in a complex web of political forces. Unions, managers, owners, lobby groups, government agencies, and so on, each with their own needs,

seek to influence decisions. There is no one central source of power, no one simple goal. The goal system of the organization is characterized by bargaining among these groups, with each winning some issues and losing others. Hence, the organization attends to a whole array of goals sequentially, ignoring the inconsistencies among them. The organization cannot make decisions to "maximize" any one goal such as profit or growth; rather it must seek solutions to its problems that are good enough, that satisfy the constraints.

2. *In the adaptive mode, the strategy-making process is characterized by the "reactive" solution to existing problems rather than the "proactive" search for new opportunities.* The adaptive organization works in a difficult environment that imposes many problems and crises. Little time remains to search out opportunities. And even if there were time, the lack of clear goals in the organization would preclude a proactive approach:

> . . . if [the strategy-makers] cannot decide with any precision the state of affairs they want to achieve, they can at least specify the state of affairs from which they want to escape. They deal more confidently with what is wrong than with what in the future may or may not be right.[11]

Furthermore, the adaptive organization seeks conditions of certainty wherever possible, otherwise it seeks to reduce existing uncertainties. It

[10] R. M. Cyert and J. G. March, *A Behavioral Theory of the Firm* (Englewood Cliffs, N.J.: Prentice-Hall, 1963), p. 118.

[11] Lindblom, op. cit., (1968), p. 25.

establishes cartels to ensure markets, negotiates long-term purchasing arrangements to stabilize sources of supply, and so on.

3. *The adaptive organization makes its decisions in incremental, serial steps.* Because its environment is complex, the adaptive organization finds that feedback is a crucial ingredient in strategy-making. It cannot take large decisions for fear of venturing too far into the unknown. The strategy-maker focuses first on what is familiar, considering the convenient alternatives and the ones that differ only slightly from the status quo. Hence, the organization moves forward in incremental steps, laid end to end in serial fashion so that feedback can be received and the course adjusted as it moves along. As Lindblom notes, ". . . policy-making is typically a never-ending process of successive steps in which continual nibbling is a substitute for a good bite."[12]

4. *Disjointed decisions are characteristic of the adaptive organization.* Decisions cannot be easily interrelated in the adaptive mode. The demands on the organization are diverse, and no manager has the mental capacity to reconcile all of them. Sometimes it is simply easier and less expensive to make decisions in disjointed fashion so that each is treated independently and little attention is paid to problems of coordination. Strategy-making is fragmented, but at least the strategy-maker remains flexible, free to adapt to the needs of the moment.

Lindblom provides us with an apt summary of the adaptive mode:

> Man has had to be devilishly inventive to cope with the staggering difficulties he faces. His analytical methods cannot be restricted to tidy scholarly procedures. The piecemealing, remedial incrementalist or satisficer may not look like an heroic figure. He is nevertheless a shrewd, resourceful problem-solver who is wrestling bravely with a universe that he is wise enough to know is too big for him.[13]

THE PLANNING MODE

In a recent book, Russell Ackoff isolates the three chief characteristics of the planning mode:

1. Planning is something we do in advance of taking action; that is, it is *anticipatory decision-making.* . . .
2. Planning is required when the future state that we desire involves a set of interdependent decisions; that is, a *system of decisions.* . . .
3. Planning is a process that is directed toward producing one or more future states which are desired and which are not expected to occur unless something is done.[14]

---

[12] Ibid., p. 25.

[13] Lindblom, op. cit., (1968), p. 27.

[14] R. L. Ackoff, *A Concept of Corporate Planning* (New York: Wiley Interscience, 1970), pp. 2–5.

Formal planning demands rationality in the economist's sense of the term—the systematic attainment of goals stated in precise, quantitative terms. The key actor in the process is the analyst, who uses his scientific techniques to develop formal, comprehensive plans.

The literature of planning is vast, and is growing rapidly. Much of the early writing concerned "operational planning"—the projecting of various budgets based on the given strategies of the organization. More recently, attention has turned to the planning of organizational strategies themselves, the more significant and long-range concerns of senior managers. Two techniques have received particular attention—strategic planning in business and planning-programming-budgeting system (PPBS) in government.

George Steiner has written what up to this point is the definitive book on business planning, entitled *Top Management Planning*. The general prescriptive flavor of the planning literature is found throughout this book. For example, "plans can and should be to the fullest possible extent objective, factual, logical, and realistic in establishing objectives and devising means to attain them."[15] Steiner outlines a stepwise procedure for business planning which begins with three studies: (1) fundamental organizational socioeconomic purpose, (2) values of top management, and (3) evaluation of external and internal opportunities and problems, and company strengths and weaknesses. Strategic plans are then devised, and these lead to the formulation of medium-range programs and short-range plans. In Steiner's opinion, comprehensive planning is important because it simulates the future, applies the systems approach, prevents piecemeal decision-making, provides a common decision-making framework throughout the company, and so on.

In PPBS, the focus is on the budget rather than the general plan (although a budget is, of course, one type of plan). The steps in the process are, by now, well known—the determination of overall governmental goals and objectives, the generation of program proposals to achieve these, the evaluation of these proposals in terms of costs and benefits, the choice of a group of proposals that will satisfy the objectives while not overextending the resources, and the translation of these into five-year and one-year budgets for implementation.

We can delineate three essential features of the planning mode:

1. *In the planning mode, the analyst plays a major role in strategy-making.* The analyst or planner works alongside the manager, and assumes major responsibility for much of the strategy-making process. His role is to apply the techniques of management science and policy analysis to the design of long-range strategies. A U.S. Senator notes the reasons for this:

I am convinced that we never will get the kind of policy planning we

---

[15] G. A. Steiner, *Top Management Planning* (New York: Macmillan, 1969), p. 20.

need if we expect the top-level officers to participate actively in the planning process. They simply do not have the time, and in any event they rarely have the outlook or the talents of the good planner. They cannot explore issues deeply and systematically. They cannot argue the advantages and disadvantages at length in the kind of give-and-take essential if one is to reach a solid understanding with others on points of agreement and disagreement.[16]

2. *The planning mode focuses on systematic analysis, particularly in the assessment of the costs and benefits of competing proposals.* Formal planning involves both the active search for new opportunities and the solution of existing problems. The process is always systematic and structured. As one business planner wrote recently:

> No doubt much of top-level management is unscientific. But by applying a systematic, structured approach to these problems, we have a better basis for analyzing them. We may identify more specifically the challenges and needs in the situation and see how they are interrelated.[17]

Formal planning follows a stepwise procedure in which particular atten-

tion is paid to the cost-benefit evaluation of proposals, where the planning methodology is best developed. The planner tests proposals for feasibility, determines their efficiency (or economic value), and relates them to each other. The planner deals best with conditions known to the management scientist as "risk"—where the uncertainty can be expressed in statistical terms. Conditions of certainty require no planning; those of pure uncertainty cannot be subjected to analysis.

3. *The planning mode is characterized above all by the integration of decisions and strategies.* Ackoff notes that "the principal complexity in planning derives from the interrelatedness of decisions rather than from the decisions themselves."[18] But this interrelatedness is the key element in planning. An organization plans in the belief that decisions made together in one systematic process will be less likely to conflict and more likely to complement each other than if they were made independently. For example, planning can ensure that the decision to acquire a new firm complements (or at least does not conflict with) the decision to expand the product line of an existing division. Thus, strategic planning is a process whereby an organization's strategy is designed essentially at one point in time in a comprehensive process (all major decisions made are interrelated). Because of this, planning forces the organization to think of global strategies and to develop an explicit sense of strategic direction.

---

[16] Quoted in R. N. Anthony, *Planning and Control Systems: A Framework for Analysis* (Boston: Harvard Graduate School of Business Administration, 1965), p. 46–47.

[17] M. F. Cantley, "A Long-range Planning Case Study," *OR Quarterly* (20, 1969), pp. 7–20.

---

[18] R. L. Ackoff, op. cit., p. 3.

To conclude, the planning mode is oriented to systematic, comprehensive analysis and is used in the belief that formal analysis can provide an understanding of the environment sufficient to influence it.

The upper part of Table 1 presents in summary form the characteristics of the three modes of strategy-making, while Figure 1 depicts these three modes in graphic form. The first figure shows the taking of bold steps consistent with the entrepreneur's general vision of direction. In the second figure, we see a purely adaptive organization taking incremental steps in reaction to environmental forces, while the third figure indicates a precise plan with a specific, unalterable path to one clear end point.

THE DETERMINATION OF MODE

What conditions drive an organization to favor one mode of strategy-making over the others? We may delineate a number of characteristics of the organization itself, such as its size and the nature of its leadership, and features of its environment, such as competition and stability. These are discussed below and are summarized in the lower portion of Table 1.

The *entrepreneurial* mode requires that strategy-making authority rest with one powerful individual. The environment must be yielding, the organization oriented toward growth, the strategy able to shift boldly at the whim of the entrepreneur. Clearly, these conditions are most typical of organizations that are small and/or young. Their sunk costs are low and

they have little to lose by acting boldly. Young organizations in particular have set few precedents for themselves and have made few commitments. The way is open for them to bunch a number of key decisions at an early stage and take them in entrepreneurial fashion. This behavior may also be characteristic of the organization in trouble—it has little to lose by acting boldly, indeed this may be its only hope. In a study of the Montreal radio industry, one student concluded that the less successful stations were predisposed to adopt an entrepreneurial approach in order to catch up and displace the leader (whose behavior was primarily adaptive).

To satisfy the condition of centralized power, the organization must be either a business firm (often with the owner as chief executive), or an institutional or governmental body with a powerful leader who has a strong mandate. The entrepreneurial mode is often found with charismatic leadership. Charles de Gaulle could have been characterized as an entrepreneur at the head of government.

Use of the *adaptive* mode suggests that the organization faces a complex, rapidly changing environment and a divided coalition of influencer forces. Goals cannot be agreed upon unless they are in "motherhood" form and non-operational (they cannot be quantified). Here we have a clear description of the large established organization with great sunk costs and many controlling groups holding each other in check. This is typical of most universities, of many large hospitals, of a surprising number of large corporations, and of many gov-

Characteristic	Entrepreneurial Mode	Adaptive Mode	Planning Mode
Motive for Decisions	Proactive	Reactive	Proactive & Reactive
Goals of Organization	Growth	Indeterminate	Efficiency & Growth
Evaluation of Proposals	Judgmental	Judgmental	Analytical
Choices made by	Entrepreneur	Bargaining	Management
Decision Horizon	Long Term	Short Term	Long Term
Preferred Environment	Uncertainty	Certainty	Risk
Decision Linkages	Loosely Coupled	Disjointed	Integrated
Flexibility of Mode	Flexible	Adaptive	Constrained
Size of Moves	Bold Decisions	Incremental Steps	Global Strategies
Vision of Direction	General	None	Specific
Condition for Use			
Source of Power	Entrepreneur	Divided	Management
Objectives of Organization	Operational	Non-Operational	Operational
Organizational Environment	Yielding	Complex, Dynamic	Predictable, Stable
Status of Organization	Young, Small or Strong Leadership	Established	Large

TABLE 1: Characteristics and Conditions of the Three Modes.

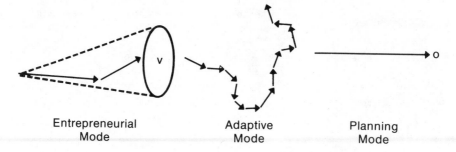

Entrepreneurial Mode   Adaptive Mode   Planning Mode

FIGURE 1: Paths of the three modes.

ernments, especially those in minority positions or composed of coalitions of divergent groups. Indeed, the American system of government has been expressly designed to create conditions of divided power, and it is, therefore, not surprising that Charles Lindblom, the chief proponent of the adaptive approach, is a student of the U.S. public policy-making process.

In order to rely on the *planning* mode, an organization must be large enough to afford the costs of formal analysis, it must have goals that are operational, and it must face an environment that is reasonably predictable and stable. (This last point inevitably raises the comment that planning is most necessary when the environment is difficult to understand. This may be true, but the costs of analyzing a complex environment may be prohibitive and the results may be discouraging. As one Latin American chief executive commented: "Planning is great. But how can you plan—let alone plan long-term—if you don't know what kind of government you'll have next year?"[19])

---

[19] Quoted by H. Stieglitz, *The Chief Executive and His Job* (New York: National Industrial Conference Board, Personnel Policy Study Number 214, 1969), pp. 46–47.

The above conditions suggest that formal comprehensive planning will generally be found in business firms of reasonable size that do not face severe and unpredictable competition and in government agencies that have clear, apolitical mandates. NASA of the 1960s is a prime example of extended use of the planning mode in government. Its goal was precise and operational, its funding predictable, its mission essentially apolitical in execution. The communist form of government with its five-year plan is another good example. The power system is hierarchical, goals can be made operational, the home environment can be controlled and made more or less stable and predictable (at least as long as the crops are good).

MIXING THE MODES

What is the relationship between our three abstractions and strategy-making reality? Clearly, few organizations can rely on a pure mode. More likely, an organization will find some combination of the three that reflects its own needs. Management students at McGill University have examined a number of business and public organizations according to these three modes, and they have uncovered a variety of ways in which organizations mix these modes. I shall discuss four combinations below, citing examples from these studies to illustrate each.

Combination 1: *Mixing the pure modes.* As we have seen, the literature tends to delineate three modes which are quite distinct in their characteristics. This trichotomy provides a convenient starting point for analysis; however, we cannot preclude the existence of other modes that mix their characteristics. Indeed, studies have revealed various combinations of the modes. We have, for example, found a number of adaptive entrepreneurs. One owned a car dealership. Reluctant to delegate authority but unable to achieve further growth without doing so, he was content to hold power absolutely, like the entrepreneur, but to avoid risk and move in incremental steps, like the adaptive strategy-maker.

We can find the two other combinations of the pure modes as well. In entrepreneurial planning, the organization takes bold, decisive steps in terms of a systematic plan for growth, while in adaptive planning the organization reaches a specific goal through a flexible path. Herbert Simon describes an example of adaptive planning found in nature:

> We watch an ant make his laborious way across a wind- and wave-molded beach. He moves ahead, angles to the right to ease his climb up a steep dunelet, detours around a pebble, stops for a moment to exchange information with a com-

patriot. Thus he makes his weaving, halting way back to his home. . . . [His path] has an underlying sense of direction, of aiming toward a goal. . . . He has a general sense of where home lies, but he cannot foresee all the obstacles between. He must adapt his course repeatedly to the difficulties he encounters . . .[20]

Combination 2: *Mixing modes by function.* Within single organizations, we have found different modes in different functional areas. One group of students carefully studied all departments of a large downtown hotel, and found evidence of all three modes. Where operations were largely routinized and predictable, as in housekeeping and the front office, the planning mode was used. In marketing, where there was room for imagination and bolder action, the hotel tended to act in an entrepreneurial fashion, while in the personnel department, which faced a complicated labor market, the mode was clearly adaptive.

Another group studied a modeling agency and found that in the area of fashion it was forced (as were all its competitors) to adapt to the dictates of the hautes couturieres of Paris, while it was free to be entrepreneurial or to plan in the areas of marketing and operations. Clearly, different parts of an organization can employ those modes which best fit their particular situations.

Combination 3: *Mixing modes between parent and subunit.* Neil

---

[20] H. A. Simon, *The Sciences of the Artificial* (Cambridge, Mass.: MIT Press, 1969), pp. 23–24.

Withers, a member of a group studying the Montreal International Airport (which comes under the purview of the Canadian Department of Transport), became interested in the relationship between a parent organization and its subunit (a division, a subsidiary, an agency, and so on). The question he addressed was: If the parent uses a particular mode, what limitations does that impose on the subunit (assuming, of course, that there is not enough decentralization to allow the subunit to operate independently)? Withers considers all nine possible combinations in which each could use one of the three modes, and he draws some interesting conclusions.

Figure 2 shows the use of the adaptive mode by both parent and subunit—a situation Withers refers to as "muddling through times two." In this case, the subunit merely follows the path of the parent, adapting to its incremental moves, and following a slightly more varied and lagged path. Withers concludes that the adaptive mode is,

in fact, always an acceptable one for the subunit, no matter what the mode of the parent.

Withers believes "entrepreneurial duets"—whereby both parent and subunit employ the entrepreneurial mode—to be "the worst possible combination." The subunit is subjected not only to its own bold moves but to the unexpected bold moves of the parent. The disruption may prove intolerable. One is led to conclude that no centralized organization is big enough for two entrepreneurs. Sooner or later one must make a bold, unexpected move that interferes with the other. (In contrast, another group described a decentralized social work agency where strategy-making was largely in the hands of the social workers. They were all entrepreneurs, acting independently to initiate original programs and seeking approval from the main office whose behavior was described as adaptive.)

Finally, Withers considers the conditions under which the subunit can

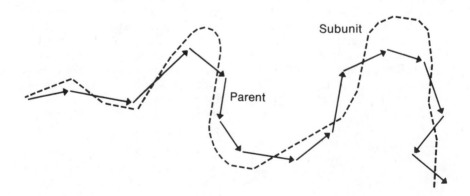

FIGURE 2: Muddling through times two.

plan. Figure 3 shows a situation where the subunit plans while the parent organization adapts. The subunit at time t_1 anticipates the trend of the parent's strategy and plans accordingly.

Up to time t_2, no difficulties are incurred, and the subunit continues to extrapolate. But soon the parent's direction begins to change, and the subunit finds itself in conflict with the

Generally, the young organization is entrepreneurial—it has few committed resources, it stands to lose little and to gain much by taking bold steps, leadership tends to be charismatic, and there is much spirit associated with its mission. This is the period of expansion and growth. But each new strategic decision commits additional resources, and gradually the organization locks itself into specific strategies, bureaucratic structures,

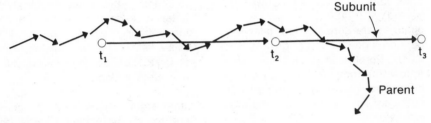

FIGURE 3: Planning in an adaptive environment.

parent. According to Withers, "The use of planning in this uncertainty may not yield sufficiently improved results over [adapting] to justify the cost of planning and the long-term commitment of resources." Withers concludes that subunit planning will work only if the parent plans and if the two planning centers are properly coordinated.

Combination 4: *Mixing modes by stage of development.* A number of writers have described the growth of organizations in terms of three or four basic stages—generally corresponding to a life cycle beginning with youth and ending with maturity. It appears that we can characterize the various stages by the mode of strategy-making employed.

and demanding pressure groups. The adaptive mode sets in. For example, one group of students studied a Montreal hospital which began in a most entrepreneurial fashion, with dramatic innovations in design and operation. Some time later, when the hospital was established, the provincial government took over increasing control of its budgets and by the time of the study these students felt that the adaptive mode was most descriptive of this organization's strategy-making behavior.

The adaptive mode may signal the final stage of maturity, or the conditions may be such that an organization can attempt to regenerate itself through a new period of entrepreneurship. In fact, it appears that the way to turn around a large, adaptive organization requiring major change is to bring in an entrepreneurial leader. Only by consolidating power in the hands of one strong newcomer will it be possible to override the established factions and the entrenched attitudes.

Some organizations appear to develop cyclical patterns in which periods of entrepreneurship are alternated with periods of adaptiveness. They make a set of bold changes in order to grow, then settle down to a period of stability in which the changes are consolidated, later embark on a new period of growth, and so on. Perhaps in some cases these follow economic cycles—an entrepreneurial mode in an expanding economy, an adaptive mode during recession.

Some time ago, I interviewed the president of a hotel chain who traced his firm's strategy through to the third distinct cycle of change and consolidation. The first stage of growth, as a real estate firm, involved the purchase of a number of older downtown hotels as property investments. Later, realizing the potential of investments, the firm entered a period of consolidation in which the properties were developed into an efficient hotel chain. Having reached this point after some years, a second wave of entrepreneurial growth began. First the firm became public in order to obtain expansion capital and then it entered into a major expansion program involving primarily the construction of a chain of modern motor hotels. Toward the end of the program, the firm found that its financial resources were overextended, partly due to higher

expansion costs than anticipated. Again growth was halted while the firm consolidated its new units, concentrating on making them efficient, and waiting until its financial reserves were sufficient to begin to grow again. About three years later, at the time of the interview, cycle three has just begun, this time with the emphasis on the construction of larger downtown hotels.

Such an approach to strategy-making may, in fact, be a sensible one. It proceeds on the assumption that it is better to keep the modes distinct, concentrating fully on one mode at a time rather than mixing them and having to reconcile the different styles of strategy-making.

Other organizations, as they mature, tend to use the planning mode—the development of new strategies by controlled, orderly change. As these organizations grow large, they commit more and more of their staff resources to planning. Indeed, this is the thesis of John Kenneth Galbraith who claims, in *The New Industrial State,* that large business firms are controlled by the planners (the "techno-structure") who use their techniques to enable the firms in turn to control their markets.

Our studies have not covered these large firms, but analyses of the strategy-making behaviors of a diverse array of smaller organizations—airlines, brokerage firms, universities, race tracks, cultural centers—suggest that virtually all start in the entrepreneurial mode, most later shift to an adaptive mode, and some move on to planning or back to entrepreneurship in their maturity.

IMPLICATIONS FOR STRATEGIC PLANNING

What can we conclude from this description of strategy-making? One point merits special emphasis. *Planning is not a panacea for the problems of strategy-making.* As obvious as this seems, there is little recognition of it in planning books or by planners. Instead, one finds a focus on abstract, simple models of the planning process that take no cognizance of the other two modes of strategy-making. Little wonder then that one finds so much frustration among formal planners. Rather than seeking panaceas, we should recognize that the mode used must fit the situation. An unpredictable environment suggests use of the adaptive mode just as the presence of a powerful leader may enable the organization to best achieve its goals through the entrepreneurial mode.

Some situations require no planning, others only limited planning. Often the planning mode can be used only when mixed with the others. Most important, planners must recognize the need for the manager to remain partially in the adaptive mode at all times. Crises and unexpected events are an important part of every strategy-maker's reality. Conventional planning requires operational goals which managers cannot always provide (the coalition may simply not agree on anything specific). Furthermore, it must be recognized that good planning is expensive, it often requires unrealistic stability in the environment, and, above all, it is the least flexible of the strategy-making modes. All this is not to conclude that planning is useless; rather, it suggests that the planner must become more realistic about the limitations of his science.

Often there is a need to redesign the formal planning process. Adaptive planning would differ from conventional planning in a number of important respects. The plans would be flexible so that the manager could adjust as the future unfolded itself. He would be able to time his moves accordingly—to begin construction on the new plant when interest rates fall, to reorganize the structure after certain executives retire. The plans would also provide for different options—alternate locations for a new plant depending on impending state legislation, different possible acquisition strategies depending on the success of recent acquisitions, and so on. In other words, like the path of the ant described earlier, strategic plans would specify end points and perhaps alternate routes, but they would also leave the manager with the flexibility necessary to react to his dynamic environment.

In addition, the planner could draw up a series of contingency plans to help the manager deal with any one of a number of possible events that could have a sudden, devastating effect on the organization. He could also be prepared to "plan in the real-time," that is, to apply his analytical techniques quickly for the manager who faces an unforeseen crisis. By preparing in this way, planners can more closely adapt themselves to the realities of strategy-making.

3

Strategy Formulation:

relating environmental forces to internal capabilities and values

Strategy Formulation:

relating environmental forces to internal capabilities and values

This chapter continues the discussion of corporate strategy begun in Chapter 2. The focus here is on the dynamic interplay between environmental forces, corporate capabilities, and personal values in the process of strategy formulation.

THE ASSESSMENT OF CAPABILITIES

The very obvious assumption underlying the discussion of environmental forces in Chapter 2 is that it is not enough for a firm merely to identify and analyze the nature and types of market opportunities that may present themselves. That process means very little if the firm cannot *capitalize* on its opportunities. In addition, the firm must be able to exploit a particular opportunity *better* than someone else. In order to resolve the first issue—whether the firm in fact can seize a new opportunity—it is necessary to conduct a resource or capability audit to determine what it is capable of doing strategically. In order to resolve the second issue—whether the firm can seize the market opportunity better than its competitors—it is necessary to further analyze the implications of the resource audit in terms of customer needs and the ability of competitors to satisfy those needs. With respect to the latter, the firm is attempting to establish a *competitive advantage* as exemplified by its ability to satisfy some customer need that is currently unfulfilled by competitors.

The Capability or Resource Audit

The basic goal of the resource audit is to generate an inventory of the firm's strengths and weaknesses which then can be used to assess the feasibility of exploiting any new product/market opportunities. The best generic approach to this problem, without reference to any particular market opportunity, is to delineate *areas* for analysis, without trying to conclude beforehand what is "good" or "bad." After all, what may be a strength or a plus factor for entering one market may be a neutral or even a negative factor in another. For example, a firm which possesses an abundance of skills in close tolerance, precision manufacturing may have an obvious strength if it is considering diversification

from watch manufacturing to production of precision control instruments, as Elgin did in the late 1950s. However, this same skill may be of no use at all if the firm is considering diversification into basic steel production. Consequently, the approach taken here is to delineate areas for analysis without making any value judgements concerning what may be a strength under the various categories. The important point is that each area must be assessed in relation to the product/market opportunity under consideration by a particular firm. The reading at the end of the chapter, "How to Evaluate a Firm," provides additional guidelines for judging the resources and capabilities of a firm. The areas of analysis appropriate for the internal resource audit are summarized in the following paragraphs.

Human resources. What are the dominant values of top management and other key personnel? What is the overall quality of personnel in the various areas? What are their special skills? Are there attitudinal problems? Are there undesirable instances of interpersonal conflict? Are work group and intergroup relationships satisfactory? Do employees identify with and support the goals and objectives of the firm? In short, what are the firm's personnel problems and weaknesses? What are its strengths?

Financial resources. What is the overall financial situation with regard to liquidity, leverage, working capital, profitability, and growth? Does the firm have the ability to raise additional capital? Is the contemplated opportunity financially feasible? What are the firm's financial strengths and weaknesses?

Physical resources and production. What types of processing are currently utilized? What is the overall condition of plant and equipment? Is plant capacity being fully utilized? What particular operating skills exist? Can the production requirements of the contemplated opportunity be in any way integrated into present processes or would they only exist "side by side" or in separate plants? What is the situation with regard to inventories, quality control, and scheduling? What are the production strengths and weaknesses?

Marketing. What are the channels of distribution utilized to implement the present strategy? What channels would be required to implement the contemplated strategy? What is the overall quality of sales personnel and managers? Are current promotional techniques effective? What are the basic skill requirements for sales and advertising? Does a market research program exist? What are the strengths and weaknesses of the marketing operation?

Research and development. Does the company emphasize basic or applied research? What are the research and development requirements associated with the present strategy? What are the requirements associated with the contemplated strategy? What are the particular technical orientations and skills of the present scientific personnel? What are the research and development strengths and weaknesses?

Organizational. What are the current structural arrangements? What modifications in structure must occur to accommodate any new strategy? Is the present structure flexible? Effective? Efficient? What are the structural strengths and weaknesses?

Present strategic posture. What are the present product mix, customer mix, geographic limits of the market(s) served, competitive emphasis, and objectives (performance criteria) of the firm? Does the potential opportunity represent a radical departure from the present posture? What would be the effects of a radical shift on company image, customer identification and loyalty, investor evaluations of the firm, employee identification, and overall firm-environment relationships? What is the overall outlook for the present strategy? What is the overall outlook for the contemplated strategy?

Environmental research capabilities. The most important assessment in this area relates to the financial and human resources currently devoted to external research. Is the firm "active" or "passive" in this area? Would the opportunity under consideration necessitate a shift in philosophy? Would it necessitate gaining a previously unexplored type of environmental knowledge? If exploited, would the idea require much more resources for market research, economic forecasting, and long-range planning than has been thus far necessary? Is the firm contemplating movement into a dynamic and unstable industry while having been in a relatively stable situation? In general, how different from the important factors in the present markets are those in the contemplated markets? Are our external research skills transferable to the new situation?

Establishing a Competitive Advantage

As indicated earlier, it is not enough for a firm to simply possess the resources to exploit an environmental opportunity or to respond to some new environmental constraint. Establishing that the firm *can* enter a contemplated market is only the first step toward success. The second step is to determine whether or not the firm can capitalize on the opportunity *better* than its potential (or existing) competitors. There are many ways in which a firm can establish a competitive advantage. Robert L. Katz has identified the following:

1. Excellence in product design and/or performance (engineering ingenuity).
2. Low-cost, high efficiency operating skill in manufacturing and/or in distribution.
3. Leadership in product innovation.
4. Efficiency in customer service.
5. Personal relationships with customers.
6. Efficiency in transportation and logistics.
7. Effectiveness in sales promotion.
8. Merchandising efficiency. High turnover of inventories and/or of capital.
9. Skillful trading in volatile price movement commodities.
10. Ability to influence legislation.
11. Highly efficient, low-cost facilities.
12. Ownership or control of low-cost or scarce raw materials.
13. Control of intermediate distribution or processing units.

14. Massive availability of capital.
15. Widespread customer acceptance of company brand name. Company reputation.
16. Product availability, convenience.[8]

The resource audit of a company should indicate the strengths *from which* a competitive advantage may be developed. It must be recognized, however, that mere possession of a particular strength does not guarantee its utility to the consumer. Therein lies the necessity to evaluate thoroughly the *needs* of the target consumers in relation to what the firm can provide. For example, prime location of manufacturing facilities much nearer to an industrial consumer than competitors can be a decided advantage for a firm, either in terms or providing more rapid deliveries and better service or providing a lower-price product because of lower transportation costs. However, if the customer does not *need* rapid delivery, and if quality, not price, is the more important variable affecting the purchase decision, then the firm has no "distinctive competence" and may have no competitive advantage at all. The key point is that possession of a strength is valuable only if that strength is important for filling a customer need and is not possessed by a competitor to the same, or to a larger, degree. Otherwise the firm possesses no "distinctive competence" which provides it with a competitive advantage.

The Concept of Synergy

A useful concept to consider in the attempt to match external opportunities with internal capabilities and resources is that of *synergy*. Positive synergy is best described as the "2 + 2 = 5" effect, or alternatively, the "whole is greater than the sum of its parts." In the process of strategy formation or change, it refers to the degree of complementarity between *present* skills and resources and the *future* skills and resources which would be required by an alteration of strategy. The higher the degree of complementarity that exists between the present strategic posture and the contemplated posture, the greater the opportunity for realizing positive synergy. This somewhat elusive concept is best explained through the consideration of different types of synergy and how they relate to the process of strategy formation. *In each of the cases below, assume that a new product/market opportunity is being considered by an existing firm.*

First, maximum *production synergy* would be achieved if the production facilities, processes, and skills currently in operation also could be utilized to produce the contemplated product. This situation, given some existing excess capacity, obviously could result in decreased unit production costs because factory overhead would be spread over a greater volume. Also, neither quality nor efficiency should suffer, as worker skills would be completely transferable

---

[8] Robert L. Katz, *Cases and Concepts in Corporate Strategy* (Englewood Cliffs, N.J.: Prentice-Hall, 1970), p. 215.

to the new production requirements. This "ideal" synergy would occur when one firm horizontally merged with another which manufactured the same or substantially similar products. In the case of internal growth, positive production synergy would occur to the extent that new products developed are compatible with existing skills and resources. On the other hand, there is little chance for production synergy if, for example, a writing instrument manufacturer diversifies into the production of copying machines and ceramics (as Scripto did in the late 1960s, with negative results). It should be emphasized that production synergy can occur if only some "common thread" between two operations can be found, regardless of the degree of market congruence insofar as end uses of the products are concerned. Chrysler Corporation's purchase of the Lone Star Boat Company illustrates this last point. Chrysler foresaw the application of its experience and skills in the mass production of automobiles to the mass production of boats. Thus, experience and skill in assembly line techniques and administration provided a common thread in operations.

Second, maximum *marketing synergy* would be achieved if the current sales force, distribution channels, physical facilities, and promotional techniques also could be utilized to market the contemplated product addition. This type of synergy differs somewhat from the production case, as a high degree of synergy may be achieved here even if the products are physically different from one another. A very high degree of marketing synergy may exist for a workshoe manufacturer adding a workglove line, whereas substantially less production synergy would occur. This is because the work gloves may be distributed through the same channels, by the same sales force (no different skills required), and supported by substantially equivalent promotional techniques; on the other hand, although some aspects of the production process may be similar, such as stitching, the degree of overlap between facilities and skills requirements in production is not nearly so great as in the marketing sphere.

Third, *research and development synergy* would be achieved if the technologies supporting the development of both the present and contemplated product lines are substantially similar. The potential in this area usually emanates either from similar research skills (for example, basic vs. applied, product vs. process orientation, chemistry vs. computer science) or from similar functional characteristics of the products.

Fourth, *financial synergy* is the one major type of synergy that is virtually unrelated to the degree of similarity between present and contemplated strategic postures. This is because the skills and techniques of financial planning and control have a high degree of transferability across both industry and institutional lines. The *opportunity* for positive synergy in this area lies in the extent to which the firm can achieve a larger capital base for investment, increased borrowing power, and greater earnings growth through the spreading of administrative overhead over a greater volume. Note that this type of synergy is frequently the *only* rationale for addition of some product lines and is the underlying reason for conglomerate growth and expansion. In essence, the conglomerate firm attempts to achieve a larger capital base and earnings growth than the sum of what could be achieved by its various product lines operating as completely separate companies. The declining fortunes of many conglomerates in the 1960s indicates all too clearly that financial synergy alone is a tenuous base for expansion.

Fifth, *general management synergy* occurs when the skills, experience, and knowledge of key managers are transferable from the present strategy to the contemplated one. Basically, knowledge requirements for *any* successful general manager are twofold: (1) general knowledge of the processes and techniques of administration (initially acquired in business school and sharpened through experience) and (2) technical knowledge about the manager's specific industry and firm (generally acquired only through on-the-job training and experience). The first type of knowledge, which is essentially a methodological base, is freely transferable to all types of industries and institutions. The second type, however, indicates that there is a definite learning period for managers moving from one firm to another. Moreover, the greater the dissimilarity between strategies of firms, the longer the learning period. A manager may have little trouble moving freely from Firm A to Firm B within the same industry. However, if the move is from Firm A in Industry A to Firm B in Industry B, then the task is progressively more difficult. In general, the further a manager moves "from home" in terms of firm and industry characteristics, the longer the learning period. The extreme cases, of course, would be encountered when a general manager moves from one broad type of institution to another (for example, from vice president of a business firm to hospital administrator).

In conclusion, it should be emphasized that the concept of synergy is useful *only* for assessing the potential complementarity of skills and resources when contemplating an alteration of strategy. One cannot conclude that potential positive synergy is directly correlated with future success, as many factors other than complementarity affect future revenues and costs. One may conclude, however, that the greater the potential for achieving positive synergy, the greater is the *probability* for success, simply because eliminating duplicate functions, spreading overhead, and utilizing similar skills are directly related to unit cost reduction.

THE INFLUENCE OF PERSONAL VALUES ON STRATEGY

The iterative, judgmental process of "matching" external opportunities and constraints with internal resources and capabilities usually results in the generation of alternative strategic postures for the firm. Up to this point, we have assumed a somewhat rational process and have not explicitly accounted for the influence of personal values on strategy. The role of *judgment* in strategic decision making has long been recognized, primarily because of three major factors:

1. All information related to the numerous external forces operating in any situation cannot possibly be gathered, assimilated, and evaluated.

2. The information which can be collected and evaluated is frequently imperfect.
3. The large number of variables related to strategic decisions cannot be "modeled" in the sense of establishing precise functional relationships which provide deterministic outputs or "correct" decisions.

It should be recognized that the *personal values* of top managers are an integral component of strategic decisions. Moreover, it will be argued that such values should be reflected and satisfied by decisions on major issues such as corporate strategy.

Culturally Derived Values

A personal value can be viewed as one's "conception of the desirable." Eduard Spranger identified six major kinds of value orientations that are useful for distinguishing among types of people:

1. *Theoretical*—dominant intellectual interest in an empirical and rational approach to systematic knowledge.
2. *Economic*—orientation toward practical affairs, the production and consumption of goods, the uses and creations of wealth.
3. *Aesthetic*—dominant interest in the artistic, in form, symmetry, and harmony.
4. *Social*—primary value is the love of people and warmth of human relationships.
5. *Political*—dominant orientation toward power, influence, and recognition.
6. *Religious*—primary orientation toward unity and creation of satisfying and meaningful relationship to the universe.[9]

All these values may be viewed as "culturally derived." As noted by William D. Guth and Renato Taguiri, values are transmitted to a person "through his parents, teachers, and other significant persons in his environment who, in turn, acquired their values in similar fashion."[10] These culturally derived values serve as guiding principles for decision making in our everyday life. Because they are such an integral and active component of one's personality structure, it is logical to expect that such values also will serve as guiding principles in making decisions on organizational issues, such as strategy, for which no predetermined "correct" solution exists.

---

[9] William D. Guth and Renato Taguiri, "Personal Values and Corporate Strategy," *Harvard Business Review* 43,5 (September–October 1965), p. 124.

[10] *Ibid.*, p. 125.

As the success of any business firm is generally measured by economic criteria,[11] the tendency has been to impute dominant economic values or orientations to decision makers. Although little research has been done in this area, the results to date reveal enormous individual variations among the value structures of U.S. executives—some have dominant economic values, while others may be primarily oriented to the aesthetic, political, social, theoretical, or religious.[12] Granted these individual variations exist, what may be the nature of their respective influences on corporate strategy? Or, to put it another way, how might executives with diverse value structures differ in their general perceptions of the most desirable course of action for the firm?

Obviously, the executive with dominant economic values would tend to emphasize strategic opportunities which promise the greatest increases in growth and/or profitability of the firm. On the other hand, an executive with dominant aesthetic values would be more prone to eschew profitable opportunities which would require, for example, "cheapening" the design of a product and thus detracting from the firm's image as the quality producer in the industry. An executive with dominant social values may well veto profitable opportunities which might threaten to upset interpersonal relationships within the organization, assuming, of course, that a reasonable return on investment is being earned with the present strategy. The individual with dominant social values also would be more favorable toward strategies which are "socially responsible" than other managers who are *primarily* concerned with increasing the profitability of the firm. An individual with a dominant political or power orientation will tend to emphasize those opportunities which promise to increase the various indicators of the size of a firm, such as sales volume, total assets, or total employees. An executive with a primary orientation toward the theoretical may be more prone to emphasize long-range research and development activities at the expense of short-run economic returns. Finally, strategic opportunities likely will be evaluated by the highly religious person in terms of their moral implications for the "nature of man" vis à vis the Creator and the total universe. The highly religious person also might evaluate opportunities in terms of ethical criteria, which are generally thought to be beyond the rightful concern of businessmen —namely those ethics which are more philosophical or religious in nature than those related to everyday business practice, such as fair trade or the independent determination of prices.

The above examples indicate that, consciously or subconsciously, our culturally derived personal values may serve as criteria for choice among competing strategic alternatives, assuming, of course, that all the alternatives satisfy minimum economic criteria for the perpetuation of the firm. The following section

---

[11] This obviously remains true today and for the near future, although growing public dissatisfaction with profits as the primary criterion for business success may eventually result in "social performance" indicators. This movement in itself represents a shift in the personal values of the larger society and was discussed more fully in Chapter 2.

[12] Guth and Taguiri, "Personal Values and Corporate Strategy," pp. 126–27.

discusses the manner in which our organizationally derived values may exert a similar type of influence.

Organizationally Derived Values

A second classification of values may be viewed as "organizationally derived." Within this general classification, it is possible to identify five major types:

1. *Production*—dominant value is cost reduction, operating efficiency, commitment to schedules, work simplification, and certainty and stability of operations.
2. *Research and development*—primary orientation toward innovation, design ingenuity, "scientific challenge," discovery of new knowledge, and technical superiority of products over those of competitors.
3. *Marketing*—dominant value is increased sales volume and market share.
4. *Financial*—dominant value is profits, return on investment, efficient cash flows, safety of assets, orderly records.
5. *Personnel*—greatest emphasis is on organizational stability and worker satisfaction and development.

These values tend to be associated with one's major role grouping within an organization. Thus, different functional area personnel tend to have different "conceptions of the desirable" for their firm with regard to product mix, customer designation, product characteristics and quality, priority of objectives, and the like. Specific market opportunities would be perceived differently by the various functional area personnel as a result of their differences in dominant or primary orientation. Each manager involved would apply different criteria to the same opportunities for the firm, consciously or not, and this would logically result in disagreements over the efficacy of the various decisions proposed. Examples of this divergence are discussed below.

Cases of Conflicting Values

The following examples illustrate cases where culturally and organizationally derived values have contributed to conflict and disagreement among top managers.

Consider first the case of a brewery located in the Midwest. It was founded in 1862 and soon established itself over a two-state area as the top producer of premium draught beer. This reputation was enhanced as further improvements in brewing techniques were developed and implemented. Then the brewing industry turned to packaged (canned and bottled) beer and found immediate consumer acceptance. By the mid-1960s, over 80 percent of national beer consumption was in canned and bottled beer. The brewery in question, however, continued to emphasize premium draught beer in the face of declining sales and despite numerous market surveys which indicated consumer preferences for packaged beer. A strategy session was called by the president and also included the vice presidents of sales, production, and finance. The subject was: What should be the future product/market scope (basic strategy) of the firm in light of the changing preference of beer consumers?

Three basic alternatives were advanced by the executives:

1. The sales vice president was in favor of switching to cans and concentrating on retail grocery outlets and packaged-liquor stores. He pointed out that this change in basic strategy would reflect consumer preferences and offered the greatest potential for increasing sales volume in the local area. He presented detailed statistics to support his proposal, including information to show that national markets were beyond the firm's capabilities at the present time.

2. The production vice president (brewmaster) argued against the preceding alternative. He strongly held the conviction that "packaged beers taste as differently from draught beer as cabbage tastes from sauerkraut. Can or bottle it and it is no longer the real thing." He favored maintaining the firm's present strategy of producing and selling premium draught beer in the two-state area.

3. The president felt that the firm should expand nationally with both canned and draught beer and that his personal skill in advertising would enable him to at least match the greater resources devoted to advertising by the national brands. Selective exploitation of restricted market areas would be necessary until a greater capital base was established; the accumulation of such efforts over the years to come would result in the brewery's becoming truly national in scope.

An examination of the alternatives reveals the influence of three differing value orientations on perceptions of *the same basic set of market data.* The sales vice president exhibits a dominant economic orientation. Note his emphasis on the strategy which "offered the greatest potential for increasing sales volume." The production vice president's idea of maintaining the status quo appears to result from his concern over the aesthetic nature (quality and taste) of the product. Finally, the president's proposed strategy exhibits a tendency toward a political or power orientation. Note the emphasis on the firm's becoming "truly national in scope."

To illustrate how organizationally derived values may conflict, consider the fact that most top management decision-making groups are composed of functional area vice presidents. Paul R. Lawrence and Jay W. Lorsch provide rich examples of such potential conflict in their discussion of differentiation and integration in organizations.[13] In the following excerpt from their book, imagine

---

[13] Paul R. Lawrence and Jay W. Lorsch, *Organization and Environment* (Homewood, Ill.: Richard D. Irwin, 1969).

that the sales manager and the research scientist are vice presidents of marketing and research and development, respectively, and that the integrator is the chief executive of the firm:

> In the plastics organization we might find a sales manager discussing a potential new product with a fundamental research scientist and an integrator. In this discussion the sales manager is concerned with the needs of the customer. What performance characteristics must a new product have to perform in the customer's machinery? How much can the customer afford to pay? How long can the material be stored without deteriorating? Further, our sales manager, while talking about these matters, may be thinking about more pressing current problems. Should he lower the price on an existing product? Did the material shipped to another customer meet his specifications? Is he going to meet this quarter's sales targets?
>
> In contrast, our fundamental scientist is concerned about a different order of problems. Will this new project provide a scientific challenge? To get the desired result, could he change the molecular structure of a known material without affecting its stability? What difficulties will he encounter in solving these problems? Will this be a more interesting project to work on than another he heard about last week? Will he receive some professional recognition if he is successful in solving the problem? Thus our sales manager and our fundamental scientist not only have quite different goal orientations, but they are thinking about different time dimensions—the sales manager about what's going on today and in the next few months; the scientist, how he will spend the next few years.[14]

It is obvious from the preceding example that the two individuals are applying quite different criteria in evaluating the feasibility of a new product proposal. The fact that many alternative strategies available to a given firm are economically sound permits the intrusion of these organizationally derived values, in addition to the fact that the "correct" decision solution at this level, however defined, is never known in advance. If a proposed alternative could satisfy *both* sets of criteria being employed in the above example, then obviously little disagreement would occur. However, when one considers that the problem is usually compounded by the presence of other functional specialties, at least production and finance, in evaluation of decisions affecting the total firm, the potential for considerable disagreement and conflict exists.

The Resolution of Conflicting Values

The preceding illustrations raise the issue of how to resolve conflicting values in the process of decision making. Although there is no easy answer to such conflict, several comments can be made. First, we must be *aware* of our own

---

[14] *Ibid.,* pp. 134–35.

values and the manner in which they affect our decisions. Second, it should be noted that although one value orientation may be dominant in an individual, other values also are possessed by that same person. Thus it may be possible to appeal to these "lower-order" values in an attempt to effect some sort of compromise when disagreement occurs over future strategy or other decision issues.

Third, we should be aware of the tendency to exaggerate value differences between ourselves and others. As shown by Guth and Taguiri's study, there is frequently a tendency to inaccurately attribute dominant value orientations to individuals based on our own stereotypes of their particular organizational roles.[15] For example, those researchers found that scientists and research personnel attributed higher economic and political value scores to a group of executives than the executives actually indicated for themselves. Similarly, the executives attributed higher theoretical values to the research personnel than the latter indicated for themselves. Thus, there may be more "common ground" for agreement than is apparent at first glance.

Fourth, we should recognize that this type of conflict is healthy for the firm. The assessment of decision alternatives from several different value perspectives lends another dimension to the advantage of obtaining a "diversity of inputs" in decisions of major importance. Such advantage is usually couched in terms of obtaining a diversity of *technical* inputs from different functional areas of expertise. It appears that a diversity of *value* inputs would contribute greatly toward illumination of the more subtle elements of decisions—namely, the extent to which the decision outcomes may be congruent with the value structures of those who will bear primary responsibility for decision implementation.

Finally, it is particularly important that the chief executive of a firm maintain a workable balance among the various types of values, those which are culturally derived and those which emanate from organizational role groupings. As noted by Katz, there can be no "separate, permanent, 'general management' set of values and criteria."[16] To effectively integrate the various cultural and organizational orientations in a manner which will ensure enterprise success and personal commitment *simultaneously* remains the responsibility of the chief executive. It is mandatory that this individual carefully examine his or her own innate bias and compensate for it in the attempt to reconcile value conflicts among immediate subordinates.

SUMMARY

Continuing the discussion begun in the previous chapter, Chapter 3 has focused on the dynamic interplay between environmental forces, corporate capabilities, and personal values in the formulation of strategic decisions by

---

[15] Guth and Taguiri, "Personal Values and Corporate Strategy," pp. 130–31.

[16] Katz, *Cases and Concepts in Corporate Strategy,* p. 19.

the firm. An outline of areas for analysis in an internal capability audit is presented, with more detailed guides for conducting that audit, in the reading entitled "How to Evaluate a Firm," which follows this chapter. The various means by which firms can establish a competitive advantage were briefly discussed, with emphasis on the interrelation of a given firm's capabilities with those of competitors.

Various types of synergy were described, as well as the means by which an organization can assess the extent to which its internal capabilities are sufficient to meet the challenges posed by a new product/market opportunity. The key areas of analysis with regard to determining synergistic potential were presented as production, marketing, research and development, financial, and general management synergy.

Finally, the role of personal values in the process of strategy formation was discussed in some detail. Emphasis was placed on distinguishing "culturally derived" and "organizationally derived" values when trying to assess underlying reasons for certain strategic moves.

This chapter concludes the discussion of overall strategy from a "formulative" perspective. Quite clearly, however, the process of strategy formulation cannot be completely separated from a discussion of its implementation and its effects on the various internal activities of the firm. Consequently, even though the following chapters primarily focus on the integrative aspects of functional area decision making within the firm, the effects of changes in product mix, customer mix, and the other components of overall strategy on those functional areas is discussed at appropriate points.

How to Evaluate a Firm

Robert B. Buchele

The sharp drops in earnings and even losses recently suffered by many so-called "growth" companies, whose stocks had been bid so high, have cast doubts upon the adequacy of the established methods which are used by investment specialists to evaluate companies.

Equally dramatic but less evident have been the serious declines of numerous companies shortly after having been rated as "excellently managed" by the best known of the evaluation systems using a list of factors covering numerous aspects of corporate management.

What has happened to render these evaluation systems so inadequate? What lessons can be learned by persons whose work requires them to do overall evaluations of companies—investors, acquisition specialists, consultants, long-range planners, and chief executives? Finally, what are the requirements for a system for evaluating firms that will function reliably under today's conditions?

After all, the decline of even blue chip companies is not a new phenome-

non. To quote from an unpublished paper recently presented by Ora C. Roehl before a management conference at UCLA:

> The Brookings Institution sometime ago made a study of the 100 top businesses in the USA in the early 1900s, and they found that after 40 years only 36 were still among the leaders.

We all look at the Dow-Jones Industrial Average practically every day and we know the companies that are a part of the Average today—from Allied Chemical, Aluminum Company of America, and American Can to U.S. Steel, Westinghouse, and Woolworth. But, as we go back in time a bit, we find names that once were important enough to be a part of the Average and which we have heard of, such as Hudson Motors, Famous Players-Lasky, and Baldwin Locomotive. It is not long, however, before we run into one-time business leaders whose names are strange to us, such as Central Leather, U.S. Cordage Company, Pacific Mail, American Cotton Oil Company, and one with

Source: Robert B. Buchele, "How to Evaluate a Firm." © 1962 by The Regents of the University of California. Reprinted from *California Management Review*, Vol. V, No. 1, pp. 5–17, by permission of The Regents.

OUTLINE FOR EVALUATION OF A FIRM

I. PRODUCT LINES AND BASIC COMPETITIVE POSITION

A. PAST

What strengths and weakness in products (or services) have been dominant in this firm's history—design features, quality-reliability, prices, patents, proprietary position?

B. PRESENT

What share of its market(s) does the firm now hold, and how firmly? Is this share diversified or concentrated as to number of customers? In what phases of their life cycles are the present chief products and what is happening to prices and margins? How do customers and potential customers regard this firm's products? Are the various product lines compatible marketing-wise, engineering-wise, manufacturing-wise? If not, is each product line substantial enough to stand on its own feet?

C. FUTURE

Is the market(s) as a whole expanding or contracting, and at what rate? What is the trend in this firm's share of the market(s)? What competitive trends are developing in numbers of competitors, technology, marketing, pricing? What is its vulnerability to business cycle (or defense spending) changes? Is management capable of effectively integrating market research, R & D, and market development into a development program for a new product or products?

II. R & D AND OPERATING DEPARTMENT

A. R & D AND ENGINEERING

What is the nature and the depth of its R & D capability? Of engineering capability? What are engineering's main strengths and weaknesses re creativity, quality-reliability, simplicity? Is the R & D effort based on needs defined by market research, and is it an integral part of an effective new product development program? Are R & D efforts well planned, directed, and controlled? What return have R & D dollars paid in profitable new products? Have enough new products been produced? Have schedules been met?

B. MARKETING

Nature of the Marketing Capability—What channels of distribution are used? How much of the total marketing job (research, sales, service, advertising and promotion) is covered? Is this capability correctly tailored to match the nature and diversity of the firm's product lines? Is there a capability for exploiting new products and developing new

OUTLINE FOR EVALUATION OF A FIRM

(continued)

markets? Quality of the marketing capability—Is market research capable of providing the factual basis that will keep the firm, especially its new product development and R & D programs, truly customer-oriented? Is there a capability for doing broad economic studies and studies of particular industries that will help management set sound growth and/or diversification strategies?

C. MANUFACTURING

What is the nature of the manufacturing processes, the facilities and the skills—are they appropriate to today's competition? How flexible are they—will they be, or can they be made, appropriate to tomorrow's competition? What is the quality of the manufacturing management in terms of planning and controlling work schedule-wise, cost-wise, and quality-wise? Is there evidence of an industrial engineering capability that steadily improves products and methods?

III. FINANCIAL ANALYSIS AND FINANCIAL MANAGEMENT

A. FINANCIAL ANALYSIS

What main strengths and weaknesses of the firm emerge from analysis of the trends in the traditional financial data: earnings ratios (to sales, to tangible net worth, to working capital) and earnings-per-share; debt ratios (current and acid tests, to tangible net worth, to working capital, to inventory); inventory turnover; cash flow; and the capitalization structure? What do the trends in the basic financial facts indicate as to the firm's prospects for growth in sales volume and rate of earnings? Does "quality of earnings" warrant compounding of the earnings rate?

B. FINANCIAL MANAGEMENT

What is the quality of financial management? Is there a sound program for steadily increasing return on investment? Do the long-range financial plans indicate

B. TOP MANAGEMENT AND THE FUTURE

What are top management's chief characteristics? How adequate or inadequate is this type of management for coping with the challenges of the future? Will the present type and quality of top management continue? Will it deteriorate, will it improve, or will it change its basic character?

C. BOARD OF DIRECTORS

What influence and/or control does the Board of Directors exercise? What are the capabilities of its members? What are their motivations?

V. SUMMARY AND EVALUATION STRATEGY

What other factors can assume major importance in this particular situation? (Use a check list.) Of all the factors studied, which if any, is

Does manufacturing management effectively perform its part of the process of achieving new products?

D. SUMMARY ON R & D AND OPERATING DEPARTMENTS

Is this a complete, integrated, balanced operation; or have certain strong personalities emphasized some functions and neglected others? What is the quality of performance of key R & D and operating executives; do they understand the fundamental processes of management, namely planning, controlling organizing, staffing and directing? Are plans and controls in each department inadequate, adequate or over-developed into a "paperwork mill?" Is there throughout the departments a habit of steady progress in reducing overhead, lowering breakeven points and improving quality? Are all departments future-minded? Do they cooperate effectively in developing worthy new products geared to meet the customer's future needs?

that management understands the cost of capital and how to make money work hard? Have balance sheets and operating statements been realistically projected for a number of years into the future? Is there careful cash planning and strong controls that help the operating departments lower breakeven points? Are capital expenditures inadequate or excessive with respect to insuring future operating efficiency? Are capital investment decisions based on thorough calculations? Does management have the respect of the financial community? Is the firm knowledgeable and aggressive in tax administration?

IV. TOP MANAGEMENT

A. IDENTIFICATION OF TOP MANAGEMENT AND ITS RECORD

What person or group constitutes top management? Has present top management been responsible for profit-and-loss results of the past few years?

overriding in this particular situation? Which factors are of major importance by virtue of the fact that they govern other factors? What are the basic facts-of-life about the economics and competition of this industry now and over the next decade? In view of this firm's particular strengths and weaknesses, what are the odds that it will succeed, and at what level of success, in this industry? What are the prospects of its succeeding by diversifying out of its industry?

a nostalgic sort of name, The Distilling and Cattle Feeding Company.[1]

What is new, however, is the current pace of such events. Stemming in part from the rise of industrial research expenditures from less than $200 million in 1930 to an estimated $12.4 billion in 1960,[2] the pace of industrial change has been accelerating for many years. It is now so rapid that firms can rise or fall more quickly than ever before.

Sophisticated technologies are spreading to many industries; in addition, as we shall see in this article, various management techniques contribute to the quickening pace of change. In consequence, the rapid rate of change now affects a great many American firms rather than just that minority known as "growth" companies.

PRESENT EVALUATION METHODS

Financial Analysis

This method typically consists of studying a "spread" of profit and loss figures, operating statements and balance sheet ratios for the past five or ten years. The underlying assumption is that the future performance of a company can be reliably projected from trends in these data. The reasoning is that these data represent the "proof of the pudding." If they're sound, the company as a whole, particularly its top management, must be sound, for a competent top management will keep a firm healthy.

Through the years this method has worked well because the basic assumption has been reasonably valid. Despite the fact that some blue chip companies have failed, it is still reasonably valid for the large firms who are thoroughly entrenched in their markets and who make substantial investments in executive development, in market development, and in any technology that promises to threaten one of their market positions.

However, the assumption is becoming less safe, especially in connection with medium-sized and small firms, as the pace of industrial change steadily accelerates. Thus, a firm whose financial record is unimpressive may be on the verge of a technological breakthrough that will send its profits rocketing ahead; conversely, a company that looks good in financial analyses may be doomed because it is being bypassed technologically or marketing-wise or because rigor mortis has taken over the executive offices.

In practice the financial analysis method is often supplemented by market research in the form of interviews with leading customers, by interviews with the firm's top executives, and by consultation with scientists capable of evaluating technological capabilities and trends. While these supplementary activities help, financial analysis still is neither adequately comprehensive nor adequately oriented to the future.

Thus, this type of market research can yield some insights into the effectiveness of past and present performance but is too superficial to tell much about the future. The interviews with top executives can be more misleading than informative simply because they are conducted by financial people inexperienced in management, marketing, or technology.[3] The use of scientists is a commendable step forward. However, it provides help in only one and possibly two of the many areas essential to a thorough evaluation.

Key Factor Ratings

Systems more comprehensive than the financial analysis method have been developed, mainly by consultants seeking to understand firms' overall strengths and weaknesses in order to be able to prescribe for them. Such systems typically involve ratings based on a series of key factors underlying the financial factors themselves. Little has been published about these systems because the consulting firms regard them as proprietary secrets. One system that has been published and, therefore, is well known is that developed by the American Institute of Management.[4] That this system is not adequately future-oriented is clearly proved by the fact that numerous companies have encountered deep trouble shortly after being rated "excellently managed" by the AIM.[5]

Professor Erwin Schell a decade ago set forth a comprehensive system with some future-oriented elements; however, he recently stated that his system should be revised to give greater emphasis to the future via more attention to the R & D function.[6]

As indicated in the outline for evaluation which accompanies this article, the evaluation of a firm, as it is at present and as it will be in the future, can be organized around a series of penetrating questions. Thorough study of the areas covered by these questions will yield a picture, oriented to the future, of the strengths and weaknesses of the firm under consideration and a reliable indication of its chances for success in the future.

There are, as the outline shows, four vital areas in a firm about which you should ask questions. They are: its product lines and basic competitive position; its R & D and operating departments; its financial position as revealed by analysis of the traditional financial data plus an estimate of the quality of its financial management; its top management with emphasis not only upon its past record, but also on its adequacy to cope with the future.

When these data have been assembled and summarized, you are in a position to evaluate both the present situation and potential of the firm under study as an investment possibility or as a management problem.

The rest of this article will be devoted to a discussion of these factors one by one. First we shall pose the questions contained in the outline; then we shall discuss the techniques professional analysts use for obtaining such data and determining what it means.

PRODUCT LINES AND COMPETITION

The first things to investigate are a firm's product lines and its basic competitive position. This involves a study of its past, present, and future. Here are the lines your inquiry should take:

Past ... What strengths and weaknesses in products (or services) have been dominant in this firm's history—design features, quality-reliability, prices, patents, proprietary position?

Present ... What share of its market(s) does the firm now hold, and how firmly? Is this share diversified or concentrated as to number of customers? In what phases of their life cycles are the present chief products and what is happening to prices and margins? How do customers and potential customers regard this firm's products? Are the various product lines compatible marketing-wise, engineering-wise, manufacturing-wise? If not, is each product line substantial enough to stand on its own feet?

Future ... Is the market(s) as a whole expanding or contracting, and at what rate? What is the trend in this firm's share of the market(s)? What competitive trends are developing in numbers of competitors, technology, marketing, pricing?

What is the vulnerability to business cycle (or defense spending) changes?

Is there the capability effectively to integrate market research, R & D and market development into a new products development program?

The past-present-future structure furnishes the material needed to deter-

mine whether the firm has presently or in-the-pipeline the type of products needed for success in the future.

A key technique here is to determine how much quantitative information the company executives have and, then, to spot-check the quality of that information by the evaluator's own research. The firm that has sound, pertinent market data usually has achieved the first step to success—a clear definition of the job to be done. Conversely, the firm that has only sparse, out-of-date, out-of-focus data and relies heavily on executives' opinions is usually a poor bet for the future. Unsupported opinions, no matter how strongly held or ably stated, can be misleading. Although top management often must rely on such opinions, failure to secure the data that are available is a serious weakness.

LIFE CYCLE CURVES FOR PRODUCTS MADE

Another device for focusing on the basic facts of life about a product line is the building of S, or life cycle curves. These curves plot sales and/or margins for a product against time. For a given firm such plots picture clearly the life expectancy of products. Composite plots can show the trends in life expectancies. Also, they can indicate developing gaps. When past data are joined to carefully projected estimates of the future, dangerous situations can be revealed. Thus, the firm that is currently highly profitable but has not provided for the future will show virtually all of its products at or near the period of peak profitability.[7]

The question of compatibility of product lines may seem too elementary for mention; however, major mistakes are made in this area, especially by firms headed by scientists. Seeing their own skill as the key one in business, scientists tend to underestimate the importance and difficulty of other management activities. In consequence, they often develop or acquire products that present marketing problems far beyond the financial or managerial capability of the firm.

One science-based and scientist-led company, after an acquisition binge, was attempting to market ten distinct product lines through one centralized marketing organization, all with a total of less than $18 million annual volume. None of the products could individually support a top-flight marketing organization; yet no two of them could be effectively marketed through the same people. The result was disaster.

Integration of market research, R & D and market development into an effective new product development program is one of the newer and more difficult arts of management. Such integration, which is the heart of profit planning, apparently accounted for much of the success of the Bell and Howell Company during the decade of the '50s.[8]

In vivid contrast to the coordinated profit planning of Bell and Howell is the case of the small glamor firm that "went public" in early 1961 for $1,000,000 and has since seen the price of its stock triple. The scientist-president and his associates have developed a dazzling array of tech-nically ingenious new products; however, they have little data on the market for the products and have not yet started to build an organization for distributing and selling them.

R & D AND OPERATING DEPARTMENTS

Having probed a firm's product lines and competitive position, the second vital area for investigation is its R & D, marketing, and operating divisions. Good questions to guide your analysis are:

R & D and Engineering . . . What is the nature and the depth of the R & D capability? Of the engineering capability? What are the main strengths and weaknesses re creativity, quality-reliability, simplicity?

Is the R & D effort based on needs defined by market research, and is it an integral part of an effective new product development program? Are R & D efforts well planned, directed and controlled? What return have R & D dollars paid in profitable new products? Have enough new products been produced, and have schedules been met?

A truly basic change in American industry since the start of World War II has been that thousands of companies have R & D programs whereas earlier only a handful of firms did so. The figures cited earlier concerning the growth of R & D expenditures indicate that sophisticated technologies and rapidly changing products and markets characterize not only electronics and defense industries but also such diverse fields as food processing, photography, communications, pharmaceuticals, metallurgy, plastics, and equipments used in industrial automation processes. The consequence is that most firms beyond the "small business" category must have R & D programs; increasingly a firm must take on the characteristics of a "growth" firm in order to survive.

HOW TO EVALUATE A FIRM'S R & D

One of the newest of management activities, R & D management, is one of the hardest to evaluate. For lack of better technique, the vogue has been to assume that the volume of dollars spent on R & D is commensurate with results achieved. However, we now know that there has been great waste; also, there has been deception by firms "padding" their reported R & D expenditures to give the impression of being more R & D oriented than they really are.

A growing literature reports useful techniques for conceiving, planning, controlling and directing R & D programs and for evaluating R & D output.[9] The truth is being established that R & D management is a capability different from and much rarer than the capability of performing straight engineering or scientific work.

The first task of the evaluator is to determine whether the selection of R & D programs is integrated with a sound overall long-range plan and is based on market research findings. The next task is to compare the nature and depth of the R & D capability with the job to be done. Can it cope with the firm's future needs in regard to maintaining and improving market position by an integrated new products program? The third job is to compare cost and output. Techniques for evaluating output include assessing the quantity and quality of patents produced, measurement of the contribution of R & D to increased (or maintained) sales volume and profit margins, and measurement of the contribution to lowered breakeven points via improved materials and methods.

ARE ITS INNOVATIONS WELL TIMED?

An evaluator needs to understand the time cycle required for research, development and introduction to application; also, he must be able to relate this understanding to the basic facts about the market being served. Such an evaluator can tell when a firm is proceeding in the vanguard of the competition or when it is jumping on a bandwagon too late—as so many electronics firms did with respect to the transistor bandwagon.

MARKETING

Closely allied with R & D and product innovation are the marketing skills of the firm under analysis. Strengths and weaknesses in this area can be uncovered by digging into the following topics.

Nature of the Marketing Capability
. . . What channels of distribution are used? How much of the total marketing job (research, sales, service, advertising, and promotion) is covered? Is this capability correctly tailored to match the nature and diversity of the firm's product lines?

Is there a capability for exploiting new products and for developing new markets?

Quality of the Marketing Capability
. . . Is market research capable of providing the factual basis that will keep the firm, especially its new product development and R & D programs, truly customer-oriented? Is there a capability for doing broad economic studies and studies of particular industries that will help management set sound growth and/or diversification strategies?

The evaluator will already have learned much about market research capability in answering the product line questions posed earlier in this article. There it was indicated that the firm that knows the facts about trends in its market and technologies is well on the way to success in the future. This clearly places great responsibility on market research, a field still neglected or abused by many science-based firms, especially those in defense work.

To cope adequately with the challenges of the future requires more than market research in the old narrow concept; rather, it requires an ability at economic analysis of entire industries. Survival and growth in a rapidly changing economy sometimes demands more than a stream of new products; often it requires diversification into substantially different fields that offer greater growth and better profits for a given time period.

Diversification strategy is another subject that is currently being developed.[10] The aircraft industry today presents a case study in which certain firms are prospering because ten years ago they started to diversify while other firms are suffering badly because they failed to do so.

The accelerating rate of change in industry is a process that feeds on itself. Thus, sophisticated methods of market research and planning not only help a firm cope with rapid change but also foster more rapid change.

The evaluator must know enough about quantitative methods of research to be able to distinguish between valid use and abuse of market research. If not so equipped, he is at the mercy of the supersalesman with a smattering of scientific lore who can spin great tales about how a given firm has made a technological breakthrough that soon will have tremendous impact upon the market.

The evaluator must also be able to distinguish between creative market research and pedestrian fact-gathering that plods along a year too late to help management conquer the future. Only when market research secures fresh quantitative data on future markets can management integrate market development with product development.

MANUFACTURING

The next area to be studied is production. Questions to be asked include:

Manufacturing . . . What is the nature of the manufacturing processes, the facilities and the skills—are they appropriate to today's competition? How flexible are they—will they be or can they be made appropriate to tomorrow's competition?

What is the quality of the manufacturing management in terms of planning and controlling work schedule-wise, cost-wise, and quality-wise? Is there evidence of an industrial engineering capability that steadily improves products and methods? Does manufacturing management effectively perform its part of the process of achieving new products?

The answers to these questions call mainly for conventional type analysis which need not be commented upon here. This is not to say that there are not now, as always, new and better techniques being developed in the manufacturing field. Certainly an alert manufacturing management will use such progressive techniques as "value engineering" to simplify product designs and, thus, reduce costs; and it will use electronic data processing and other modern industrial engineering methods of controlling the work pace and other cost elements.

But, basically, manufacturing management still is, and long has been, evaluated on the basis of performance schedule-wise, cost- and quality-wise, and techniques for such evaluations are among the oldest and best-developed tools of management consultants and others concerned with industrial engineering.

The quickening pace of technological change does, however, require special attention to the ability of the engineering and manufacturing departments to cooperate effectively in bringing new products into production and in utilizing new processes. Also, it requires special caution with respect to firms with heavy investments in inflexible capital equipment because such investments might be susceptible to almost sudden obsolescence.

SUMMARY ON R & D AND OPERATIONS

To make the most of information acquired about a firm's operating departments and R & D, it is well at this point to pull all this sometimes diffuse information together into a sight summary that pulls the whole picture of operations into focus. Questions running along lines such as these help clarify it.

The Overall Picture . . . Is this a complete, integrated, balanced operation; or have certain strong personalities emphasized some functions and neglected others?

What is the quality of performance of key R & D and operating executives; do they understand the fundamental processes of management, namely planning, controlling, organizing, staffing, and directing? Are plans and controls in each department inadequate, adequate, or over-developed into a "paperwork mill"?

Is there throughout the departments a habit of steady progress in reducing overhead, lowering breakeven points and improving quality?

Are all departments future-minded; do they cooperate effectively in developing worthy new products geared to meet the customer's future needs?

Finance is the third area of a corporation which should be analyzed carefully in appraising its present and future development. In this connection, both the men handling a company's finances and the figures on the balance sheet should be studied. Beginning inquiries could be:

Financial Analysis . . . What main strength and weaknesses of the firm emerge from analysis of the trends in the traditional financial data: earnings ratios (to sales, to tangible net worth, to working capital) and earnings-per-share; debt ratios (current and acid tests, to tangible net worth, to working capital, to inventory); inventory turnover; cash flow; and the capitalization structure?

What do the trends in the basic financial facts indicate as to the firm's prospects for growth in sales volume and rate of earnings? Does "quality of earnings" warrant compounding of the earnings rate?

Although this article has already pointed out limitations of financial analysis standing alone as a method of evaluating firms, its importance as one of the key elements of an evaluation should never be overlooked. Because financial analysis has been so important for so long, its techniques have been well developed. Therefore, it is not necessary to discuss them here.

One concept concerning "growth" companies, however, does require comment. The technique of evaluating a growth firm on the basis of an assumption that it will "plow back" its earnings and thereby achieve a compounded rate of increase in earnings per share is of questionable validity. By compounding earnings on a straight-line (or uninterrupted) basis, financial analysts arrive at estimates of future earnings that justify stock prices from 40 to 100 times present earnings per share.

NO FIRM PROGRESSES EVENLY

The concept of straight-line progress just doesn't square with the facts of life as observed by students of management. Especially in small and medium-sized companies, progress typically occurs in a sawtooth, rather than a straight-line pattern. This phenomenon is based partly on the experience of business cycles and partly on the fact the firms are affected by the strengths and limitations of the humans in key positions. There are stages in which the typical growing firm requires managerial talents greater than—or, possibly, only different from—those talents essential to its start.

At these critical periods the earnings per share may slow down or even turn into losses. Such events devastate the compounding process; if one compounds a more realistic 5–10 percent rate of growth per year, the result is far less sensational than is secured by compounding a 20–25 percent rate. It is exceedingly rare that a firm achieves the higher percentages for any sustained period; Litton Industries and IBM appear to be the exceptions that prove the rule. The reference to quality of earnings is meant to shed light on the sustainability of the rate of improvements in earnings. Here the evaluator must distinguish between continuous, sustainable improvement and isolated events (such as a single acquisition or securing an especially favorable contract) or cyclical events (a period of high profitability certain to be followed by a corresponding low).

THE MONEY MEN

Figures alone don't tell the complete financial story of a firm. Its money management must be rated and this involves an evaluation of both policies and men, not only those in the financial division but also the men in charge of planning and top management. You need to know their attitudes about . . .

Financial Management . . . Is there a sound program for steadily in-creasing return on investment? Do the long-range financial plans indicate that management understands the costs of capital and how to make money work hard? Have balance sheets and operating statements been realistically projected for a number of years into the future?

Is there careful cash planning and strong controls that help the operating departments lower breakeven points? Are capital expenditures inadequate, adequate, or excessive with respect to insuring future operating efficiency? Are capital investment decisions based on thorough calculations?

Does management have the respect of the financial community?

Is the firm knowledgeable and aggressive in tax administration?

While many financial departments function only as record keepers and rules-enforcers, some play a truly creative role. Financial management can today contribute as much or more to improvement in earnings per share as can any other part of management.[11] In fact, in recent years bold use of the newer forms of financing have in many cases contributed as much to the rapid rise of companies as have technological innovations. And, alas, bold but unwise financing has ruined many a promising young company.

The questions here are designed to help the evaluator discover whether or not the financial people are vigorously contributing in a number of ways to the steady improvement of earnings currently and in the long run.

RATING TOP MANAGEMENT

All study of management invariably and understandably leads to a searching examination of the top management men. Here there are pitfalls for the unwary. The analyst must first identify the true top management before he can examine their performance record. Things, in terms of who actually runs the show, are not always what they seem on the organization chart. So key topics are:

Top Management and Its Record . . . What person or group constitutes top management? Has present top management been responsible for profit-and-loss results of the past few years?

The problem is to determine the individual or group of individuals who contribute directly and regularly to those decisions that shape the basic nature of this business and significantly affect profit and loss results. This usually cannot be determined reliably by direct questions to persons in key positions; few men are objective about themselves on these matters.

WATCH THEM WORK

Rare is the top executive who will admit that he is a one-man rule type; rare is the vice president or department head who will admit that he is a highly paid errand boy. Accordingly, direct observation of management at work is needed. Some additional information can also be gained through examination of minutes of meetings and files of memos.

After top management has been identified, the evaluator must ask whether this management has had time to prove itself one way or the other. The criterion is whether or not major decisions and programs put forth by this top management have come to fruition. It is not simply a matter of looking at profit and loss figures for a few years. We all know that in certain situations factors other than top management capability (for example, an inherited product line that is unusually strong) can produce good profits for a number of years.

Next comes consideration of:

Top Management and the Future . . . What are top management's chief characteristics? How adequate or inadequate is this type of management for coping with the challenges of the future?

Will the present type and quality of top management continue, or will it deteriorate, will it improve, or will it change its basic character?

We must ask how and why top management has achieved the results that it has achieved so that we can judge how adequate it will be for meeting tomorrow's challenges. Exploring the how and why gets the evaluator into the subject of types of management and their effects on profitability—the thorniest area of contemporary management theory. Over the past twenty years a tremendous literature has accumulated on such subjects as participative leadership, autocratic vs. bureaucratic vs. democratic types of management, and related subjects.

Some writers have claimed or implied great virtues for participative-democratic methods; others have attacked such methods as wasteful and ineffective, wholly inappropriate in industrial life and have advocated "benevolent autocracy." The confusion recently reached a zenith with the almost simultaneous publication of conflicting views by eminent professors from the same university.[12]

Industrial psychologists and sociologists have provided valuable insights into management practices and their effects upon profitability. While a skilled social scientist could contribute importantly to the evaluation of a firm's top management, there is a more direct way of evaluating top management's capability for coping with future challenges.

The direct method is to determine how top management has in the past coped with the future. This technique is based on the idea that management is essentially the process of planning to achieve certain goals and, then, controlling activities so that the goals are actually attained. It is in the processes of planning and controlling that top management does its major decision-making. Since planning and controlling are the heart of the managerial process, it is in these activities that top management most fully reveals its vital characteristics.

The evaluator can probe deeply into the content of the firm's past and current long-range and short-range plans, into the methods by which the plans are formulated, and into the controls used to bring those plans to fruition. This technique gets away, to

a considerable extent, from subjective judgments; it deals with such facts as what was planned, how it was planned and what actually happened.

Fortunately these activities can be studied without great difficulty and by persons who do not have formal training in the behavioral sciences. A simple yet highly informative procedure is to compare succeeding sets of old long-range plans with one another, with present plans and with actual events.

DO THEIR PLANS WORK?

First, a firm that is effectively tomorrow-minded will have long-range plans. These may not be neatly bound in a cover labeled "long-range plans"; however, they will exist either in minutes of meetings, in memos, in reports to stockholders or in other places. Second, the old plans will contain evidence as to whether top management truly has studied the future to determine and anticipate the nature of the opportunities and threats that will inevitably arise.

Third, the old plans will contain evidence of the nature and quality of the solutions developed for meeting the challenges of the future—how creative, aggressive and realistic management has been in initiative matters such as selecting R & D programs, establishing diversification strategy and program, developing new markets, planning the organizational changes needed to keep fit for new tasks, and effectively utilizing advanced techniques (e.g., operations research, automation, etc.) when feasible.

Special attention to initiative matters will indicate whether or not top management is creative and aggressive enough to keep up with an accelerating rate of change.

Fourth, comparison of succeeding sets of plans will indicate whether consistent progress has been made or top management is recklessly aggressive in that it undertakes unrealistic, ill-conceived, unachievable plans.

The same technique can be applied to short-range plans such as annual budgets, sales forecasts and special developmental programs of many types. This study will indicate whether or not forecasts are typically accurate, whether or not plans typically are successfully completed, whether or not new products are developed on schedule, and whether or not they are supported by marketing, finance, and management programs ready to go at the right time. Again, as in the case of long-range plans, the inquiry will reveal whether decision-making is mature or immature. Has management made profitability a habit, or just a subject of wishful thinking?

A management that knows how to bring plans to fruition builds into every plan a set of controls designed to give early warning of problems and an indication that corrective action is needed. Examination of the controls and the ways in which they are used will indicate whether or not top management is on top of its problems or vice versa.

WHO MAKES THE PLANS?

Investigation of the methods by which plans are formulated and control is exercised will reveal a great deal about whether top management is autocratic, bureaucratic or democratic. This inquiry holds more than academic interest; the extent to which lower levels of management contribute to the formulation of plans and the extent to which they are held accountable for results will tell much about the firm's down-the-line strength.

EXECUTIVE TURNOVER

Also, these factors are particularly important indicators of whether top management will retain its vigor, will improve or will deteriorate. Thus, they indicate whether or not top management is making sincere efforts to recruit and develop middle management that will become a new and better generation of top management. Other insights into whether management is bringing in too little or too much new blood can be gained by examining age patterns and statistics on turnover in executive ranks, by reviewing formal executive development efforts and by interviews with some of the men.

YARDSTICK TO GAUGE GROWTH FACTORS

In summary, the technique of probing deeply into the firm's actual plans and controls and methods of planning and control can yield abundant evidence to indicate whether or not top management has the characteristics of a growth firm. Their characteristics have been set forth in a major study by Stanford Research Institute of the factors that usually distinguish growth from nongrowth firms. They are:

- Affinity for growth fields.
- Organized programs to seek and promote new opportunities.
- Proven competitive abilities in present lines of business.
- Courageous and energetic managements, willing to make carefully calculated risks.
- Luck.

Incidentally, this study found that high growth companies had twice the earning power of low growth companies, while maintaining four times the growth rate.[13]

THE BOARD OF DIRECTORS

Rounding out the top management of every corporation is an enigmatic, unpublicized group of men about whom a competent analyst should be most curious. They are the Board of Directors. Questions such as these should be asked about them: What influence and/or control does the Board of Directors exercise? What are the capabilities of its members? What are their motivations?

In the author's experience one of the most frequent and serious errors of small and medium-sized firms is failure to have and use effectively a strong Board of Directors. Too often the entrepreneurial types who start firms disdain help until they are in deep trouble.

Especially in firms headed by a scientist or a supersalesman, a strong and active Board can be invaluable in helping make up for the top executives' lack of rounded managerial training and experience. Except in a few unusual situations, a Board must be an "outside," or nonemployed Board to be strong.

DUMMIES OR POLICY MAKERS

To be active and helpful, an "outside" Board must have some motivation, either financial or the psychic motivation involved in being confronted with real problems and being able to contribute to their solution. Examination of files and minutes of Board meetings will reveal whether or not there is a good flow of information to the outside directors and a contribution by them to the solution of significant problems.

ADDING UP THE FACTS

With all the data in about the four vital areas of a firm, products and competition, operations and R & D, finance, and top management, the analyst ends his task by posing one more set of questions which might be called Summary and Evaluation Strategy. They should run something like this:

What other factors (use a checklist)[14] can assume major importance in this particular situation?

Of all the factors studied, which, if any, is overriding in this particular situation? Which factors are of major importance by virtue of the fact that they govern other factors?

What are the basic facts of life about the economics and competition of this industry now and over the next decade? In view of this firm's particular strengths and weaknesses, what are the odds that it will succeed and at what level of success, in this industry? What are the prospects of its succeeding by diversifying out of its industry?

DETERMINING OTHER VITAL FACTORS

There is a purpose behind every evaluation study. That purpose or the particular nature of the firm and its industry might place importance upon any of an almost infinite number of factors. Accordingly, the evaluator must thoughtfully run through a checklist containing such considerations as: personnel management practices (e.g., labor relations, profit-sharing, compensation levels), valuation questions (e.g., valuation of fixed or real assets or inventory or unique assets), geographical location as related to labor markets, taxes, cost of distribution, seasonality factors, in-process or impending litigation, or any matter footnoted in the financial reports so that the auditing firm is, in effect, warning of an unusual circumstance.

The purpose of a particular evaluation study often will determine which factor, if any, is overriding. Logically, the quality of top management should usually be the overriding factor. By definition a highly competent top management group can solve the other problems such as securing competent scientists and other personnel, developing new products, getting financing, etc. However, there may be an investment or acquisition situation in which the product line, for example, is the overriding factor because it is so obsolete that even the finest management could not effect a recovery within existing time and financial parameters.

MATCHING BUYER AND ACQUISITION

If the evaluation is being done to help decide the advisability of an acquisition, many additional considerations come into play. The problem is one of matching the acquiring and acquired firms; many firms have acquired grief rather than growth because they have neglected this point. At one extreme, acquisition of one healthy company by another may be unwise because the two are so different that the acquirer may mismanage the acquired company. At the other extreme, it may be wise for one unhealthy company to acquire another unhealthy one if the strengths of one remedy the weaknesses of the other, and vice versa.

THE CHARACTER OF THE COMPANY

The acquirer must precisely define his objectives in acquiring. Also, he must carefully consider the "character," or "climate," of the other firm in relation to his own. The subject of "company character" has not been well developed in management practice or literature.[15] Nevertheless, a consideration of the "character" of the two companies is highly relevant, and the outline presented in this article will help the evaluator consider some of the more obvious elements of "company character" such as the nature of its engineering and manufacturing skills, the type of distribution channels and marketing skills required, the type of managerial leadership practiced and top management's aggressiveness and the quality of its decisions in initiative matters.

In sum, the evaluation of a firm requires a clinical judgment of the highest order. The purposes of the evaluation study set the criteria for the judgment. Except in a few instances in which conditions are highly stable, the day is rapidly passing when simple financial analyses, or even financial analyses supplemented by a few interviews and judgments of scientists will suffice for evaluation of a firm.

REFERENCES

(The author, while retaining full responsibility for the content of this article, wishes to express thanks to Drs. Harold D. Koontz, William B. Wolf, J. F. Weston, and Mr. Ora B. Roehl for suggestions that have been most helpful. R. B. B.)

1. "Evaluating Your Company's Future," an unpublished paper presented at the Fourth Annual Management Conference, UCLA Executive Program Association, Los Angeles, October 20, 1960, p. 2.

2. Data from the National Science Foundation, cited in: *Research Management,* Autumn, 1960, Volume III, No. 3, p. 129.

3. Lee Dake explains in detail a case in which a financial analyst and a management consultant arrived at opposite conclusions about a firm's prospects in "Are Analysts' Techniques Adequate for Growth Stocks?" *The Financial Analysts Journal,* Volume 16, No. 6, Nov.–Dec., 1960, pp. 45–49. Dake's thesis can be confirmed many times over in the present author's experience. Particularly distressing was the case where a persuasive but incompetent chief executive persuaded three investment firms to recommend his stock less than six months before declaration of losses exceeding the firm's tangible net worth!

4. The factors are: (a) Economic Function; (b) Corporate Structure; (c) Health of Earnings; (d) Services to Stockholders; (e) Research and Development; (f) Directorate Analysis; (g) Fiscal Policies; (h) Production Efficiency; (i) Sales Vigor; (j) Executive Evaluation. The factors and their use are explained in detail in a series of ten reports: *The Management Audit Series* (New York: The American Institute of Management, starting in 1953).

5. Most dramatic was the case of the Douglas Aircraft Company whose "excellently managed" rating for 1957–8–9 was followed by staggering losses in late '59 and '60. Among numerous other examples that can be cited are the 1957 ratings of Olin Mathiesen Chemical Co. and Allis-Chalmers Manufacturing Company, both of whom, soon after receiving "excellently managed" ratings, suffered serious declines that have been openly discussed in business magazines. For the ratings, see: *Manual of Excellent Managements* (New York: The American Institute of Management, 1957). For accounts of the tra-

vails of these firms see *Business Week,* April 15, 1961, pp. 147–149 and April 9, 1960, p. 79.

6. "Industrial Administration Through the Eyes of an Investment Company," *Appraising Managerial Assets—Policies, Practices and Organization,* General Management Series #151 (New York: American Management Association, 1950). The new emphasis is suggested in a postscript to a reprint published in 1960 by the Keystone Custodian Funds, Inc. (Boston, Mass.: 1960, p. 13). Professor Schell suggested increased emphasis on tax administration, too. The original factors were: (a) Breadth and variety of viewpoint in administration; (b) Vigor and versatility in operating management; (c) Clarity and definiteness of long-term objectives; (d) Vigilance in matters of organization; (e) Dependence upon far-reaching plans; (f) Maintenance of integrated controls; (g) Upkeep in harmony with an advancing art; (h) Improvement as a normal expectancy; (i) Creativeness through high morale; (j) Effectiveness of managerial attitudes; (k) Resources for consistently distinguished leadership in a specific industry.

7. For an illustration and discussion of use of life-cycle curves, see C. Wilson Randle, "Selecting the Research Program. A Top Management Function," *California Management Review,* Volume II, No. 2 (Winter, 1960), pp. 10–11.

8. The Bell and Howell methods are described in two articles: "How to Coordinate Executives," *Business Week,* September 12, 1953, p. 130 ff., and "How to Plan Profits Five Years Ahead," *Nation's Business,* October 1955, p. 38.

9. An invaluable review of this literature up to early 1957 is given in: Albert H. Rubenstein, "Looking Around: Guide to R & D," *Harvard Business Review,* Volume 35, No. 3, May–June, 1957, p. 133 ff. Among the most pertinent articles since Rubenstein's review are: Ora C. Roehl, "The Investment Analyst's Evaluation of Industrial Research Capabilities," *Research Management,* Volume III, No. 3, Autumn, 1960, p. 127 ff.; Maurice Nelles, "Changing the World Changers," a paper presented at the Ninth Annual Management Conference, The Graduate School of Business Administration, University of Chicago, March 1, 1961; C. Wilson Randle, "Problems of R & D Management," *Harvard Business Review,* Volume 37, No. 1, January–February 1959, p. 128 ff.; James B. Quinn, "How to Evaluate Research Output," *Harvard Business Review,* Volume 38, No. 2, March–April 1960, pp. 69 ff.; and "Long-Range Planning of Industrial Research," *Harvard Business Review,* Volume 39, No. 4, July–August 1961, pp. 88 ff.

10. H. Igor Ansoff, "Strategies for Diversification," *Harvard Business Review,* September–October, 1957.

11. For an exposition of this thought as applied to large firms, see: "The New Power of the Financial Executive," *Fortune,* Volume LXV, No. 1, January 1962, p. 81 ff. See also the new text by J. Fred Weston, *Managerial Finance* (New York: Holt, Rinehart & Winston, 1962).

12. Rensis Likert, reporting on a decade of social science research into patterns of management, makes a case for participative management in *New Patterns of Management* (New York: McGraw-Hill Publishing Company, 1961). George Odiorne, reporting on studies of successful managements, warns strongly against the views of social scientists and makes

a case for the more traditional, somewhat autocratic, business leader in *How Managers Make Things Happen* (New York: Prentice-Hall, Inc., 1961). Both authors are professors at the University of Michigan.

13. *Environmental Change and Corporate Strategy* (Menlo Park, California: Stanford Research Institute, 1960), p. 8. A more recent report on this continuing research project is given by Robert B. Young, "Keys to Corporate Growth," *Harvard Business Review,* Volume 39, No. 6, Nov.–Dec., 1961, pp. 51–62. Young concludes: "In short, the odds for corporate growth are highest when the top executives of a firm treat their future planning as a practical decision making challenge requiring personal participation, and direct their planning efforts toward the origins of opportunity itself. Such an approach can make the difference between having constantly to adapt to day to day crises and enjoying profitable future growth."

14. For one such checklist, see: Robert G. Sproul, Jr., "Sizing Up New Acquisitions," *Management Review,* XLIX, No. 1, Feb. 1960, pp. 80–82.

15. A new textbook brings together for the first time the few and scattered writings on the subject of "company character." See William B. Wolf's *The Management of Personnel* (San Francisco: Wadsworth Publishing Company, Inc., 1961), pp. 8–43.

4

Marketing:

the interdependent nature of decision making

Marketing:

the interdependent nature of decision making

There is no universal agreement as to what marketing is.[17] It can be described as: (1) a group of related business activities—including product development, pricing, personal selling, advertising, physical distribution, and marketing research; (2) a structure of institutions including manufacturing, wholesaling, and retailing; (3) an economic process dealing with the exchange or transfer of ownership of products; (4) social behavior, because it involves interaction between buyers and sellers, as well as adaptive and formative behavior by marketing institutions to meet changing consumer life-styles and demands and to influence their buying behavior; (5) a macro process involving a view of marketing as an institution (pervasive behavior) in a society; (6) a micro process performed by the firm or the consumer; and (7) a management process involving the planning, organizing, and controlling of marketing activities.

Therefore, people can view marketing differently depending on their vantage points and the dimension of concern to their study. Because of the general management nature of strategy formulation and implementation, we should adopt the same view of marketing. Marketing management can be described as

> the analysis, planning, implementation, and control of programs designed to bring about desired exchanges with target audiences for the purpose of personal or mutual gain. It relies heavily on the adaptation and coordination of product, price, promotion, and place (programs) for achieving effective response.[18]

The above definition is general in nature in order to account for the broad and pervasive nature of marketing.[19] For example, marketing functions are per-

---

[17] Marketing Staff of the Ohio State University, "A Statement of Marketing Philosophy," *Journal of Marketing* 29 (January 1965), pp. 43–44.

[18] Philip Kotler, *Marketing Management: Analysis, Planning, and Control,* 2nd ed. (Englewood Cliffs, N.J.: Prentice-Hall, 1972), p. 13.

[19] Philip Kotler and Sidney Levy, "Broadening the Concept of Marketing," *Journal of Marketing* 33 (January 1969), pp. 10–15.

formed and its technology is used to promote and to enhance not only the image of products and services but also:

1. *Organizations*—the church, police department, NASA
2. *Persons*—political candidates, celebrities
3. *Places*—tourism in states and nations, museums
4. *Social causes*—family planning, defensive driving, and anti-smoking

Therefore, in case analyses involving strategy for non-business and non-profit organizations, the student should also look for strategic marketing problems. Indeed, one may ascribe the failure of some organizations to a top management view of the organization as a government agency or a philanthropic concern without considering it as a marketing institution as well.

Not only is the student encouraged to examine strategic marketing programs that pertain to the firm's or organization's product or service offering to its customers, but also to make sure that the firm or organization has developed marketing programs designed to relate to *all* of its publics.[20] An example of this would be the advertisement of a firm's attempt to abate environmental pollution, contribute to urban renewal efforts, or train the hard-core unemployed. Another example of such a marketing campaign would be that of a non-profit, family planning organization who must (1) promote the family planning concept to potential users of birth control methods; (2) relate to private foundations providing financial and technical assistance; (3) relate to a hostile church and/or minority community concerned with religious premises or race genocide; and (4) relate to a hostile medical society and community concerned with the ramifications of the organization's success in the promotion of socialized medicine.[21]

MARKETING DECISION VARIABLES

Chapter 1 established a distinction between C_1, C_2, C_3, and C_4 decision variables. C_1 and C_2 variables are those decisions which provide the strategic and coordinative constraints on the marketing function of the firm. The C_3 variables are those decisions which heavily depend on other functional area inputs as well as on marketing inputs. A summary of the C_3 marketing variables and their determinants must be presented before the detailed discussion of them can be initiated. This is expressed in terms of functional equations where, for example, the dependent variable "product research and development" is a function of production technology, financial strength, marketing feasibility, and

---

[20] Philip Kotler, "A Generic Concept of Marketing," *Journal of Marketing* 36 (April 1972), pp. 46–54.

[21] Adel El-Ansary and Oscar E. Kramer, Jr., "Social Marketing: The Family Planning Experience," *Journal of Marketing* 37 (July 1973), pp. 1–7.

C_1 (strategic) variables. It should be clear, however, that the dependence and independence expressed in these functional equations is only relative. For example, financial strength is expressed as an independent variable which partially determines the nature and direction of product research and development (equation 1) and marketing research (equation 2). From a financial perspective, however, financial strength becomes a variable dependent on product research and development and marketing research. The marketing decision variables to be discussed in this chapter are:

1. *Product research and development* = f (financial strength, marketing feasibility, production technology, C_1 and C_2 variables).
2. *Marketing research and information systems* = f (financial strength, production equipment and facilities, financial and accounting information needs, C_1 and C_2 variables).
3. *Distribution channel structure* = f (nature of the market, product characteristics, availability of middlemen and other channel specialists, financial requirements, firm's market position, C_1 and C_2 variables).
4. *Price* = f (cost structure, product quality, stage of product life cycle, target market share, functional discounts, quantity discounts, ROI objective, C_1 and C_2 variables).
5. *Discounts: type and structure* = f (production planning, financial arrangements and cash flows, expectations of channel intermediaries, C_1 and C_2 variables).
6. *Promotion* = f (production capacity and planning, financial strength, channel intermediaries capacity, C_1 and C_2 variables).
7. *Credit* = f (channel intermediaries requirements, cash flow requirements, C_1 and C_2 variables).
8. *Product package and protective packaging* = f (product characteristics, production equipment and facilities, material and product handling equipment, middlemen needs, environmental pressures for environmental protection, transportation modes, C_1 and C_2 variables).
9. *Physical distribution warehouse location* = f (plant location, transportation modes, customer location, customer geographic distribution [concentration], service level requirements, C_1 and C_2 variables).
10. *Inventory levels* = f (demand forecast, customer service level, warehouse and plant location, financial strength, production capacity and production planning and scheduling, C_1 and C_2 variables).

Each of these marketing decision variables is discussed more fully below.

Product Research and Development (R&D)

Most firms adopt growth goals at different rates. These goals usually are dictated by heavily competitive environments in which a firm that does not plan for growth, in all probability, will not survive. In addition, stockholders generally expect firms to grow, and the personal aspirations of many executives for prestige

I. INTENSIVE GROWTH STRATEGIES

A. Market Penetration (Increasing Use of Present Products in Present Markets)

1. Increasing the unit of purchase

   (a) Increasing the unit of purchase
   (b) Increasing the rate of product obsolescence
   (c) Advertising other uses
   (d) Giving price incentives for increased use

2. Attracting competitors' customers

   (a) Establishing sharper brand differentiation
   (b) Increasing promotional effort

3. Attracting nonusers

   (a) Inducing trial use through sampling, price inducements, and so on
   (b) Pricing up or down
   (c) Advertising new uses

B. Market Development (Selling Present Products in New Markets)

1. Opening additional geographical markets

   (a) Regional expansion
   (b) National expansion
   (c) International expansion

2. Attracting other market segments

   (a) Developing product versions to appeal to other segments
   (b) Entering other channels of distribution
   (c) Advertising in other media

C. Product Development (Developing New Products for Present Markets)

1. Developing new product features

   (a) Adapt (to other ideas, developments)
   (b) Modify (change color, motion, sound, odor, form, shape)
   (c) Magnify (stronger, longer, thicker, extra value)
   (d) Minify (smaller, shorter, lighter)
   (e) Substitute (other ingredients, process, power)
   (f) Rearrange (other patterns, layout, sequence, components)
   (g) Reverse (inside out)
   (h) Combine (blend, alloy, assortment, ensemble; combine units, purposes, appeals, ideas)

2. Developing quality variations

3. Developing additional models and sizes (product proliferation)

FIGURE 4-1: Major growth strategies.

SOURCE: Philip Kotler, *Marketing Management: Analysis, Planning, and Control* (Englewood Cliffs, N.J.: Prentice-Hall, 1972), p. 237.

and power generally promote expansion plans, as well. The avenues for growth are numerous—as is shown in Figure 4-1.

II. INTEGRATIVE GROWTH STRATEGIES

A. Backward Integration

B. Forward Integration

C. Horizontal Integration

1. Extension to related products
2. Extension of company technology or know-how
3. Extension of company materials
4. Extension of plant utilization
5. Extension of company sales force and/or channels
6. Extension of brand name and goodwill
7. Lateral conglomeration

III. CONGLOMERATIVE GROWTH STRATEGIES

A. Financial Development

B. Skill Development

C. Stability Development

FIGURE 4-1: (continued)

Growth may require the addition of new product lines and a redefinition of the nature of the corporate business. For example, Avon added ceramics, costume jewelry, and needlepoint kits to its door-to-door selling of cosmetics and also entered into the marketing of family fashions by direct mail and plastic housewares through a "party plan."

Product development strategy is shown in Figure 4-1 as one of the major intensive growth strategies. Philip Kotler notes that:

One of the fastest-growing budgets in this generation has been the nation's research and development budget. In 1928, R&D expenditures totaled less than $100 million. By 1953, it had grown fifty times larger, to $5 billion, and by 1970, R&D stood at over $27 billion, or almost 3 percent of gross national product (GNP). R&D has grown much faster than GNP.[22]

The reasons for the heavy emphasis on internal product research and development are numerous. They include the antitrust implications of integrative growth

---

[22] Kotler, *Marketing Management,* p. 72.

strategies, the desirability of developing new products, and the need to acquire firsthand experience of the problems of R&D.

Determinants. As indicated earlier, investment in product research and development is a function of the financial strength of the firm, of marketing feasibility, and of the availability of production technology and skills. When an individual company lacks the necessary *financial strength,* it may join forces with one or more other firms to pursue a joint-development strategy. The advantages of joint R&D efforts include risk-sharing and reduction and the potential synergistic effects of combining resources and skills that would otherwise be unavailable. On the other hand, joint R&D projects also can suffer from the disadvantages of reduced profits for each firm (as they become shared profits), possible conflicts in goals, and the difficulties inherent in any cooperative undertaking which requires agreement on issues for which there are no clear answers.

Normally, marketing-oriented firms pursue product R&D when feasibility studies point to potential profitable marketing. However, some technology-based companies may pursue basic research not directly intended for immediate product development. This type of technological research is ultimately conducive to product R&D but requires financial strength.

The availability of *production technology and skills* is also necessary for successful implementation of product R&D results. Mass production and marketing are not possible without production resources, including capacity and skills.

Another one of the major problems encountered in product R&D is the necessity of having a pool of engineering, marketing, and finance personnel; and the coordination and communication problems that arise because of their different orientations.[23]

Beyond the point of R&D completion, a product is usually market-tested and then introduced. But it is not necessarily true that marketing decisions are the controlling decisions throughout the life cycle of a product. For example, research and development decisions may predominate at the introduction stage, production decisions at the growth stage, marketing decisions at the maturity stage, and financial decisions at the decline stage. One can readily see that at the growth stage, the concern is one of keeping up with the rapidly expanding demand and minimizing stock-out conditions. At the maturity stage, promotion becomes a vital factor in order to sustain sales volume. As the decline and saturation stages are reached, the concern becomes one of maintaining vigilant control over return on investment and cost reduction procedures.[24] Figure 4-2 should be examined in conjunction with Figure 4-3 to help understand the product life cycle.

---

[23] David Luck and Theodore Nowak, "Product Management—Vision Unfulfilled," *Harvard Business Review* 43 (May–June 1965), pp. 143–57.

[24] Theodore Levitt, "Exploit the Product Life Cycle," *Harvard Business Review* 43,6 (November–December 1965), pp. 81–94.

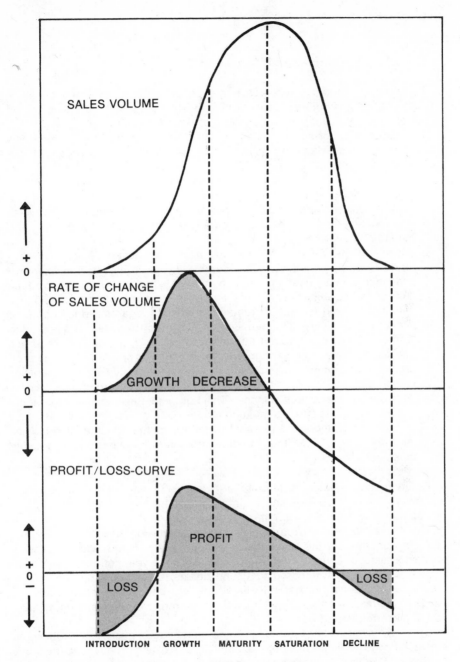

FIGURE 4-2: Development and interrelation of pertinent product life cycle curves.

SOURCE: Eberhard E. Schewing, "The Product Life Cycle as an Aid in Strategy Decisions," *Management International Review*, 1969, p. 115.

Marketing Research and Information Systems

Traditionally, marketing research had a project and/or problem orientation; however, the contemporary perspective emphasizes information systems geared to the continuous collection and analysis of environmental data.

The marketing information system consists of four component subsystems for gathering, processing, and utilizing data collected from the organization's macro environment:

1. *Internal accounting*—This subsystem supplies management with information on current operations and performance. For example, it provides sales volume and cost data by product, salesmen, customer groups, and geographic region.
2. *Marketing intelligence*—This subsystem includes data collected from secondary and primary sources concerning the environment. For example, management may need information about competitors' plans to introduce new products, shifts in consumer life-styles, current work on technological innovations, and federal government intentions regarding price controls.
3. *Marketing analysis*—This subsystem is project-oriented. Its task is to gather, evaluate, and report information needed by marketing executives for decision making regarding *specific projects* or problems. These project-oriented studies may include sales forecasts, evaluation of advertising effectiveness, consumer attitude surveys, and brand preference studies.
4. *Marketing management-science*—This subsystem task involves the application of sources such as queuing models, brand-switching models, sales territory design models, and statistical tools to complex marketing problems and operations. The intent of this subsystem is to optimize marketing operations.

Determinants. Marketing information systems require significant financial investment for development and maintenance. Therefore, their development hinges upon the financial strength of the firm.

The marketing research conducted by Samsonite for their "Travel Bureau Line" is illustrative of the functional dependence and cooperation necessary for a successful outcome. The project involved three years of high-level teamwork and cost several hundred thousand dollars. The group that worked on product and marketing research included the marketing vice president and the heads of the merchandising, cost analysis, research, product planning, design, and engineering departments.

Often, the availability of production and marketing capacity is conducive to research on the feasibility of market expansion for existing products or additional products. Normally, undertaking research for new markets and/or products requires at least some assurance of availability of production capacity when needed. The role of marketing research and its relationship to the overall process of strategy formation was discussed more fully in Chapter 2.

	Introduction	Growth	Maturity	Saturation	Decline
Sales Volume	Growing slowly as initial resistance is hard to overcome and diffusion requires time.	Booming sales volume.	Tapering increase in sales volume.	Decreasing sales.	Rapidly decreasing sales that reach zero at the end of the stage.
Rate of Change in Sales Volume	Growing slowly at the beginning. Growing faster toward the end of the stage.	Fast increase is continued. Toward the middle of the stage it peaks then starts to decrease because of competition.	Continued decrease. Reaches zero at the end of this stage.	Negative rate of change in sales volume.	Continued negative rate of change.
Profit/Loss	Total loss because of the high initial research and development cost. However, high profit margins because of novelty.	Profits are realized at the beginning of the stage. They increase sharply toward the middle of the stage then starts declining.	Continued decrease in profits at a relatively constant rate. Profit margins tend to decline because of increased competition.	Continued decrease in profits at the same rate. Profits reach zero at the end of the stage.	Loss is realized at the beginning of the stage and continues thereafter. Profit margins continue to decline.
Managerial Emphasis and Controlling Factors	Research and Development	Production	Marketing	Financial	Financial

FIGURE 4-3: Basic changes at different stages of the product life cycle.

As indicated earlier, the internal accounting system is one of the components of the marketing information system. Naturally, the internal accounting system also serves financial and fiscal information needs. Therefore, these needs are important determinants of the marketing information system.

Distribution Channel Structure

Many variables can influence the determination of the firm's channels of distribution. From a top management perspective, though, the channel decisions will be constrained by product, customer, and geographic concentration policies and by competitive emphasis. More specifically, they are greatly influenced by the product mix, the markets and market segments concentrated on, the company's primary markets, and the basis upon which it has chosen to compete. Thus, major changes in the channels of distribution will come as a result of a change in one of these strategic variables.

Determinants. Some of the most important determinants, or constraints, that must be considered when channel decisions are made include:

1. *Customer characteristics*—including the number, geographical dispersion, purchasing patterns, and susceptibility to different selling methods.
2. *Product characteristics*—including perishability, bulk, degree of product standardization, service requirements, and unit value.
3. *Middleman characteristics*—including the strengths and weaknesses of the intermediaries handling the tasks.
4. *Competitive characteristics*—especially the channels that competitors use.
5. *Company characteristics*—including size, financial strength, product mix, and past channel experience.
6. *Environmental characteristics*—including economic conditions and legal regulations and restrictions.[25]

It readily can be seen that some of the important determinants of channels already have been defined by product policy, customer policy, competitive emphasis, and geographic limits. The decision on these commitments have, in turn, defined the environment within which the firm operates. In examining the determinants and functions, it is evident that production supplies the multifunctional aspect of the variable. Perishability, bulk, and service requirements are, in most cases and to some degree, capable of being influenced by production.

Financial considerations also represent an important determinant of distribution channels. Different channels require varying amounts of capital from the manufacturer. For example, if the manufacturer elects to distribute directly to retailers, this would involve wholesaling functions that require greater capital investment than using the services of wholesalers. Ideally, the manufacturer

---

[25] Kotler, *Marketing Management,* pp. 566–68.

should consider the "opportunity cost" of investing capital in performing marketing functions versus using the capital in the manufacturing process. If a greater return on investment can be generated by deploying capital in manufacturing, then wholesalers should be used for distribution.[26]

The John Deere case is illustrative of the multifunctional, interdependent nature of channel decisions. When it introduced its new consumer and heavy industrial product lines, the company did not expect all of the current dealers handling its agricultural products to carry the new products as well. Handling the new industrial lines might require redesigning service areas, expanding inventories and parts departments, and adding more personnel. In addition, urban dealers would be more likely to handle the new lines because of their proximity to potential customers.

Price

The most common pricing approaches include cost-, demand-, and competition-oriented approaches; and "ball park," product line, and for a new product, skimming and penetration pricing. The use of one of these approaches in favor of another depends, in part, on the specific price objectives of the firm as discussed below. It also should be noted that under the conditions of raw material and product shortages that prevailed in the early 1970s, more and more pricing decisions became market- or value-oriented rather than cost-oriented.

Determinants. Regardless of the specific approach, the fact is that there are certain components of the price over which the marketer has no control—the fixed and variable costs of production.[27] These are a function of the product design and various other characteristics, including quality, material, size, shape, and the like. Such costs determine the minimum price that must be charged if the firm is to recover what was incurred in order to make the items.

Allowances and deals, distributors' and retailers' mark-ups, and discount structure are additional factors that must be considered before the final price of the product can be determined. They are only a portion of the total cost of the product and are determined within the boundaries of the cost floor, set by production, and the pricing policy developed by top management, as discussed in Chapter 1. Most likely, the pricing policy will be in the form of well-defined pricing objectives. One study of 20 of the largest corporations in the United States found that their most typical pricing objectives are: (1) to achieve a target return on investment; (2) to stabilize price and margin; (3) to realize a target market share; and (4) to prevent or meet competition.[28]

---

[26] Kotler, *Marketing Management,* pp. 575–578.

[27] For example, taxes, building and equipment depreciation, power, heat and light, material and labor are a few of these costs.

[28] Robert F. Lanzillotti, "Pricing Objectives in Large Companies," *American Economic Review* 48 (December 1958), pp. 921–40.

It should be noted that pricing objectives may change, depending on the product life cycle. The price objective at the introductory stage might be to skim the market. Later, at the growth stage, it could change to market penetration. For example, when it was first introduced, the Polaroid SX-70 was selling for $179. Less than a year after its introduction, the SX-70 was selling for as low as $129 at some major discount mass-merchandising chains.

Given all objectives except number three, decisions on allowances and deals, distributor and retailer mark-ups, and discount structure must be made in light of (1) the cost to produce the product and (2) the selling price necessary to achieve either a target return, a stable price and margin, or a price that meets or prevents competition. Even with pricing to realize a target market share, there is a need to price in order to realize a share of the market without incurring a loss. This again would set definable limits on the magnitude of cost associated with the price variables.

It should be clear, then, that decisions on the price variables of the marketing department must be made within the limits set by production costs and the pricing objectives set by top management. These limits define an amount that can be "spent" on allowances and deals, distributor and retailer mark-ups, and discount structure.

Some might argue that the final price of a product is, at times, dictated by the necessity to distribute it through certain market channels. This possibly may be the case, but if the company is adhering to strict pricing objectives, the channel should be altered to meet the objectives.

Under conditions of rising costs and tough competition some companies pull detail pricing responsibility from the field and move it up in the corporate organization—sometimes all the way up to the chief executive officer. Some companies even bring specialists in production, finance, and marketing research together to examine pricing decisions.

It can be concluded that price variables depend on product policy, customer policy, geographic limits, and pricing policy, as well as on the product itself—including the cost to produce it, the customers and target markets that the product serves, and the geographic locations that must be reached. Production supplies yet another input to these multifunctional variables, although decisions on price also will be dependent on a financial input (cash flow). Because all the price variables can have significant impact on the firm's cash flow, financial inputs concerning the timing and magnitude of future inflows and outflows must receive consideration before final decisions are made.

Discounts: Type and Structure

Different types of discounts exist in different industries. However, the pervasive types include quantity, cash, trade, seasonal, and geographic discounts.

Determinants. Quantity discounts are partially determined by production planning, which, in turn, determines inventory levels. A manufacturer may find it advantageous to make larger production runs, as the setup cost may exceed the cost of carrying the inventory. Also, manufacturers may grant quantity discounts to avoid inventory carrying costs which exceed the discount granted.

Cash discounts are used to accelerate the incoming cash flow. Normally, there is a cost involved in financing sales and carrying receivables. Also, dollars tied up in receivables cannot be used in production or inventories.

Trade discounts are generally determined by the expectations of the channel members involved in product distribution. Seasonal discounts generally are utilized to help even out production times. They enable the manufacturer to produce for the whole year and simultaneously move inventories forward in the channel. The seasonal discount compensates the channel members for their inventory carrying costs for the extended period.

Geographic discounts allow the supplier to even out customer location differences by varying the list price on the basis of geographic proximity of customers to points of distribution.

Promotion

Promotion involves advertising, personal selling, sales, and public relations efforts. The importance of advertising lies in the fact that it is an extremely effective way to present information to potential buyers. It can be persuasive to some extent, and also can reinforce or even create buyer preference for company products.

Advertising becomes bewildering when the firm attempts to accurately determine its effects on sales and the amount of funds that should be allocated to advertising budgets. Although some models have been developed that attempt to measure the effects of advertising on sales and thus help to determine advertising expenditures, firms have, for the most part, relied on simple rules, such as a percentage of sales or a fixed amount the company can afford.

In addition to determining the amount of money to be allocated to advertising, decisions also involve:

1. What message and mode of presentation should be used?
2. What media should be used?
3. How should the advertising be phased during the year?[29]

When making these decisions, the objective(s) that the advertising is intended to accomplish must be kept in mind. Some of the possible objectives or tasks might be:

1. To create or point out a need,
2. To link the need to the possibility of fulfilling it with a general product,

---

[29] Kotler, *Marketing Management,* p. 666.

3. To differentiate the particular product and the company from other products which may satisfy the need approximately as well, or
4. To connect the particular product with the place and conditions under which it can be obtained.[30]

Sales promotion can be described as a variety of tools directed at different people, from the manufacturer's own sales force to the final consumer and including all the people in between. Samples coupons, money refund offers directed at consumers, free goods, merchandise allowances, and dealer-listed promotions directed at the trade, bonuses, sales force contests, and sales meetings directed at the firm's own sales force are all examples.

Personal selling may take several forms, including field, retail, and executive selling. Furthermore, it has certain qualities that distinguish it from other components of the promotion mix.

1. *Personal Confrontation*—an alive, immediate, and interactive relationship between two or more persons.
2. *Cultivation*—all kinds of relationships can spring up, ranging from a matter-of-fact selling relationship to a deep personal friendship.
3. *Response*—makes the buyer feel under some obligation for having listened to the sales talk or using up the salesman's time.[31]

Product publicity has been defined as the activity "for securing editorial space, as divorced from paid space, in all media read, viewed, or heard by a company's customers and prospects, for the specific purpose of assisting in the meeting of sales goals.[32] Publicity can have far-reaching effects in terms of media coverage at relatively little cost to the company. Because of this, many firms have placed greater emphasis on this component of the promotion mix in the form of public relations agents. These agents can tailor public relations releases to fit the various target markets and customers.

Some of the distinctive qualities of publicity are:

1. *High veracity*—News stories and features seem to most readers to be authentic, media-originated reports. Therefore, readers are likely to regard such stories about products and companies as having a higher degree of truth than those directly sponsored by a seller.

---

[30] Edmund D. McGarry, "The Propaganda Function in Marketing," *Journal of Marketing* (National Quarterly Publication of the American Marketing Association) 23, no. 2 (October 1958): pp. 131–39.

[31] Kotler, *Marketing Management,* p. 648.

[32] George Black, *Planned Industrial Publicity* (Chicago: Putnam Publishing, 1952), p. 3. Cited in Arthur M. Merims, "Marketing's Stepchild: Product Publicity," *Harvard Business Review* 50,6 (November–December 1972), p. 107.

2. *Penetration*—Publicity can reach many potential buyers who otherwise avoid salesmen and advertisements. This is because the message is packaged as news rather than as a sales-directed communication.
3. *Dramatization*—Publicity, like advertising, has a potential for highlighting a company or product.[33]

Determinants. The decisions concerning promotional objectives and budgets are limited by certain strategic variables. First of all, resource allocation decisions by top management may be the essential constraining factor on promotion decisions. How top management has chosen to allocate promotion funds will affect the choice of media, which, in turn, may affect the message and mode of presentation. In addition, a smaller budget may call for only one advertising campaign where a relatively larger budget, all other factors the same, may call for a number of campaigns throughout the year, placed monthly or weekly. Also, production capacity and the capacity of channel intermediaries to handle varying levels of sales volume influence promotional objectives and budgets.

The message and mode of presentation, and to some extent the choice of media, are also a function of the product, the specific characteristics of the potential buyers of the product, and the geographic location of the potential customers. The message content also may be a function of the company's basis for competition. For example, if a competitive advantage is quality, this factor should be stressed in advertisements.

Credit

It is debatable whether credit is a finance or a marketing function, which should clearly indicate the functional interdependence of credit decisions.[34]

Determinants. Regardless of whether credit is a marketing or a finance function, credit extension is governed by return on investment and cash flow criteria. For example, if credit to consumers is used to promote sales volume, the return on investment for credit extended should be equal to or exceed the return on investment in alternative marketing program components such as promotion. Furthermore, the period for which credit is extended is determined on the basis of anticipated cash outflows. Cash inflows from accounts receivable, arising from the extension of credit, are needed to finance cash outflows for accounts payable.

The price of the product, the buying power of the customers, and expectations of the distributors and the retailers who handle the product influence credit

---

[33] Kotler, *Marketing Management,* p. 649.

[34] Robert Bartels, "Credit as a Marketing Function," *Journal of Marketing* 28 (July 1964), pp. 59–61.

type and policy. For example, high-priced items and low consumer buying power necessitates installment credit.

Packaging

Packaging decisions begin with determining, among other things, what the package basically should *be* or *do* for the product. The task of establishing this has been referred to as the "packaging concept."[35] These functions may reflect certain qualities about the product as well as the company.

Determinants. The packaging concept is an outgrowth of the product and customer policies, or strategy, of the enterprise. Clearly, the characteristics of the product/market provide constraints within which it must be developed. Consequently, the functions which the package is intended to fulfill also are dependent on the products of the company and the markets served. For example, under certain situations, such as industrial products, the major objectives may be *protection* and *economy,* or what may be termed a purely functional package. Other policies may demand that the prime aspect of the package be *convenience,* such as ease of opening. In the consumer goods field, the primary factor may be the *promotional* objective that the package fulfills.

After marketing management decides on a particular packaging concept, the component elements of the package design, such as size, shape, materials, color, text, and brandmark, must be determined. Because these decisions are often interrelated—for example, size suggests certain things about colors—they frequently are made by marketing personnel in conjunction with technical specialists from the production department. Here, production equipment and facilities are usually an important determinant. When the purpose of the package is purely functional and does not necessitate technical expertise—for example, when product characteristics, such as fragility, perishability, and weight are not crucial—the packaging decision may be made independently by either the production or marketing department, depending on the locus of responsibility for this function in a particular firm.

Pressure for environmental protection is another element in the packaging decision. Environmental factors, because of their importance, and particularly the urgency of the environmental pollution problem, may overrule other considerations. For example, the use of biodegradable material for packaging may preclude the use of multiple colors for shelf promotion and display.

Physical Distribution and Inventory Levels

Both the location of the physical distribution warehouse and the variable dealing with inventory levels are in the domain of logistics. Logistics involves the integration of the responsibilities of the functions of both materials manage-

---

[35] Kotler, *Marketing Management,* p. 495.

ment and physical distribution under the auspices of one manager. These functions include:

1. Plant and warehouse location
2. Transportation of inputs and outputs
3. Purchasing
4. Material handling
5. Warehousing of inputs and outputs
6. Inventory levels for inputs and outputs
7. Order processing

Some would add to this list production planning and scheduling.

Figure 4-4 illustrates the integration of material management and physical distribution into logistics. This type of organization typifies some large corporations such as Pillsbury and Xerox. Prior to adopting the logistics organization, these companies had materials management under the jurisdiction of production, as it dealt with inputs necessary for production. By the same token, physical distribution was under the jurisdiction of the marketing manager. Transportation and traffic management for both inputs and outputs were under the jurisdiction of production.

The integration was necessary to provide for *coordination* among these functions and to provide for the optimal utilization of resources. For example, the logistics manager may decide to use the space in the warehouse designated for raw material to temporarily accommodate the extra finished goods inventory which is beyond the capacity of the finished goods warehouses.

Determinants. Figure 4-5 clearly demonstrates the nature of the conflict that can arise between the functional areas when logistics functions are diffused and no effort is undertaken to coordinate them. For example, if the location of the physical distribution warehouse were determined exclusively by plant location factors, this might result in higher total distribution cost because of customer location and geographic concentration, available transportation modes, and service level requirements. Second, if inventory levels were determined by financial considerations alone, the financial manager could reduce inventory levels in order to cut part of the cost of carrying inventory. However, this might result in (1) higher production costs because of shorter production runs and (2) lost sales because of shorter production runs and stock-out conditions. The production cost increases and the cost of lost sales may exceed savings from carrying lower inventory levels. Therefore, in determining inventory levels, the trade-offs between the costs involved in inventory carrying, production, and stock-outs must be recognized. It is evident that inventory levels are affected by financial and production capacity, production planning and scheduling, demand forecast, desired customer service level—that is, the period elapsed between placement of order and receipt of goods—and warehouse and plant location.

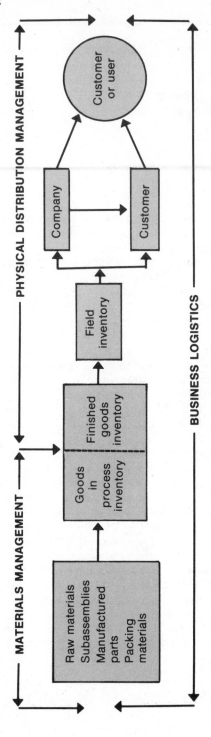

FIGURE 4-4: Alternative orientations of integrated distribution management.

Source: B. J. LaLonde, "Integrated Distribution Management—The American Perspective," *Long Range Planning,* December 1969, Pergamon Press Ltd.

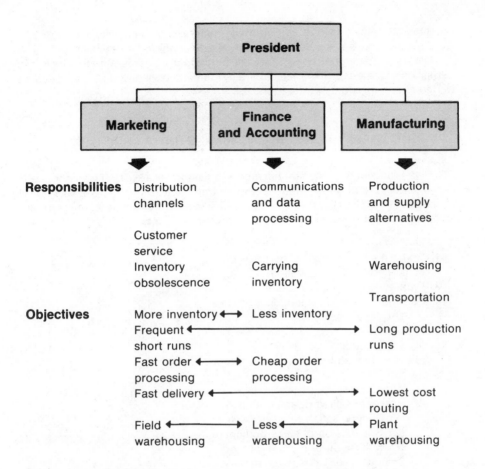

FIGURE 4-5: Traditional organization for physical distribution.

SOURCE: John F. Stolle, "How to Manage Physical Distribution," *Harvard Business Review* 45,4 (July–August 1967): 95.

It is evident from the organization of this text that it adopts the traditional view of handling physical distribution as a marketing function and materials management as a production function. This emphasis is utilized for three reasons. First, strategy focuses on the interdependence among functional areas and the traditional structure is more suitable for this focus. Second, the majority of firms still operate in this way. Certainly, the logistics organization is not a panacea for all firms. Third, the main objective of adopting the logistics concept in organizations is to provide for coordination in decision making for these functionally interdependent decisions. The spirit of the logistics concept is that of the systems approach, where effects on the total system are considered when decisions pertaining to one part are being made.[36] This coordination and systems perspective is consistent with a general management perspective.

Given this traditional orientation, all functionally interdependent decisions pertaining to materials management are treated in the following chapter devoted to operations (production) decisions.

FUNCTIONALLY INDEPENDENT MARKETING VARIABLES

Class 4 functionally independent marketing variables are not of major concern to the strategic and general management orientation of this text, as was noted in Chapter 1. Therefore, they will not be discussed in detail here. Instead, the following is a list of some of the more significant C_4 marketing variables:

1. Brand names and branding decisions
2. Marketing budget allocation
3. Promotion budget allocation
4. Selection of sales promotional activities
   (a) Displays
   (b) Shows
   (c) Exhibitions
   (d) Demonstrations
5. Personal selling
   (a) Allocation of sales territories
   (b) Personal selling operational management
       (1) Compensation of sales personnel
       (2) Supervision of sales personnel
       (3) Motivation of sales personnel
   (c) Evaluation of sales personnel
6. Advertising decisions
   (a) Selection of advertising types
       (1) Product and institutional
       (2) National and local
   (b) Selection of media
   (c) Evaluation of advertising programs
   (d) Selection of message
   (e) Timing of advertising effort
   (f) Selection of advertising agency
   (g) Adjusting the advertising agency
7. Specific channel decisions

---

[36] Lee Adler, "Systems Approach to Marketing," *Harvard Business Review* 45,4 (May–June 1967), pp. 105–18.

   (a) Selection of specific channel intermediaries
   (b) Determination of middlemen margins
   (c) Evaluation and termination of channel intermediaries
8. Specific credit decisions

SUMMARY

This chapter has examined marketing from a general management perspective. Since C_1 and C_2 variables were discussed in previous chapters, this chapter was devoted to a discussion of C_3 multifunctional marketing decision variables. These included product research and development, marketing research and information systems, distribution channel structure, price, discount type and structure, promotion, credit, product package and protective packaging, physical distribution warehouse location, and inventory levels.

The following article by Lee Adler, "A New Orientation for Plotting Marketing Strategy," demonstrates the strategic nature of some marketing decisions. Adler deals with a broad range of decisions and provides several examples from major corporations. More importantly, Adler warns of pitfalls in strategic decision making and prescribes approaches to effective management.

A New Orientation for Plotting Marketing Strategy

Lee Adler

Since World War II ever intensifying competition and the need for profits have prompted alert companies to forge a number of new and productive marketing strategies, concepts, and tools. Unfortunately, however, there are signs that a grave illness affects many managements, preventing their effective use of these modern marketing instruments. Among the symptoms are:

1. A tendency to engage in bloody, knock-down-drag-out fights with entrenched competitors. Examples abound, especially in the packaged goods industries.
2. Haphazard or sophomoric application of theoretically sound marketing strategies—market segmentation, selection of companies for merger or acquisition and, above all, product differentiation. Products without truly demonstrable points of difference meaningful to the consumer are legion. Ask any advertising agency copywriter.
3. Devoted marriage to an existing business pattern despite evidence that it is in a declining phase. In the beauty aids business, for example, a famous company jealously guarded its department and drug store trade while sales volume in their product categories relentlessly shifted to supermarkets. To make matters worse, this company persisted in holding onto its older customers, despite ample evidence that women under thirty-five are the heavy users and are also becoming a larger proportion of the entire female population.
4. Emotional attachment to products that have outlived their viability. Take the case of the packaged breakfast food. It had been the foundation item in the original line, and, though tastes in breakfast foods had shifted and new products had been successful competitors for years, its manufacturer, like an indulgent parent, could find no fault with it. Or, when pressed to justify its continued existence, the company rationalized that the brand was a symbol for the company and that its old-time trade was still loyal to it.
5. A passion for the cachet conferred by volume without reckoning the cost of attaining that volume. This bit of irrationality leads to a drive for volume for the sake of volume, rather than volume at a profit.

Source: Lee Adler, "A New Orientation for Plotting Marketing Strategy," *Business Horizons,* Winter, 1964.

6. Failure to consider alternate routes to profitable volume. Thus, some companies continue to regard the United States as their sole territory while their peers are also vigorously expanding abroad where product potentials are easier to tap. Similarly, some marketers maintain safe advertising-to-sales ratios in fields where advertising makes a powerful contribution to total sales effect. In the meantime, their rivals have learned not to regard advertising as a cost, an inhibiting, negative viewpoint, but rather as an investment that can produce fabulous returns.

MARKETING VISION

What is the nature of this illness that so inhibits creative marketing effort? Levitt called it "marketing myopia."[1] He argued that failure to define a business broadly enough leads to

"preoccupation with products that lend themselves to carefully controlled scientific experimentation, improvement, and manufacturing cost reduction."[2]

Several other considerations that seem also to interfere with the achievement of marketing breakthroughs can be added to Levitt's discussion. The concern here is not so much with a whole industry as with the growth of individual companies, divisions, and brands.

Trapped in the Square

The problem is basically lack of vision and self-imposed limitations. There is no better analogy than to the nine-dot square, the familiar puzzle requiring the player to connect all nine dots arranged in the form of a square with no more than four lines, without lifting his pencil from the paper.

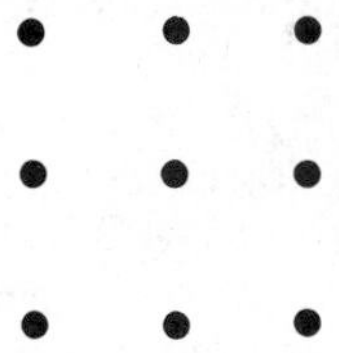

FIGURE 1: Nine-dot square (solution in figure 2).

premature senescence. Levitt noted four conditions which tend to foster decay in the midst of apparent bounty: reliance on population growth, confidence in the infallibility of one's current product, reliance on the cost efficiencies of mass production, and

Most players do not succeed at first because, even without being told, they think that they have to remain within the square. It's only the bolder and more deeply reasoning who immediately realize that they must go outside the square in order to succeed.

[1] Theodore Levitt, "Marketing Myopia," *Harvard Business Review* 38 (July–August 1960), pp. 47–48.

[2] Ibid.

Another factor responsible for this near-sightedness is the overdetailing of objectives. It used to be that if a man was asked what his business goal was he would say, "to make money." More likely, he would not even have been asked the question in the first place. A corporate manager today will give some fancy responses, such as:

—To implement the marketing concept
—To build my share of market by five percentage points by January 1966
—To assure maximum use of our manpower, financial, and productive resources
—To widen our distribution to 90 per cent of all supermarkets
—To achieve an advertising penetration of 62 per cent by the end of the campaign, and so on.

It is vital to have goals. A steady parade of marketing experts are calling for businesses to lay down both broad corporate and divisional goals, and specific marketing objectives. But we should be aware of a danger inherent in setting objectives. To be workable a given objective must be concretized and aimed at a single target. While doing so, however, one tends to block his broader thinking. Thus, the objective of building brand X's share of market from 18 per cent to 23 per cent within two years leaves out such other considerations as, "Maybe we should launch another brand in this market," or "Would franchising help broaden our market, lessen our competitive burden?" or, "Our technical people say they can obsolete our brand and those of our competitors with a radically new idea. Should we market the idea, or suppress it for the time being?"

Although the process of detailing objectives is necessary, it tends at the same time to scatter objectives. The setting of numerous, detailed targets for an existing business bearing on advertising, sales management, sales channels, expense control, and so on may not add up to an integrated system of goals leading to market breakthroughs. On the contrary, this process may perpetuate the status quo because it obscures the need for fresh approaches, because its benchmarks and building blocks all emerge from the existing situation, and because it administratively entangles marketers in today to the neglect of tomorrow.

Two other factors abet this tendency to blind business vision. The first is decentralization. Not decentralization itself, to be sure, for when unit managers are given the freedom and responsibility to operate, the spirit of innovation often flourishes. The trouble is with those managements who cannot keep their hands off the divisional steering wheels and insist that profit responsibility belongs to headquarters. When only lip service is paid to decentralization, both practical and psychological obstacles are raised to the free-thinking of divisional personnel.

The brand manager system, with all its merits, is an even worse offender in this respect. While acceptable in concept, in practice brand managers are often turned into production schedulers, inventory controllers, budget preparers, sales analysts, and expense control clerks. They are so busy with the mechanical details of their jobs that they have no time for its vital aspects—market planning, improving the creativity of their advertising, expanding their brands' domains. The growing roles of marketing consultants, package designers, sales promotion creators, and other outside business services testify to the sterility inside.

This problem is a serious one. It leads to such ill-advised actions as discordant mergers, copy-cat brands, and futile attacks on well-fortified positions. Or it leads to no action at all. The results are failure to grow and to manage change, and increased vulnerability to competition. This is a useless waste when powerful and proven marketing weapons are waiting to be deployed.

Breaking Out the Square

To take advantage of opportunities, management needs a vision of the business.[3] This vision, McKay observes, should be spelled out in terms of (a) customers and markets, (b) products and services, (c) technology and production capability, and (d) corporate personality and character—all geared to the satisfaction of customer wants and needs.

Development of this vision enables a company or a division to apply marketing strategies in an orderly, consistent manner. It helps to plan and program marketing innovation. In a more detailed fashion, it guides the selection and use of each marketing

weapon geared to the desired direction, pace, and timing of growth.

Put another way, this vision helps marketers break out of their nine-dot squares. It arises from a holistic view of a business's raison d'être, a return to fundamentals. And of all the fundamentals, the most basic is: a company is in business to make money by providing consumer gratifications. Within reason, it does not matter how the company makes money. No law says it must make money with brand *A* if brand *A* simply no longer has the capacity to make money. Brand *B* might do a much better job. Or, similarly, if market *C* is exhausted, market *D* may be wide open.

The vision necessary to grasp this fundamental reality has two dimensions. For breadth, according to Levitt,[4] industries should define their spheres broadly enough to assure continuing growth and to head off competition or, at least, to be fully prepared to deal with it. Thus, it is not sufficient for an oil company to conceive of itself as being in the oil business; it is far healthier if it regards itself as being in the fuel or energy business, or in the even broader petro-chemicals business.

The second dimension is depth. Every company has an essential being, a core, the commercial equivalent of a soul. Deep-thinking managers learn to look for, identify, and capitalize on the essence of a company—that which gives it vitality and

---

[3] Edward S. McKay, "The Marketing and Advertising Role in Managing Change," in an address before the 54th meeting of the Association of National Advertisers, November 10–13, 1963.

[4] "Marketing Myopia," *Harvard Business Review*, pp. 52–53.

makes the crucial difference in dealing with rivals and making money.

Consider the Coca-Cola Company. It can be described as a manufacturer of a popular soft drink, or, more correctly, as the manufacturer of syrup used as the base of the soft drink. Or, more recently, as the parent of a whole line of soft drinks—Coca-Cola, Tab, Sprite, Fanta. But a definition of the Coca-Cola Company as a remarkable distribution network may be much closer to the truth. The company's great leader, Robert Woodruff, laid down the policy in the 1920s of putting Coca-Cola "within an arm's length of desire." Today, Coca-Cola is distributed in 1,600,000 outlets, more than any other product in the world. Every kind of retail outlet carries the brand. It is put into these outlets by over 1,000 local franchised bottlers in the United States. Because

manufactures soaps and detergents. To define their business in broader terms, as they keep adding products by internal development and by acquisition, P&G is in the household cleaner business, the food business, the health and beauty aids business, or in short, in the personal and household products business—a broad enough definition to keep even P&G going for years.

But P&G can also be viewed as a marketing management philosophy embodying such vital elements as careful market testing, the assurance of genuinely good products, a high order of merchandising skill, and well-supported brand managers. The application of these elements in a determined and unified manner brings marketing success whether the product is a detergent, a dentifrice, or a decaffeinated coffee.

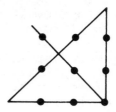

FIGURE 2: Solution to nine-dot square.

these bottlers, guided by the parent company, have created this extraordinary distribution, it is easier for the company to market new brands. So, with increasing competition on all sides, the heart of this success is the means of achieving widespread availability.

Procter & Gamble Company furnishes another good example. Sure, P&G

Still another example is the Alberto-Culver Company, a manufacturer of hair preparations that has lately been broadening its line to include a headache remedy, a first-aid item, a dentifrice, and so on. Its president, Leonard Lavin, has said: "If you judge us to be successful (the company went from sales of $400,000 in 1956 to over $80,000,000 in 1963), chalk it up to innovator products, excellent packaging, premium pricing, hard-driving promotions, and heavy TV backing of effective creative commercials."[5] Many marketers have innovator products and excellent packaging, and the rest, but not many have the kind of heavy TV backing Lavin refers to. For in my opinion the essence of Alberto-Culver is really a courageous media investment policy that results in their profit rate out-distancing their sales rate. The company has said as much:

> We have found an astounding fact: the more we invest in advertising, the less our advertising-to-sales ratio becomes. The sales for our established brands are growing at a greater rate than their substantial advertising budgets. Where a million dollars in advertising used to buy for us $1 to $2 million in gross sales, for our leading brands it now buys added millions of dollars worth of sales, and the ceiling hasn't been reached. Our aggressiveness continues with the added incentive that once we get a brand off the ground, its ability to grow and return profits to the company accelerates at a much greater rate than the increased advertising expenditure.[6]

A company's definition of itself is at the root of marketing success. Only the company with unobstructed vision can use the marketing weapons with maximum effect.

---

[5] Leonard Lavin, in an address before the New York Marketing Executives Association, April, 1962.

[6] John S. Lynch, "Turmoil in Toiletries—the Rise of Alberto-Culver," *Food Business* (November, 1962), p. 19.

MARKETING WEAPONS SYSTEM

There are an even dozen marketing weapons and together they make up a weapons system. They have been isolated by a qualitative analysis of the operations of many firms, mainly in the consumer, nondurable packaged-goods industries. Utilization of one or more of these marketing weapons was found to run as a common thread through the marketing practices of the successful companies in these fields. But these weapons were not used in a vacuum. Rather, an underlying philosophy gave them power and impact. By contrast, haphazard utilization of these weapons consistently characterized the less-able marketers.

The End Run

The purpose of the end run is to avoid unnecessary, costly, time-consuming, or otherwise undesirable battles with entrenched competitors or other nearly insuperable obstacles. The objective is to create the arena rather than uncritically accept one made by the competitor. The following examples show how to do battle in one's own arena.

Those tobacco companies that are outflanking the serious problem of government regulation, public outcries, and negative publicity revolving around the health issue are practicing the end run. A number of possible end runs are available to the industry. Defining oneself as being in the tobacco business, not just the cigarette business, leads to more vigorous activity in cigars and pipe tobaccos, which do not have the serious problem of cigarettes. The self-definition can refer to a technology-based firm using the tobacco plant as raw material. R. J. Reynolds' development of a fertilizer from tobacco stems is a step in this direction. The next step is to become a chemical processor of other vegetable matter.

Increased overseas marketing to escape or soften the strictures of the U.S. scene is another illustration. So, too, is a tobacco company's viewing itself as an expert in mass distribution rather than as a cigarette manufacturer. Philip Morris exemplifies this approach, as shown in their acquisition of Burma-Vita Company, American Safety Razor Company, and Clark Chewing Gum Company, all different products that rely on the same channels of distribution.

During the late 1940s and early 1950s, Lever Brothers Company made a number of unsuccessful assaults on P&G's solid position in the heavy-duty detergent field.[7] Finally, in 1957, Lever acquired "All" from Monsanto for the automatic washing machine market. In this way, Lever succeeded in outflanking P&G in a high-volume segment of the laundry market.

Not to be outdone, P&G counterattacked "All" frontally with Dash. This tactic worked for a time, but by 1961 "All" had regained its lost ground. Then P&G launched its own end run—Salvo low-sudsing tablets. What P&G could not accomplish directly, it accomplished indirectly. Between

Dash and Salvo P&G won half the low-sudsing business in several years. By 1963, P&G was well ahead of Lever with a 16.1 per cent share of the heavy-duty soap and detergent market with two brands as against only 12.7 per cent for Lever's "All" and Vim low-sudser combined.[8]

Thus, acceptance of the boundaries of a marketing battlefront, or of the weapons to be used, does not nurture the development of competitive advantage. But a penetrating vision of one's business strips away these restrictive definitions and leads to refreshing new horizons.

Domination

The principle of domination calls for sufficient concentration of effort, funds, manpower, or creativity (within the limits of one's resources) in one area to "own" that area rather than to spread oneself thin over a wider sector. Application of this principle calls for realistic self-perception. For example, one manufacturer of deodorants recognized that in his field, crowded with multi-million dollar advertisers relying heavily on television, his own modest resources would be insufficient. He, therefore, elected to use a medium then largely ignored by his competitors—radio. Put into radio, his budget was large enough to make him the dominant deodorant brand for radio listeners. This advertiser understood that it was not absolute dollars only that mattered but *share* of dollars too. Moreover, he

---

[7] Spencer Klaw, "The Soap Wars: A Strategic Analysis," *Fortune* (June, 1963), p. 123ff.

[8] *The Gallagher Report,* Vol. 12 (May 13, 1964).

saw that domination brought not only extra dollar volume but important psychological advantages in leadership and in the surety of a solid position, as well as a good jumping-off point to seize another segment of the business.

Market Segmentation

The concept of market segmentation is well known, and need not be discussed here. Its purpose is to identify and concentrate on fractions of a total market capable of yielding a disproportionate volume and profit. The key point of focus is on the skill with which factors that truly divide markets are identified, vital target groups are defined, marketing programs are tailored according to their motivations and needs, and segments harmonizing with a company's own talents are selected.

Some companies in the cosmetic industry, for instance, have developed an almost uncanny skill at grasping the psychology of beauty-conscious American women. The essence of their business is selling beauty rather than certain chemicals made up into cosmetics. "In the factory, we make cosmetics," says Charles Revson, president of Revlon, "in the drugstore, we sell hope." The subtle sale of hope has led to a profitable segmentation of the total cosmetics market.

Other companies have developed a flair for segmenting markets on a price basis. The heart of their business is efficient, low-cost production combined with low-margin marketing effort. Price segmentation also works at the other end of the scale—some

firms have the taste for opulence that leads to success in "class" selling.

In this manner, insight into the heart of a business leads to use of the principle of market segmentation in ways that are uniquely right for the individual marketer. Market segmentation is no longer necessarily an unenlightening slicing of populations in terms of demographic and socioeconomic characteristics. It becomes a creative approach to markets that leads to real benefits.[9]

Consider what manufacturers of make-up and skin-care preparations have achieved. Once upon a time there was a simple product called cold cream. Segmenting in terms of specialized consumer needs and desires, manner and occasion of use, age, motivation, and attitude, cold cream manufacturers now market foundation, cleansing, vanishing, nourishing, conditioning, hormone, astringent, lanolin, marrow, and wrinkle creams.

The vision of a business as a money-making operation also helps to secure concentration on key target groups, rather than dissipation of effort over a broad front. And so beauty aids companies zero in on young women, beer marketers direct their attention to young men, laxative and tonic producers to older, lower-income people, soft drink bottlers to teenagers, floor wax makers to suburban housewives, cigarette manufacturers to men, and so on through all the heavy users in each field.

---

[9] Daniel Yankelovich, "New Criteria for Market Segmentation," *Harvard Business Review* 42 (March–April 1964), pp. 83–90.

At the same time, this vision of a business reduces the dangers of the misuse of market segmentation. Three misapplications frequently observed are described below.

Pursuing the wrong segment. One Western brewer, having won a good hold on the heart of the beer market—younger, lower-income male drinkers—aspired to win the favor of a more elegant, upper-income audience. Not only did his effort fail, but he also managed to alienate his original market. Contrast this with the cases of other brewers who appeal to different social class and price segments with different brands. Thus, Anheuser-Busch now offers two premium beers, Michelob and Budweiser, and one popular-priced brand, Busch Bavarian. Schlitz has two regional popular-priced brands, Burgemeister and Old Milwaukee, along with its premium-priced Schlitz.

Oversegmentation. This phenomenon manifests itself in more specialization than the market requires. The deodorant industry is a case in point. Until the mid-1950s, women were the heart of the market and all products were named and promoted with feminine appeal uppermost. Men used women's products. By the early 1960s the female market was saturated and much had been done to evolve brands with a masculine appeal. Gillette's Right Guard was a prominent example. Then Gillette discovered that other family members were using Right Guard, too. Now the brand is being promoted for the whole family. Since men are willing to use "women's" deodorants and women are willing to use "men's" deodor-

ants, one wonders whether segmentation by sex may not be overdone.

Overconcentration. Sometimes companies, indeed whole industries, learn to concentrate too well. The brewery industry, for instance, has concentrated for many years on young men and justifiably so, in light of their heavy usage. But this has led to a sameness in advertising themes and subjects, media, and sports associations, and to near-maximum penetration of the young male market at the expense of other segments worthy of further development. This may help to explain a static per capita level; annual gallons consumed per person were 18.0 in 1946, 16.8 in 1952, and 15.1 in 1962.

In the malt beverage field additional cultivation could include many other segments. The segments suggested in Table 1 are necessarily an incomplete catalog and do not purport to be a set of recommendations to brewers. Rather, they are cited to demonstrate the potential in building new segments where competition is low-key or nonexistent, while not neglecting established segments.

Soundly used, with guidance provided by a vision of the business, market segmentation is a creator of new markets rather than a constrictor of established markets.

Market Stretching

New Markets are created in many different fashions; the one a business uses depends on how it identifies itself. For example, it is becoming

Upper social class, "snob" appeal	via	Ale, imported beers
"With-meals" market	via	Advertising and store promotions depicting with-meals use
With snack foods	via	Promotion such as Coca-Cola's "Nothing beats a Coke 'n' Pizza," or "Coke 'n' Burger" promotions
Women	via	Feminine appeal brand-name, small package sizes, recipes using beer, as the wine industry does*
Those who prefer strong beers	via	Malt liquor, some imports
Draught beer lovers	via	Bottled draught beer (for example, Michelob)

* These measures would be introduced to foster greater consumption of beer by women, in addition to the fact that they buy most of the beer sold in grocery stores (now over 40 percent of total beer volume—and growing steadily) as their families' purchasing agents.

TABLE 1: Possible malt beverage market segments for additional cultivation.

more common for industrial chemical producers to "go consumer." This can only come about from a redefinition of a business. Dow Chemical Company, for example, has broadened its horizon with plastic food wraps, oven cleaners, even Christmas tree decorative materials, among a long list of consumer products. A number of makers of hair care products have gone consumer another way; specialists serving the beauty salon trade, Helene Curtis, Rayette, Ozon, Breck, Clairol, and VO-5, have all made their mark by selling direct to the consumer.

Paradoxically, market segmentation can lead to the broadening of markets. Zealous specialization evokes a countervailing force: a strong desire is born for all-purpose products sold to and used by practically everyone. The detergent industry is ripe for one; now there are specialized products for heavy-duty laundering, fine laundering, manual dishwashing, automatic dishwashing, cleaning floors, kitchens, bathrooms, and so on. As a result, uses for even the most general cleansers are narrowing. The floor wax business is also setting the stage for an all-purpose product with its profusion of pastes, waxes, polishes—including a product that removes the other products. In this context, the recent burgeoning of one-step cleaning and waxing in floor waxes and one-step dusting, waxing, and polishing in furniture waxes may be the industry's way of broadening user segments. Thus, the sharp strategist recognizes when the time has come to throw the gears into reverse and use the tool of product or line simplification.

Multibrand Entries

Underlying this marketing strategy is a basic premise: two brands tend to capture more of the available sales than one. Marketers with a broad conception of their business have learned to overcome their passionate devotion to one brand. Their vision grants them detachment; they can see that their role in life is not to nurture their brand regardless of cost, but rather to maximize profitable volume. They can then also see that there will always be a few contrary consumers who will persist in buying a rival brand. So they reason that the other brand might just as well be theirs too. They know there may be some inroads into sales of the original brand, but that there will be a *net* gain in volume with two brands instead of one.

Many packaged-goods industries provide examples of the application of this strategy. In deodorants, Bristol-Myers has four brands and seven product variants: Ban (roll-on and cream), Mum (including Mum Mist and Mum Mist for Men), Trig, and Discreet. In soaps and detergents and tobacco products, examples of this strategy abound. Alberto-Culver has enunciated multibrand competition as a policy, and has begun to send second brands into markets in which they already compete.

Perhaps the shrewdest extension of this strategy, particularly applicable when a company is first with a truly new product and can realistically anticipate competition, is to lock out rivals by bringing out multiple offerings at the time of product introduction. One food manufacturer used this approach recently in a product category segmented by flavor. Similarly, a housewares producer applied this strategy to preempt the key position with different-features models in a market that segments by price. The cigarette field also furnishes current examples: Philip Morris brought out no less than four new charcoal filter brands virtually at the same time—Philip Morris Multifilter, Galaxy, and Saratoga; and Liggett & Myers introduced two—Lark and Keith.

Brand Extension

Marketers' emotional attachment to products often includes the brand-name. With brand extension strategy, too, a wholesome and realistic view of the business precludes the imposition of artificial and unnecessary limitations on the use of brand-names. There is nothing holy about a brand-name, and if extension of it can bring about marketing good, while not discrediting or cheapening the original product or confusing the consumer, then extension can serve as a potent instrument. Thus, Dristan, first a decongestant tablet, is now a nasal spray, cough formula, and medicated room vaporizer. Lustre Creme, in addition to ignoring the literal meaning of its name and coming out as a liquid and a lotion shampoo, is now also a rinse and conditioner and a spray set.

Ivory, as homey and hoary a brand-name as any, is as vital as ever in Ivory Flakes, Ivory Snow, Ivory Soap, and Ivory Liquid.

Product Change

As in the case of market segmentation, the crucial importance of product innovation is so clear and so well understood that it requires no description here. Product change lies at the heart of many market strategies and is capable of application in a marvelous variety of ways. The essential prerequisite is a conception of a business that permits free scope to product change and, indeed, urgently demands ceaseless product change. The exact form and pattern of change will be conditioned by the nature and goals of the individual business.

End-run candidates—and the concomitant avoidance of me-tooism —are evident in the development of essentially new products, such as cold water detergents, hair sprays, electric toothbrushes, low-calorie foods and beverages, sustained-release cold tablets.

Flank attacks are also possible by what might be called extra-benefit innovation, as contrasted with straight innovation. The typical example is in the use of an additive, for instance, lanolin, hexachlorophene, fluoride. The less typical example is the double-duty product; shampoos may also provide a color rinse, such as Helena Rubinstein's Wash 'n' Tint.

Product differentiation is the usual means of seeking a demonstrable point of difference. Taste, packaging size, and ways of using established products are the customary variations, as in orange-flavored analgesics for children, spray antiseptics, aerosol oven cleaners, liquid aspirin, mint-flavored laxatives, roll-on lipsticks, powdered deodorants, and travel-size packages of dentifrice.

To outflank competition or to carve out new segments, the ultimate in products must come from a policy of deliberate obsolescence. But this policy is applied reluctantly, and as a result, change is forced on companies by bold innovators, or by new competitors who have no vested interest to preserve. P&G changed the detergent industry with the introduction of Tide synthetic detergent in 1946, and thus widened the future of its own soap brands. Armstrong Cork Company entered the consumer field with a one-step floor cleaner and wax and had no compunctions about upsetting the established order. Gillette joined the stainless-steel razor blade fray to protect its enormous franchise; because it was less than enthusiastic about it, the firm also demonstrated the high cost of being late.[10]

Overseas Expansion

Not only can the definition of a business be product-based, saying, "We

---

[10] Walter Guzzardi, Jr., "Gillette Faces the Stainless Steel Dragon," *Fortune* (July, 1963), p. 159ff.

are in the railroad industry, not the transportation industry," or conceptual in foundation, believing, "The strength of our company lies in the skillful use of media of communication rather than in our experience in this or that segment of the food trade," but the definition may also be geographic. Therefore, the vision of a business can also be liberating in this respect. Most American companies have, until recently, regarded themselves as serving the American market. The foreign market was truly foreign to their thoughts.

In contrast, companies that have the vision to see both the vast potential of the foreign market for basic goods, and their own role in supplying it, have profited enormously. In the case of Colgate-Palmolive, for instance, while its headquarters happens to be in New York, its spirit is global. This self-image is reflected in its sales and profit story. Faced with savage competition in most of its markets in the United States, Colgate has pushed its business abroad. Thus, its 1952 foreign sales were 36 per cent of its worldwide total; by 1962 this ratio had risen to 51 per cent. But the profit contribution from abroad soared from 45 per cent of total earnings in 1952 to a whopping 89 per cent in 1962. True, Colgate's overseas divisions do not have to absorb any of the costs of product development and testing, all of which are borne by the U.S. division. Nonetheless, the disproportionate overseas profit role is eloquent testimony to the benefit of this liberating vision. Another kind of corporate vision is working here in providing the extra margin necessary to overcome cost differentials, tariff

barriers, and so forth, permitting overseas business to become feasible.

Investment Philosophy

The packaged-goods world provides a sad, almost daily spectacle of products being sent into ferociously competitive markets by their loving . . . but niggardly parents. To prevent nearly certain slaughter, products, especially new ones, require continued substantial support. But again it takes a certain vision to see beyond the tendency to hold down on spending and seek as rapid as possible a return on investment. The vision includes a financial aspect in seeing the company as investor, not spender, and a temporal aspect in realizing that the company is going to be around for a long time and, if necessary, can wait for its money. It is surely going to have to wait longer as marketing rivalries intensify and greater resources are brought to bear. In the packaged-goods field, a realistic vision is frequently identified by three policies:

> *Heavy weight* in advertising, sales promotion, merchandising, and distribution-building, particularly in the introductory phase

> *Substantial share* of weight in whatever media and segment(s) one competes in

> *Prolongation* of payout periods from a "traditional" three years to four or five years, where necessary, while maintaining a firm hold on future profit by sharp sales forecasting and margin control. (Ob-

viously, this can't be done in fields where product life-cycles are growing shorter.)

To challenge so well established a brand as Listerine is a formidable undertaking. When Johnson & Johnson entered the market with Micrin, their investment in traceable advertising expenditures alone gave evidence of their awareness of these realities of the market place. Similarly, a deodorant brand of fairly recent vintage bought position by both heavy weight and deferment of profit taking to four and one-half years after launching. As the president of Alberto-Culver has observed, very heavy advertising appropriations build volume and market share to the point where, in that rarefied atmosphere where few marketers venture, the return becomes disproportionately higher than dollars invested, and the advertising-to-sales ratio actually drops.[11]

Distribution Breakthroughs

Almost as limiting in its effect on the vision of a business is being wedded to a given distribution system. It is also almost as frequent a manifestation of marketing backwardness because the forces of inertia, tradition, and myopia all exert their pull in the same direction. Helene Curtis' acquiring Studio Girl and Bristol-Myers' acquiring Luzier to tap the rich house-to-house sales channel are positive examples. So, too, is Chock

Full o' Nuts' signing up local licensees for door-to-door selling. Cosmetics lines nationally sold to main-line department stores and Class A drug stores that have now extended distribution to grocery stores are also cases in point. (Indeed, one must credit supermarkets more than manufacturers for breaking out of the traditional mold of being only food outlets and creating a vast enterprise in health and beauty aids and in packaged household necessities. Moreover, one must credit retailers in general for the positive effects of scrambled distribution in all manner of goods.) If a national beer brand were to franchise local brewers, taking a leaf from the book of the parent, soft drink companies, they would be acting on this principle.

Merger and Acquisition

The growing tide of mergers and acquisitions testifies to industry's awareness of the potential benefits of corporate marriages. Yet many curious matings raise questions about the vision of the corporations initating them. This is not to argue against a most unlikely merger of a business whose vision is management talent for buying depressed situations and upgrading them or a business whose core is financial wizardry. But these are special circumstances. For most companies, mergers are a serious drain on manpower, time, and resources. Blind worship at the shrine of the Great God Diversification may hinder or arrest opportunities to blend the benefits of diversification with logical extensions of a business. Sound mergers take sound vision.

---

[11] Leonard Lavin, in an address before the New York Marketing Executives Association, April, 1962; and Alberto-Culver's *1963 Annual Report*, p. 4.

Chiclets are quite different from Bromo-Seltzer, Richard Hudnut Shampoo, Anahist, and DuBarry cosmetics, yet the purchase of American Chicle by Warner-Lambert marries dissimilar products with similar characteristics of packaging, rapid purchase-repurchase cycles, channels of merchandising, and advertising response. By the same principles, the subsequent merger of American Chicle with Smith Brothers cough drops is a further logical development of the Warner-Lambert vision.

The merger of Coca-Cola with Minute Maid and Duncan Coffee simultaneously with soft drink line extensions in different flavor categories with Sprite and Fanta and the low-calorie category with Tab represents the application of a two-fold vision of the business. One aspect of the vision has already been noted—an extraordinary distribution skill that Coca-Cola management can contribute to the acquired companies, though outside the bottler network, of course. The second is the definition of the firm as being not in the carbonated cola beverage field, nor even in the soft drink field, but rather in the refreshment business, or indeed, in the beverage business. To these instances of horizontal mergers can be added vertical ones, such as cosmetics companies acquiring chemical interests or, more frequently, chemical and ethical drug producers entering cosmetic and proprietary drug fields. Philip Morris has effected mergers in both direc-

tions—horizontally with shaving cream and razor blades and vertically with Milprint.

Moreover, creativity and imagination in realizing a business' vision can lead to interesting symbiotic relationships. (Here I borrow the concept of symbiosis from biology where it refers to the living together of two dissimilar organisms in a mutually beneficial relationship.) International Breweries, for example, has undertaken to manufacture the product requirements of a small Cleveland brewer, at one of International's own plants. The added volume will help amortize a goodly share of plant overhead and, at the same time, the Cleveland firm will become the distributor in that market for International's brands. The two companies remain independent while enjoying the benefits of a merger.

Iconoclasm

One of the hallmarks of practical application of a creative vision of a business is a willingness to depart from customary ways, to seek unorthodox solutions to orthodox problems. This iconoclasm runs as a common thread through the success stories of the period after World War II. Icon-breaking is necessary even in applying the most sophisticated marketing strategies. For example, it is by now axiomatic to concentrate on heavy users; yet this is not always the wisest strategy. In the wine industry, for example, a careful analysis of the characteristics of heavy users reveals a diverse assemblage of consumer segments. Marketing to each segment requires different tools and can be quite costly. Moreover, many confirmed users require only reminder advertising, but it is well worth promoting to the occasional user who can be cultivated to a greater frequency of usage.

To illustrate further, it is customary for national marketers to have advertising agencies serving them nationally. But Carling Breweries chose a quite different method to help bring the company from forty-ninth place to fourth place between 1950 and 1960. Reasoning that much of the beer business is local in character and competition, and that local advertising agencies are best suited to understand local circumstances, Carling worked up a network of eight local agencies, each of which serves the brewer in one of its marketing divisions, and is coordinated by the agency in the home city.

The advantages of marketing vision should be apparent. It is a mind-opening, horizon-stretching way of business life, keeping industries in the growth camp or converting them into growth situations. It fosters industry leadership, enabling companies to bypass competition and to manage change rather than to be managed by it. It helps decentralization to live up to its promise. Moreover, in providing a systematic framework for exploring new profit avenues, marketing vision is especially valuable in fields with built-in limitations. Some industries have trouble in new product development. Dentifrice manufacturers, for example, despite many efforts to give toothpaste companions in powder,

liquid, and tablet forms, still find the paste in the collapsible tube owning the business. In their case, marketing vision found its practical expression in additives, including chlorophyll, antienzymes, hexachlorophene, and, most recently, the brilliantly successful fluoride development.

For another field, marketing vision might call for overseas expansion, diversification, or new distribution channels. But for each industry, for each company, for each division, and for each brand or line there is often one success factor that is more appropriate than any other. The utilization of these marketing weapons cannot be generalized. What works well for one business will not work for another; what works well for one set of competitive circumstances will not work for another. Also, what works well at one point in time will not work at another. On the other hand, in some situations, two or more strategies may be applicable concurrently. Thus, a chart depicting various strategies at work in a multi-division, multibrand company might present a most haphazard appearance and yet make sense for each unit and harmonize with overall corporate goals. To exemplify this point, Figure 3 shows the strategies at work over a recent five-year period for some of the components of one company. Some of these strategies can be developed within a brand management group; others, for example the acquisitions, have been worked out by top management.

It should be evident that these marketing strategies *interlock*. Segmenting a market helps one to dominate

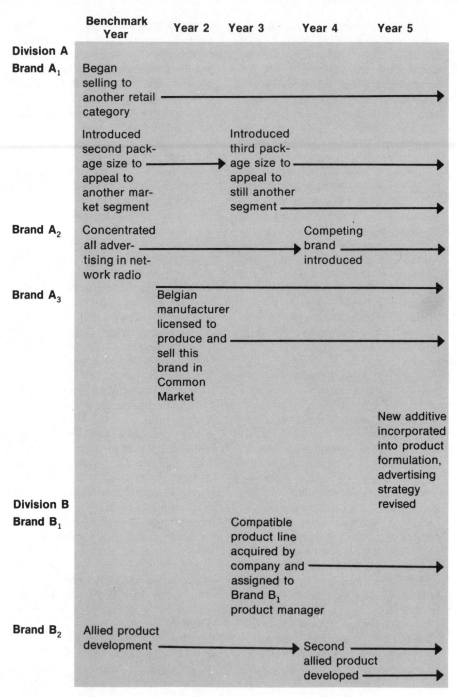

FIGURE 3:   Multibrand deployment of marketing strategies.

it. Product change is often an essential for segmentation. Brand extensions can lead to new distribution channels. And, in the final analysis, all other strategies are end runs, and all break with the rhythm and style of the past. It is this systematic yet bold imposition of a fresh image of a business that provides insurance against decay and a foundation for growth.

5

Production/Operations:

a multifunctional view

Production/Operations:

a multifunctional view

This chapter views the production/operations area from the perspective of top or general management. Therefore, it focuses on those production/operations decision variables that depend heavily on inputs from other functional areas of the firm such as marketing and finance. This emphasis on interdependency is in keeping with the important coordinative aspect of top management and is consistent with the focus of a policy course.

"Production/operations" is a relatively new term associated with the expanded application of the principles and techniques traditionally associated with the functional area of production. Production/operations has broadened the scope of production from primarily manufacturing situations to any organized undertaking—private or public, profit or non-profit. This function involves the transformation of a set of inputs to predetermined outputs in accordance with the objectives of the organization. Figure 5-1 gives some examples of the inputs,

System	Inputs	Transformation Process	Output
Factory	Raw materials and supplies	Change shape or form by fabrication and assembly	Completed product
Hospital	Patients	Health care (examinations, tests, operations, etc.)	Discharged patient
Department Store	Customers	Fill customers' need, receive payment	Customers with purchase, less cash
College or University	High school graduates	Impart knowledge and skills	Educated individual

FIGURE 5-1: Inputs, transformations, and outputs for various types of organizations.

transformations, and outputs that occur in various types of organizations. Production/operations management encompasses the design, implementation, operation, and control of systems made up of workers, materials, capital equipment, information, and money to accomplish some set of objectives.

Because the primary goals of this chapter are to identify and to describe how inputs from the other functional areas may be determinants in production/operations decisions, a preliminary overview of such inputs is desirable. The following list is not intended to be exhaustive and not all of these factors are used in the discussion below, but they should aid the student when he or she must decide on the determinants of production/operations decisions in the particular situation being analyzed.

Inputs from marketing include:
1. Size of potential market
2. Volume of production to meet anticipated market needs
3. Desired finished goods inventory
4. Pertinent data on sales orders—namely quantity, location, and timing
5. New products or processes
6. Customer quality requirements
7. Packaging needs
8. Customer feedback on products
9. Special characteristics to be stressed in marketing program

Inputs from finance include:
1. Budgetary information (allocations)
2. Investment analysis (current information about constraints and advice)
3. Provision of money for improvements
4. Provision of information covering general condition of firm (accounting)

The following production/operations decision areas (C_3 decision variables) are described in this chapter along with their determinants:

1. *Plant location and capacity* $= f$ (long-range forecast of the size and location of the market, capital structure, environmental conditions, state of existing operations and logistics system, production technology, C_1 and C_2 variables).
2. *Facilities layout* $= f$ (medium- and long-range forecast of demand and stability of product line, production technology, physical facilities constraints, safety considerations, C_1 and C_2 variables).
3. *Planning of aggregate output* $= f$ (short-range forecast of demand, finished goods inventory levels, cash flow, employment policy, plant capacity, state of production/operations system at the time of the decision, C_1 and C_2 variables).
4. *Raw materials and work-in-process inventory levels* $= f$ (forecast of demand, cash flow, supplier reliability, C_1 and C_2 variables).
5. *Process planning and job design* $= f$ (demand forecasts, product engi-

neering, production technology, labor force, design stability, C_1 and C_2 variables).

TYPES OF PRODUCTION/OPERATIONS SYSTEMS

The determinants of some of the decision variables described below are influenced by the type of production/operations system being examined. Two basic production/operations systems exist—continuous and intermittent. These classifications represent the ends of a continuum that is based on the flow of materials or services through a system. In a continuous production/operations system, a predetermined sequence of operations is followed that is relatively static over a period of time. A primary example of this is an assembly line such as those used in the automobile industry. On the other hand, in an intermittent flow system, each order (input) may require that a different set of operations be performed—as in a manufacturing job shop or in a hospital. Figure 5-2 illustrates some general distinctions between these two basic types of systems.

Basic Characteristics	Type of Production Operations System	
	Continuous	Intermittent
Unit cost of product or service	lower	higher
Work-in-process inventories	smaller	larger
Lead time	shorter	longer
Investment	higher	lower
Type of facilities	special purpose	general purpose
Material handling equipment	fixed-path	variable-path
Scheduling and control efforts	less	greater
Product line	standardized	flexible
Training efforts	less	greater

FIGURE 5-2: Basic characteristics of continuous and intermittent systems.

The discussion below deals with the ways in which each type of system can influence the determinants of a production/operations decision. By knowing the characteristics of the two basic types, the student can get an idea of where the particular system being analyzed falls on the continuum. The student should then be in a position to decide how the set of decision determinants must be altered to accommodate the system under study.

PRODUCTION/OPERATIONS DECISION VARIABLES

This section describes each C_3 production/operations decision variable, and how each component in its set of determinants can influence that decision variable.

Plant Location and Capacity

This decision involves location and determination of the size of an operating facility or facilities so that the objectives of the organization are optimized. Although it is usually an infrequent decision, it is vitally important because the organization probably will have to operate in the selected environment for some time in the future. It is also a dynamic decision because what appears to be a good location at one point in time may not be later because of changes that occur.

From an economic standpoint, the decision may be based on an objective such as maximizing long-run return on investment. (Long-run return on investment $(R) = (SR-TC)/TA$ where SR = long-run sales revenue, TC = long-run total cost and TA = total assets employed.) This incorporates many of the quantifiable factors but ignores many intangible costs and benefits that could override an economic analysis. Ultimately, the selected objectives for this decision would depend on factors such as management values and the particulars of the situation being analyzed. For example, economics may indicate the best location to be near a small town, but because of the type of industry involved, the ire of the townspeople is aroused. Thus, management may decide that this intangible factor surpasses the economic and locate elsewhere.

Some typical reasons why the decision on plant location may arise are:

1. New venture or business
2. Change in either the level or geographic location of key resources
3. Costs such as raw materials, services, and labor may increase because of price or depletion of that resource
4. Opportunity cost of an existing site
5. Legal constraints such as regulation of pollution
6. Community and/or union relations
7. Fire or other catastrophe
8. Prestige

Some alternatives available when making this decision include:

1. Adding capacity at present location or subcontracting
2. Adding needed capacity at one or more new locations
3. Selling off the plant at existing location(s) and relocating all needed capacity at one or more new locations
4. Not expanding and allowing growth to go to competitors

Determinants. As mentioned previously, the determinants of this decision are long-range forecasts of the size and location of the market, capital structure, environmental conditions, state of existing production/operations and logistics system, production technology, and C_1 and C_2 variables. The nature of the influence exerted by each of these determinants is discussed below.

A long-range forecast[37] of the size and location of the market is necessary because of the magnitude of both one-time and continuing costs dictated by the decision on location. If the forecast or planning horizon is too short, suboptimization occurs because most organizations cannot afford to react to short-term fluctuations in the location and size of the market by continually changing the size and/or location of their facilities.

For organizations that are ultimate consumer- and/or service-oriented (restaurants, banks, department stores, theaters, etc.) location greatly affects revenue and consequently, the location decision takes on more of a marketing flavor. For other firms (warehouses, processors and manufacturers, and so on), location does not greatly influence revenue. Therefore, costs and total assets employed play an important role in this decision. For instance, location of the production facility relative to the market *does* affect transportation costs. Depending on the product and the industry, this cost could be a critical competitive factor. Similar arguments also could be made for the supply side of the organization.

An example of a change in location because of supply problems is the coal industry. In the eastern United States, recoverable coal supplies contain too much sulfur to meet the standards set by the federal Clean Air Act, which took effect in July 1975. In the western United States, the sulfur content of the coal is lower, and it is easier for coal companies to acquire long-term leases. These and other reasons related to the supply of coal have forced the industry to move west.

The debate is more than academic, for the industry is already trekking West, like an eager prospector in Gold Rush days. Western coal, most of it strip-mined, now accounts for more than 10% of the 600-million tons of coal the U.S. produces annually, up from 5% in 1966. In Wyoming, for instance,

---

[37] The time span covered by a long-range forecast is dependent on the type of industry. For instance, a short-range forecast in the lumber industry may be two to four years; however, this would be considered a long-range forecast in some segments of the electronics industry.

coal production has jumped from three-million tons in 1968 to 14-million tons last year and may reach 40-million tons by 1980 and 100-million tons by 2000. Meanwhile, production in West Virginia has fallen from 145-million tons in 1968 to 115-million tons last year and may drop further. In all, says a study made by the Atomic Energy Commission, Western strip-mined coal will provide 55% of the 1.8-billion tons of coal produced in the U.S. by 1985.[38]

The size or capacity decision could be affected by the flexibility the organization wants and can afford. A company may feel that it would be more economical to build a plant with a capacity 25 percent greater than the long-range forecast, rather than have to expand at a later date. Inflationary building costs could be the rationale for such a decision. Of course, the company must support this idle space for some time and face the risk of the idle capacity never being needed.

The existing and desired capital structure of the organization is the second determinant. In the case of expansion, will the capital structure support an increase in this type of asset? The question is especially pertinent if the firm is seeking external funds to finance this effort. As capacity is increased, there is usually an increase in working capital requirements because items such as inventories—that is, raw material, work-in-process, transit and finished goods—and accounts receivable increase, along with the obvious investment in the additional facilities, such as bricks, mortar, equipment.

There are a variety of environmental conditions that directly or indirectly affect the location and capacity decision. In many cases, these circumstances take precedence over economic factors. The availability, wage rate, and productivity of the labor supply can directly influence costs. Labor attitudes and traditions also can affect costs indirectly. This would be particularly true for a foreign location. Often the attractiveness of a low hourly wage in a foreign country is greatly diminished when lower productivity is considered.

The textile industry was originally located in the southeastern United States to take advantage of the raw material and labor supply. The labor picture has now changed, as is illustrated by the predicament in which Burlington Industries found itself:

Like other textile makers, Burlington is especially troubled by increased competition for labor from higher-wage industries in its primary operating area in the Southeast. Textile companies pay an average $3 an hour, compared with $4 for all manufacturing. Charles A. McLendon, a Burlington executive vice-president, cites an example in Fayetteville, N.C. There, he says, Burlington was once the major employer, but it now competes for workers with DuPont, Rohm & Haas, and Black & Decker.

"We've got a tough labor problem," Chairman Myers concedes. In some communities where Burlington has mills, the unemployment rate is down to

---

[38] "The Coal Industry's Controversial Move West," *Business Week,* 11 May 1974, p. 134.

1%, and that, Myers says, is "awfully close to being the unemployables." The pinch is particularly painful in the Piedmont section of Virginia and the Carolinas. "For every worker we've got, we have another job we'd like to fill," says Lewis S. Morris, chairman and president of Cone Mills. Worse yet, textile companies are also having trouble keeping their workers. Burlington's turnover rate is about 65% annually, five points better than the industry average. The rate tends to be highest in the lowest-skilled jobs.[39]

Are service facilities, such as heat, electricity, water, rail, truck and/or air freight, available at capacities required and at what rates? Recreation facilities, housing, schools and churches, climate and natural phenomena are examples of social and cultural factors to be considered. The political environment in terms of tax rates, zoning, and traditional relationships with business is another environmental determinant.

Recently Xerox Corporation acquired a 104-acre site in Greenwich, Connecticut for its corporate headquarters. Greenwich is an affluent community located near New York City. The residents were outraged at the prospect of having a corporation headquarters located in their community and fought zoning changes.[40] Another example where the environment could influence the location decision is the new state constitution passed by Louisiana.

Last month, a new constitution was adopted aimed at straightening out some of the property tax problems. Far from doing so, it has left many businessmen uncertain and fearful of having to pay heavier taxes than before. "There isn't any question that the new constitution is more antibusiness in attitude than the present one, which is already substantially antibusiness," says Edward Steimel, executive director of the non-profit Public Affairs Research Council in Baton Rouge.

"It's certainly going to hurt us in attracting additional firms into Louisiana," says John G. Phillips, chairman of Louisiana Land & Exploration Co., a $160-million oil and gas producer with headquarters in New Orleans.[41]

Many states and cities use their tax structure and/or zoning policies to entice industry to locate there.

The location and capacity of the existing facilities are important inputs to this decision because a new or expanded facility will affect the manner in which the outputs of existing facilities are allocated to the market and possibly where inputs are obtained. This reallocation could increase or decrease costs, and therefore influence the decision. A similar argument holds for the logistics

[39] "Giant Burlington Faces Trying Times for Textiles," *Business Week,* 2 March 1974, p. 49.

[40] "The Battle of Greenwich," *Newsweek,* 5 June 1972, pp. 80–81.

[41] "The Louisiana Tax Swamp," *Business Week,* 25 May 1974, p. 85.

system. Presumably, the logistics system is designed around the present set of facilities. When new or expanded facilities are placed in the system, costs and/or customer service may be affected.

In some cases, the production of the product or service may require special technology or services that are only available in certain geographical areas. An illustration of this determinant can be found in the aluminum industry:

> Aluminum's energy bill now accounts for 25% of production costs, and the tab is rising fast. "The cost of energy, even nuclear energy, for a new smelter is now about eight mills per kilowatt hour," says James S. Apostolina, president of Ormet Corp., the country's fifth largest aluminum producer. That is about four times the price of hydroelectric power in the Pacific Northwest, around which much of the country's aluminum industry is built. And availability of the huge quantities of new power is even more of a problem.[42]

New technological developments in the aluminum industry could alter the influence power availability has on their location decision. The Alcoa Smelting Process is a new process developed by Aluminum Company of America that will require 30 percent less energy than Alcoa's newest and most efficient electrolytic cells.[43]

Another example is the National Cash Register (NCR) response to a basic technological change in its product line that led to a change in its production technology, which, in turn, led to a change in location.

> NCR's biggest cost saving—and most traumatic change—has been in manufacturing. The switch to electronic production was well under way when Anderson arrived. Some 80 per cent of NCR production had been in Dayton, where the average wage rate was $4.95 an hour. The United Automobile Workers had organized NCR and was pushing for equality with Detroit auto plant pay scales.

> Now, only 30 per cent of NCR's production is in Dayton, and wage rates at other plants range from $2.50 to $3. Both Oelman and Anderson stress that moving production out of Dayton was not a reaction to the UAW or the long 1971 strike by NCR workers. Rather, it was dictated by the transition from metal-working to electronic production, because large numbers of skilled machinists were replaced by lower-paid electronics assemblers.[44]

Facilities Layout

Facilities layout describes the arrangement of departments, machines, storage areas, and so forth, usually within the confines of some physical structure such

---

[42] "Aluminum Prosperity is Riddled with Troubles," *Business Week,* 1 September 1973, p. 54.

[43] "A Revolutionary Alcoa Process," *Business Week,* 20 January 1973, p. 92.

[44] "The Rebuilding Job at National Cash Register," *Business Week,* 26 May 1973, p. 86.

as a factory, office, or hospital. The objective is to provide the most effective and efficient arrangement of physical facilities that, at the same time, will provide adequate flexibility to cope with future changes in product design, processes, levels of sales volume, and product mix.

Similar to the continuum involving continuous and intermittent production/operations sytems presented previously, there are two basic types of layouts—product and process. The product layout is an arrangement of work stations that has been set up specifically to manufacture a particular product or group of highly similar products—that is, a continuous system. Before this type of layout is selected, one should consider the following points:

1. The rate and duration of output volume must be large enough and stable enough to justify the time and cost of designing, setting up and operating a special arrangement
2. There must be complete prior knowledge of what is to be produced and how
3. Material being transferred through the layout must be moveable
4. The product should be uniform and the components interchangeable

By balancing or equalizing the work performed at each station, idle time is minimized—and that is the objective in designing a product layout.

The process or functional layout groups similar operations, equipment, personnel, or material in a common area to facilitate moving the work, to provide increased utilization of workers and equipment, and increased flexibility and control. This type of layout is appropriate for intermittent-flow systems. When a product or service has insufficient volume or stability of design, the process layout is used because one could not economically justify devoting a separate set of facilities to that product or service. Usually, when determining the spatial relationship between these groups, the objective is to minimize material-handling costs.

The decision in an "on-going" concern with an established layout usually does not center on determining the basic type of layout to use, but on whether the savings and benefits derived from rearranging the existing type of layout can justify the cost of rearrangement.

Determinants. Medium-range[45] as well as long-range forecasts of demand and stability of product line, production technology, physical facilities constraints, safety considerations, and the C_1 and C_2 variables are the determinants for this decision variable.

The primary determinant of the type of layout selected is medium- and long-range forecast of the level of demand and the stability of the product or product line. This forecast will give an indication of the degree of flexibility needed in a layout. If the maturity of the product and/or the competitiveness of the market suggests that the product or product line will change frequently in the future, it would be difficult to economically justify designing and implementing

---

[45] A medium-range forecast is defined as covering one to three years in the future.

an entirely new layout every time a change occurred. In this case, the layout would be designed with flexibility in mind. This forecast also would be used to estimate the size of inventories (raw materials, work-in-process, and finished goods) necessary; therefore, the storage space requirements for these inventories could be provided for in the layout.

Many companies that are forced to use a process layout would like to take advantage of a product layout but cannot because of uncertainty of demand. Rowe Furniture Corporation has attempted to circumvent this problem. Warehouse dealers carry the same furniture as conventional retailers, but their heavier volume allows them to buy and sell more cheaply. Small independent dealers have retaliated by dropping the lines of manufacturers who sell to mass merchandisers.

Rowe hopes to walk a middle ground. It supplies the warehouse showrooms with the lines they want, but Rowe determines styles, quality, and price ranges. Meantime, Rowe encourages the conventional dealers to adopt the warehousers' methods or to develop other competitive innovations. Specifically, Rowe urges the independents to place sizeable orders for furniture well in advance of delivery, which is what the warehouse showrooms do. Big advance orders eliminate uncertainty and last-minute production changes, thus sweetening Rowe's profit margins.[46]

This reduction of uncertainty in production requirements allowed Rowe to alter its plant layout.

Rowe Furniture is now adding capacity at both its framemaking and assembly facilities in Salem while doubling the capacity of its Poplar Bluffs (Mo.) assembly plant.

Traditionally, upholstered furniture has been manufactured on a so-called roundtable, with five or six craftsmen combining their talents to turn out a single piece. Rowe has gone to an all-out assembly line approach, including such niceties as automatic stapling guns. On the line, each worker performs just one simple task.[47]

Production technology can influence the layout decision in terms of the ease of flexibility of the facilities, the likelihood of new or revised processes, and material handling techniques. The production of some goods requires heavy, relatively stationary facilities while others can use lightweight, general purpose facilities. Obviously, the cost of relocating a piece of heavy equipment such as a hydraulic press or a die casting machine is much greater than moving an engine lathe. In the former case, the layout would remain rather stable, while in the latter case, the arrangement would be flexible.

---

[46] "Rowe Furniture's Strategy for Profits," *Business Week,* 18 November 1972, p. 49.

[47] *Ibid.,* p. 51.

The probability that the transformation processes could be revised or replaced and if so, how long before this change would occur, also can influence whether a layout revision is justified. Previously, we discussed a change in the product line that could mean a change in production technology. Another source of change could be the development of new processes and technology for the same product. Some industries, such as electronics, are characterized by such developments, while in other industries, such as steel, the production technology is relatively stable. The essential point is that if the production technology is likely to change in the near future, flexibility is desired in the layout.

The material handling techniques that are available and required for an operations system can be a determinant of the layout decision. The size, weight, or configuration of the product could exclude some material handling techniques. The amount of flexibility desired in the system also could limit the choice of material handling techniques. In either case, the number of layout alternatives is reduced.

The physical constraints of the site, building, and grounds also can dictate and/or limit the layout alternatives. For example, the location of transportation facilities, such as railway sidings and highways, would determine where the shipping and receiving area should be located. Considerations such as building columns, foundations, noise control, ventilation, pollution, and high bay areas definitely serve as constraints as to where certain departments can be located. By the same token, safety regulations given by federal, state, and local regulations, union contracts, and the firm's insurance company serve as limitations in rearranging layouts. A prime example of federal legislation that influences the layout decision, as well as the next decision variable, is the Occupational Safety and Health Act (OSHA) of 1970.

Process Planning and Job Design

Process planning is the designation of the processes required and their sequence. This phase of designing a production/operations system is usually performed after what is to be made and how many have been determined. Job design consists of specifying two components—work content and work design. Work content defines what must be accomplished at a station. Work design indicates what methods, procedures, and work area layouts are to be used to perform that work. There are a variety of techniques available for making both decisions. These range from relatively simple and inexpensive charting techniques to detailed, costly computer analysis.

Determinants. Determinants for this decision variable include a forecast of both the level of demand and stability of design, product engineering, production technology, labor force, and C_1 and C_2 variables.

A forecast of the level of demand and stability of product design is a critical determinant of what processes and facilities should be selected. If the forecast projects high volume and stable design, the processes and facilities selected would differ from those selected if the forecast projects low volume and unstable design. In the former case, expensive, special purpose facilities with greater speed and precision could be justified, whereas in the latter case, less expensive, general purpose facilities with flexibility would be better. Break-even analysis can be helpful in determining this changeover or critical volume.

This forecast also would determine the amount of job design effort that can be justified. Use of detailed, relatively expensive techniques such as micromotion analysis would be advisable only for a product with a forecast of high demand and design stability. In the case of a low-volume product, only inexpensive methods such as charting or the judgment of the first-line supervisor can be justified.

The remaining three determinants—product engineering, production technology, and labor force—will be discussed together. The efforts put forth for process planning and job design will depend on the complexity of the product, an input from product engineering, on the complexity of the production technology, and on the skills possessed by the labor force. Obviously, more effort must be devoted to planning the processes involved in producing semiconductor memory chips, which require four weeks and 112 separate steps that must be performed in sequence,[48] than for producing paper clips. Presumably, if the labor force the organization is drawing from possesses certain desired skills, the job design task will be easier than if only an unskilled labor force is available.

Here are some examples of how process planning and job design are affected by these three determinants: Motorola produces a small radio receiver used to summon someone from a distance—for example, a doctor from the golf course. The product has changed because of microcircuitry, and this allowed Motorola to change its manufacturing process and job design.

A cut in number of parts from 210 to 80 is the key, not only to the unit's small size, but also to a significant change in Motorola's manufacturing philosophy. The company has set up a major operation in which each assembly worker puts together and tests the entire product.[49]

Automation has been used at Zenith Radio Corporation to hold down assembly costs of color televisions and at the same time maintain flexibility of its production facilities.

Several TV makers who tried to automate their lines failed because of this fast rate of change. "Technology is changing so rapidly that by the time you've built an automated plant, it's obsolete," says George Konkol, senior vice-president and general manager of GTE Sylvania's Entertainment Products Group.[50]

---

[48] G. Bylinsky, "How Intel Won Its Bet on Memory Chips," *Fortune,* November 1973, p. 143.

[49] "Motorola Creates a More Demanding Job," *Business Week,* 4 September 1971, p. 32.

[50] "Bringing TV Assembly Back to the U.S.," *Business Week,* 18 August 1973, p. 41.

By standardization and an assembly machine called an automatic sequencer, Zenith has overcome these problems.

Zenith jealously guards the data on the productivity of its new assembly line, but observers figure that the automated machinery cuts by half the total labor involved in building a TV chassis. Output per worker, they estimate, is 20 to 30 times greater than before.[51]

This change in manufacturing processes had an interesting relationship with the marketing function. Previously, Zenith advertising had emphasized such things as "hand-wiring" and "hand craftsmanship," "the extra care that makes the quality difference." With the automated production techniques, a different tactic had to be initiated.

Another case where automation modified the production process involves the film for the Polaroid SX-70 camera.

But Polaroid decided to innovate in manufacturing as well as in the product. It designed its production line to be run by minicomputers. And having proved to his satisfaction that the minis can handle their separate tasks, Booth is now deep in planning to hook them together in a hierarchical network, with a large EDP system at the top.

In Polaroid's case, the decision to automate the factory was not aimed at labor savings or increased productivity, says Booth. "The fact is," he says, "that we have a terribly finicky product." Indeed it is. The film must be coated precisely with nine different layers of chemicals. Going to computer control, Booth explains, was the only way to be sure that the plant would continuously turn out film, made exactly to formula. "The more opportunity that people have to change things," he says, "the more trouble we have in reproducing an exactly similar product."[52]

Levi Strauss hopes to use automation to overcome a decrease in the availability of labor in the clothing industry, which has traditionally depended on low-wage labor.

In the fragmented, low-profit apparel industry, which traditionally depends on low-wage labor, automation is normally considered an expensive burden, rather than a potential blessing. But next month, Levi Strauss & Co., the world's largest manufacturer of trousers, takes the first major step toward fully automating its assembly lines by mating an electro-optical control system to a sewing machine. By 1978, the company predicts that this unit, and other

---

[51] *Ibid.*

[52] "Minicomputers That Run the Factory," *Business Week,* 8 December 1973, p. 78.

automation innovations will increase its productivity by 50 per cent, and help double its sales to $1-billion.

The $1,500 Servo-Sewer is one example of an impressive array of machinery that Levi Strauss believes will eventually increase worker productivity at a time when the company faces a decline in the availability of skill labor.[53]

Planning of Aggregate Output

The decisions made here include the aggregate or total work force, aggregate production level, and the aggregate inventory level over a planning horizon or future time periods. The problem arises when an organization faces seasonal or fluctuating demand. The organization has many alternatives available to it to meet this type of demand—overtime, idletime, hire or fire workers, carry inventory, incur backorders, or subcontract are typical options available. However, with the selection of any of these alternatives, penalty costs are incurred. The objective of aggregate output planning is to examine what trade-offs are available between these costs along with the forecast of demand and to make a decision which will minimize, or at least reduce, the sum of these penalty costs over the planning horizon. When facing a seasonal increase in demand, a typical trade-off might involve working the existing force overtime and paying a 50% direct labor premium versus hiring additional personnel and paying to train them versus building inventory in the previous slow or slack period and paying inventory carrying charges versus incurring backorders and/or lost sales and their associated costs.

This decision area is also known as "production smoothing" because the decision maker can look ahead, through the use of a forecast, and by anticipating the fluctuations in demand, can make decisions in the present that will lead to a "smooth" production plan. Many techniques are available to aid the manager in this decision, ranging from simple graphic representations to highly complex, mathematically optimal algorithms.

Determinants. As listed in the introduction to this chapter, the determinants for this decision variable are a short-range forecast of demand, finished goods inventory levels, cash flow, employment policy, plant capacity, state of production/operations system at the time of the decision, and C_1 and C_2 variables.

The two inputs from the marketing sector include a short-range forecast of demand and desired finished goods inventory levels. The short-range forecast usually covers the next year or the length of a seasonal cycle and is the primary input to this decision. The finished goods inventory level serves as a minimum level the aggregate plan is constrained to maintain.

From a financial standpoint, the flow of cash to implement the plan should be analyzed. If cash needs are critical in other areas of the organization, cash flow considerations could be a constraint. These might include payroll and inventory costs.

---

[53] "Levi Strauss Legs It Toward Automation," *Business Week*, 21 July 1973, p. 62.

The two additional constraints on the plan include the organization's employment policy and the capacity of its facilities. If the company has an explicit or implicit policy of maintaining a stable workforce, the alternative of changing its size is limited. This means that fluctuations in demand must be absorbed by some other means, such as inventory or overtime. A similar argument can be made for customer service policy. The capacity constraint is obvious and if it is continually encountered, this points up a capacity problem.

A final determinant of this decision is the state or status of the production/operations system, with regard to inventory, workforce, and production level, at the time the decision is made. The state of the system can increase or decrease the alternatives a decision maker has available. For example, if there is a large inventory, as opposed to little or none, then the decision maker's alternatives are increased.

Raw Materials and Work-in-Process Inventory Levels

The production/operations function usually has the responsibility of obtaining raw materials and maintaining them at sufficient levels to ensure the smooth operation of the system. This also is true of work-in-process inventories. Inventories serve the primary purpose of decoupling stages of operations from each other. If inventories cost nothing, the inventory level decision would be easy, but such is not the case. Production/operations stands in the middle with the sales people on one side demanding immediate deliveries and/or a wide variety of products and models and the finance people on the other side telling production/operations not to tie up financial resources in inventories. This decision variable involves the trade-off that must be made.

Determinants. The determinants of this decision variable include forecast of demand, cash flow, supplier reliability, and C_1 and C_2 variables.

The forecast of demand, in terms of a marketing forecast or delivery promise—or the output of the previous decision variable (aggregate output plan)—must be converted to raw materials, subassembly, and assembly requirements. Adjustments must be made for time lags such as delivery times of materials and processing time in the production/operations system. What is ordered today could be used for finished goods to be delivered four to six months from now. Needless to say, an accurate forecast of demand is essential.

Because deviation from a forecast is inevitable, the production/operations manager could be tempted to provide a "cushion" against these uncertainties by ordering a little extra and carrying more inventory. Unfortunately, the inventory must be paid for, either by paying the vendor for the raw materials or by paying wages to transform these raw materials and this creates a drain on the cash flow. Furthermore, the finance function does not like to see the organization's money tied up in inventories that are earning little, if any, return. For this reason, cash flow considerations affect inventory levels.

Another determinant of raw materials inventory levels would be the reliability of the suppliers with regard to providing the proper quantity and quality of materials or services at the best price. Although a deficiency in either of these areas could suggest a change in suppliers, this may not be economically justifiable or feasible. Raw materials inventory levels would have to be adjusted upward to account for these circumstances—namely, an increased buffer between supplier and user so that changes in supplies are not felt immediately by the user. A similar argument could be presented concerning the user of the raw materials and work-in-process inventories. If the scheduling and/or information system of an organization is not adequate, additional raw materials and work-in-process inventories may have to be carried to take care of unanticipated demands being placed on them.

Speculative buying may be a reason to increase raw materials inventories, especially in the face of inflation. Burlington Industries' president Horace C. Jones faced problems of obtaining raw materials at the right price.

Meanwhile, Jones has other priorities, such as insuring that Burlington continues to get the 2-billion lb. of natural and synthetic fibers that its 35 divisions and 167 plants gobble up each year. Last year the value of its raw materials inventory jumped 55%, to $93-million. Says a competitor, with a touch of envy: "My guess is that the increase is a lot of cotton at about 41¢ per lb. Raw materials purchasing is one of the things they do well." At one point last year, cotton shot up to 95¢ and now sells at around 65¢ a lb. Asked if Burlington had bought cheap cotton in anticipation of a run-up in price, Jones chuckles. "Let's just say we don't look upon the increase in our raw materials inventory as a minus," he says.[54]

FUNCTIONALLY INDEPENDENT PRODUCTION/OPERATIONS DECISION VARIABLES

The production/operations decision variables listed below are not greatly influenced by factors in other functional areas of an organization. Under particular circumstances, any one of these areas might be classified as a C_3 variable. For example, if the student is dealing with an intermittent production/operations system, a determinant of the scheduling system employed may be the delivery promises made by the sales force. Thus, the scheduling system becomes a C_3 decision variable. In a continuous system, the scheduling system is not necessarily a C_3 decision variable. It is up to the student to decide if the conditions in the case being analyzed warrant moving a C_4 variable to a C_3 variable or vice versa.

C_4 variables include the selection and control of:

1. The maintenance system.
2. Scheduling.
3. Quality.
4. Inventories.
5. Purchasing.

---

[54] "Giant Burlington Faces Trying Times for Textiles," *Business Week,* 2 March 1974, p. 47.

SUMMARY

This chapter began with a brief review of the production/operations area and the distinctions between continuous and intermittent systems. It touched on five C_3 decision variables that require and/or are influenced by inputs from sources external and internal to the organization. These variables include plant location and capacity, facilities layout, process planning and job design, planning of aggregate output, and raw materials and work-in-process inventory levels. The chapter described the determinants of each of these decision variables and provided examples to illustrate how various factors have influenced particular decisions. The chapter concluded with a list of functionally independent decision variables.

Whereas the present focus has been on the coordinative elements of the production/operations function, the reading immediately following focuses on the "link" between corporate strategy and various production/operations decisions.

Manufacturing—missing link in corporate strategy

Wickham Skinner

A company's manufacturing function typically is either a competitive weapon or a corporate millstone. It is seldom neutral. The connection between manufacturing and corporate success is rarely seen as more than the achievement of high efficiency and low costs. In fact, the connection is much more critical and much more sensitive. Few top managers are aware that what appear to be routine manufacturing decisions frequently come to limit the corporation's strategic options, binding it with facilities, equipment, personnel, and basic controls and policies to a noncompetitive posture which may take years to turn around.

Research I have conducted during the past three years reveals that top management unknowingly delegates a surprisingly large portion of basic policy decisions to lower levels in the manufacturing area. Generally, this abdication of responsibility comes about more through a lack of concern than by intention. And it is partly the reason that many manufacturing policies and procedures developed at lower levels reflect assumptions about corporate strategy which are incorrect or misconstrued.

MILLSTONE EFFECT

When companies fail to recognize the relationship between manufacturing decisions and corporate strategy, they may become saddled with seriously noncompetitive production systems which are expensive and time-consuming to change. Here are several examples:

Company A entered the combination washer-dryer field after several competitors had failed to achieve successful entries into the field. Company A's executives believed their model would overcome the technical drawbacks which had hurt their competitors and held back the develop-

Source: Wickham Skinner, "Manufacturing—Missing Link in Corporate Strategy," *Harvard Business Review.* May–June, 1969.© 1969 by the President and Fellows of Harvard College; all rights reserved.

ment of any substantial market. The manufacturing managers tooled the new unit on the usual conveyorized assembly line and giant stamping presses used for all company products.

When the washer-dryer failed in the market, the losses amounted to millions. The plant had been "efficient" in the sense that costs were low. But the tooling and production processes did not meet the demands of the marketplace.

Company B produced five kinds of electronic gear for five different groups of customers; the gear ranged from satellite controls to industrial controls and electronic components. In each market a different task was required of the production function. For instance, in the first market, extremely high reliability was demanded; in the second market, rapid introduction of a stream of new products was demanded; in the third market, low costs were of critical importance for competitive survival.

In spite of these highly diverse and contrasting tasks, production management elected to centralize manufacturing facilities in one plant in order to achieve "economies of scale." The result was a failure to achieve high reliability, economies of scale, or an ability to introduce new products quickly. What happened, in short, was that the demands placed on manufacturing by a competitive strategy were ignored by the production group in order to achieve economies of scale. This production group was obsessed with developing "a total system, fully computerized." The

manufacturing program satisfied no single division, and the serious marketing problems which resulted choked company progress.

Company C produced plastic molding resins. A new plant under construction was to come on-stream in eight months, doubling production. In the meantime, the company had a much higher volume of orders than it could meet.

In a strategic sense, manufacturing's task was to maximize output to satisfy large, key customers. Yet the plant's production control system was set up—as it had been for years—to minimize costs. As a result, long runs were emphasized. While costs were low, many customers had to wait, and many key buyers were lost. Consequently, when the new plant came on-stream, it was forced to operate at a low volume.

The mistake of considering low costs and high efficiencies as the key manufacturing objective in each of these examples is typical of the oversimplified concept of "a good manufacturing operation." Such criteria frequently get companies into trouble, or at least do not aid in the development of manufacturing into a competitive weapon. Manufacturing affects corporate strategy, and corporate strategy affects manufacturing. Even in an apparently routine operating area such as a production scheduling system, strategic considerations should outweigh technical and conventional industrial engineering factors invoked in the name of "productivity."

Shortsighted Views

The fact is that manufacturing is seen by most top managers as requiring involved technical skills and a morass of petty daily decisions and details. It is seen by many young managers as the gateway to grubby routine, where days are filled with high pressure, packed with details, and limited to low-level decision making—all of which is out of the sight and minds of top-level executives. It is generally taught in graduate schools of business administration as a combination of industrial engineering (time study, plant layout, inventory theory, and so on) and quantitative analysis (linear programming, simulation, queuing theory, and the rest). In total, a manufacturing career is generally perceived as an all-consuming, technically oriented, hectic life that minimizes one's chances of ever reaching the top and maximizes the chances of being buried in minutiae.

In fact, these perceptions are not wholly inaccurate. It is the thesis of this article that the technically oriented concept of manufacturing is all too prevalent; and that it is largely responsible for the typically limited contribution manufacturing makes to a corporation's arsenal of competitive weapons, for manufacturing's failure to attract the top talent it needs and *should* have, and for its failure to attract more young managers with general management interests and broad abilities. In my opinion, manufacturing is generally perceived in the wrong way at the top, managed in the wrong way at the plant level, and taught in the wrong way in the business schools.

These are strong words, but change is needed, and I believe that only a more relevant concept of manufacturing can bring change. I see no sign whatsoever that we have found the means of solving the problems mentioned. The new, mathematically based "total systems" approaches to production management offer the promise of new and valuable concepts and techniques, but I doubt that these approaches will overcome the tendency of top management to remove itself from manufacturing. Ten years of development of quantitative techniques have left us each year with the promise of a "great new age" in production management that lies "just ahead." The promise never seems to be realized. Stories of computer and "total systems" fiascoes are available by the dozen; these failures are always expensive, and in almost every case management has delegated the work to experts.

I do not want to demean the promise—and, indeed, some present contributions—of the systems/computer approach. Two years ago I felt more sanguine about it. But, since then, close observation of the problems in U.S. industry has convinced me that the "answer" promised is inadequate. The approach cannot overcome the problems described until it does a far better job of linking manufacturing and corporate strategy. What is needed is some kind of integrative mechanism.

PATTERN OF FAILURE

An examination of top management perceptions of manufacturing has led me to some notions about basic causes of many production problems. In each of six industries I have studied, I have found top executives delegating excessive amounts of manufacturing policy to subordinates, avoiding involvement in most production matters, and failing to ask the right questions until their companies are in obvious trouble. This pattern seems to be due to a combination of two factors:

1. A sense of personal inadequacy, on the part of top executives, in managing production. (Often the feeling evolves from a tendency to regard the area as a technical or engineering specialty, or a mundane "nuts and bolts" segment of management.)

2. A lack of awareness among top executives that a production system inevitably involves trade-offs and compromises and so must be designed to perform a limited task well, with that task defined by corporate strategic objectives.

The first factor is, of course, dependent in part on the second, for the sense of inadequacy would not be felt if the strategic role of production were clearer. The second factor is the one we shall concentrate on in the remainder of this article.

Like a building, a vehicle, or a boat, a production system can be designed to do some things well, but always at the expense of other abilities. It appears to be the lack of recognition of these trade-offs and their effects on a corporation's ability to compete that leads top management to delegate often-critical decisions to lower, technically oriented staff levels, and to allow policy to be made through apparently unimportant operating decisions.

In the balance of this article I would like to . . .

—sketch out the relationships between production operations and corporate strategy;

—call attention to the existence of specific trade-offs in production system design;

—comment on the inadequacy of computer specialists to deal with these trade-offs;

—suggest a new way of looking at manufacturing which might enable the nontechnical manager to understand and manage the manufacturing area.

STRATEGIC IMPLICATIONS

Frequently the interrelationship between production operations and corporate strategy is not easily grasped. The notion is simple enough —namely, that a company's competitive strategy at a given time places particular demands on its manufacturing function, and, conversely, that the company's manufacturing posture and operations should be specifically designed to fulfill the task demanded by strategic plans. What is more elusive is the set of cause-and-effect factors which determine the linkage between strategy and production operations.

Strategy is a set of plans and policies by which a company aims to gain advantages over its competitors. Generally a strategy includes plans for products and the marketing of these products to a particular set of customers. The marketing plans usually include specific approaches and steps to be followed in identifying potential customers, determining why, where, and when they buy, and learning how they can best be reached and convinced to purchase. The company must have an advantage, a particular appeal, a special push or pull created by its products, channels of distribution, advertising, price, packaging, availability, warranties, or other factors.

Contrasting Demands

What is not always realized is that different marketing strategies and approaches to gaining a competitive advantage place different demands on the manufacturing arm of the company. For example, a furniture manufacturer's strategy for broad distribution of a limited, low-price line with wide consumer advertising might generally require:

- Decentralized finished-goods storage.
- Readily available merchandise.
- Rock-bottom costs.

The foregoing demands might in turn require:

- Relatively large lot sizes.
- Specialized facilities for woodworking and finishing.
- A large proportion of low- and medium-skilled workers in the work force.

- Concentration of manufacturing in a limited number of large-scale plants.

In contrast, a manufacturer of high-price, high-style furniture with more exclusive distribution would require an entirely different set of manufacturing policies. While higher prices and longer lead times would allow more leeway in the plant, this company would have to contend with the problems implicit in delivering high-quality furniture made of wood (which is a soft, dimensionally unstable material whose surface is expensive to finish and easy to damage), a high setup cost relative to running times in most wood-machining operations, and the need to make a large number of nonstandardized parts. While the first company must work with these problems too, they are more serious to the second company because its marketing strategy forces it to confront the problems head on. The latter's manufacturing policies will probably require:

- Many model and style changes.
- Production to order.
- Extremely reliable high quality.

These demands may in turn require:

- An organization that can get new models into production quickly.
- A production control group that can coordinate all activities so as to reduce lead times.
- Technically trained supervisors and technicians.

Consequently, the second company ought to have a strong manufacturing-methods engineering staff; simple, flexible tooling; and a well-trained, experienced work force.

In summary, the two manufacturers would need to develop very different policies, personnel, and operations if they were to be equally successful in carrying out their strategies.

Important Choices

In the example described, there are marked contrasts in the two companies. Actually, even small and subtle differences in corporate strategies should be reflected in manufacturing policies. However, my research shows that few companies do in fact carefully and explicitly tailor their production systems to perform the tasks which are vital to corporate success.

Instead of focusing first on strategy, then moving to define the manufacturing task, and next turning to systems design in manufacturing policy, managements tend to employ a concept of production which is much less effective. Most top executives and production managers look at their production systems with the notion of "total productivity" or the equivalent, "efficiency." They seek a kind of blending of low costs, high quality, and acceptable customer service. The view prevails that a plant with reasonably modern equipment, up-to-date methods and procedures, a cooperative work force, a computerized information system, and an enlightened management will be a good plant and will perform efficiently.

But what is "a good plant"? What is "efficient performance"? And what should the computer be programmed to do? Should it minimize lead times or minimize inventories? A company

cannot do both. Should the computer minimize direct labor or indirect labor? Again, the company cannot do both. Should investment in equipment be minimized—or should outside purchasing be held to a minimum? One could go on with such choices.

The reader may reply: "What management wants is a combination of both ingredients that results in the lowest *total* cost." But that answer, too, is insufficient. The "lowest total cost" answer leaves out the dimensions of time and customer satisfaction, which must usually be considered too. Because cost *and* time *and* customers are all involved, we have to conclude that what is a "good" plant for Company A may be a poor or mediocre plant for its competitor, Company B, which is in the same industry but pursues a different strategy.

The purpose of manufacturing is to serve the company—to meet its needs for survival, profit, and growth. Manufacturing is part of the strategic concept that relates a company's strengths and resources to opportunities in the market. Each strategy creates a unique manufacturing task. Manufacturing management's ability to meet that task is the key measure of its success.

TRADE-OFFS IN DESIGN

It is curious that most top managements and production people do not state their yardsticks of success more precisely, and instead fall back on such measures as "efficiency," "low cost," and "productivity." My studies suggest that a key reason for this phenomenon is that very few executives realize the existence of trade-offs in designing and operating a production system.

Yet most managers will readily admit that there are compromises or trade-offs to be made in designing an airplane or a truck. In the case of an airplane, trade-offs would involve such matters as cruising speed, take-off and landing distances, initial cost, maintenance, fuel consumption, passenger comfort, and cargo or passenger capacity. A given stage of technology defines limits as to what can be accomplished in these respects. For instance, no one today can design a 500-passenger plane that can land on a carrier and also break the sonic barrier.

Much of the same thing is true of manufacturing. The variables of cost, time, quality, technological constraints, and customer satisfaction place limits on what management can do, force compromises, and demand an explicit recognition of a multitude of trade-offs and choices. Yet everywhere I find plants which have inadvertently emphasized one yardstick at the expense of another, more important one. For example:

An electronics manufacturer with dissatisfied customers hired a computer expert and placed manufacturing under a successful engineering design chief to make it a "total system." A year later its computer was spewing out an inch-thick volume of daily information. "We know the location of every part in the plant on any given day," boasted the production manager and his computer systems chief.

Nevertheless, customers were more dissatisfied than ever. Product managers hotly complained that delivery promises were regularly missed—and in almost every case they first heard about failures from their customers. The problem centered on the fact that computer information runs were organized by part numbers and operations. They were designed to facilitate machine scheduling and to aid shop foremen; they were not organized around end products, which would have facilitated customer service.

How had this come about? Largely, it seemed clear, because the manufacturing managers had become absorbed in their own "systems approach"; the fascination of mechanized data handling had become an end in itself. As for top management, it had more or less abdicated responsibility. Because the company's growth and success had been based on engineering and because top management was R&D-oriented, policy-making executives saw production as a routine requiring a lower level of complexity and brainpower. Top management argued further that the company had production experts who were well paid and who should be able to do their jobs without bothering top-level people.

Recognizing Alternatives

To develop the notion of important trade-off decisions in manufacturing, let us consider *Exhibit 1,* which shows some examples.

In each decision area—plant and equipment, production planning and

Decision area	Decision	Alternatives
PLANT AND EQUIPMENT	Span of process	Make or buy
	Plant size	One big plant or several smaller ones
	Plant location	Locate near markets or locate near materials
	Investment decisions	Invest mainly in buildings or equipment or inventories or research
	Choice of equipment	General-purpose or special-purpose equipment
	Kind of tooling	Temporary, minimum tooling or "production tooling"
PRODUCTION PLANNING AND CONTROL	Frequency of inventory taking	Few or many breaks in production for buffer stocks
	Inventory size	High inventory or a lower inventory
	Degree of inventory control	Control in great detail or in lesser detail
	What to control	Controls designed to minimize machine downtime or labor cost or time in process, or to maximize output of particular products or material usage
	Quality control	High reliability and quality or low costs
	Use of standards	Formal or informal or none at all
LABOR AND STAFFING	Job specialization	Highly specialized or not highly specialized
	Supervision	Technically trained first-line supervisors or nontechnically trained supervisors

EXHIBIT 1: Some important trade-off decisions in manufacturing—or "you can't have it both ways."

Decision area	Decision	Alternatives
	Wage system	Many job grades or few job grades; incentive wages or hourly wages
	Supervision	Close supervision or loose supervision
	Industrial engineers	Many or few such men
PRODUCT DESIGN/ ENGINEERING	Size of product line	Many customer specials or few specials or none at all
	Design stability	Frozen design or many engineering change orders
	Technological risk	Use of new processes unproved by competitors or follow-the-leader policy
	Engineering	Complete packaged design or design-as-you-go approach
	Use of manufacturing engineering	Few or many manufacturing engineers
ORGANIZATION AND MANAGEMENT	Kind of organization	Functional or product focus or geographical or other
	Executive use of time	High involvement in investment or production planning or cost control or quality control or other activities
	Degree of risk assumed	Decisions based on much or little information
	Use of staff	Large or small staff group
	Executive style	Much or little involvement in detail; authoritarian or nondirective style; much or little contact with organization

EXHIBIT 1: (continued)

control, and so forth—top management needs to recognize the alternatives and become involved in the design of the production system. It needs to become involved to the extent that the alternative selected is appropriate to the manufacturing task determined by the corporate strategy.

Making such choices is, of course, an on-going rather than a once-a-year or once-a-decade task; decisions have to be made constantly in these trade-off areas. Indeed, the real crux of the problem seems to be how to ensure that the continuing process of decision making is not isolated from competitive and strategic facts, when many of the trade-off decisions do not at first appear to bear on company strategy. As long as a technical point of view dominates manufacturing decisions, a degree of isolation from the realities of competition is inevitable. Unfortunately, as we shall see, the technical viewpoint is all too likely to prevail.

TECHNICAL DOMINANCE

The similarity between today's emphasis on the technical experts—the computer specialist and the engineering-oriented production technician—and yesterday's emphasis on the efficiency expert—time-study man and industrial engineer—is impossible to escape. For 50 years, U.S. management relied on efficiency experts trained in the techniques of Frederick W. Taylor. Industrial engineers were kings of the factory. Their early approaches and attitudes were often conducive to industrial warfare, strikes, sabotage, and militant unions,

but that was not realized then. Also not realized was that their technical emphasis often produced an inward orientation toward cost that ignored the customer, and an engineering point of view that gloried in tools, equipment, and gadgets rather than in markets and service. Most important, the cult of industrial engineering tended to make top executives technically disqualified from involvement in manufacturing decisions.

Since the turn of the century, this efficiency-centered orientation has dogged U.S. manufacturing. It has created that image of "nuts and bolts," of greasy, dirty, detail jobs in manufacturing. It has dominated "production" courses in most graduate schools of business administration. It has alienated young men with broad management educations from manufacturing careers. It has "buffaloed" top managers.

Several months ago I was asked by a group of industrial engineers to offer an opinion as to why so few industrial engineers were moving up to the top of their companies. My answer was that perhaps a technical point of view cut them off from top management, just as the jargon and hocus-pocus of manufacturing often kept top management from understanding the factory. In their isolation, they could gain only a severely limited sense of market needs and of corporate competitive strategy.

Enter the Computer Expert

Today the industrial engineer is declining in importance in many companies. But a new technical expert, the computer specialist, is taking his place. I use the term "computer specialist" to refer to individuals who specialize in computer systems design and programming.

I do not deny, of course, that computer specialists have a very important job to do. I do object, however, to any notion that computer specialists have more of a top management view than was held by their predecessors, the industrial engineers. In my experience, the typical computer expert has been forced to master a complex and all-consuming technology, a fact which frequently makes him parochial rather than catholic in his views. Because he is so preoccupied with the detail of a total system, it is necessary for someone in top management to give him objectives and policy guidance. In his choice of trade-offs and compromises for his computer system, he needs to be instructed and not left to his own devices. Or, stated differently, he needs to see the entire corporation as a system, not just one corner of it—i.e., the manufacturing plant.

Too often this is not happening. The computer is a nightmare to many top managers because they have let it and its devotees get out of hand. They have let technical experts continue to dominate; the failure of top management truly to manage production goes on.

How *can* top management begin to manage manufacturing instead of turning it over to technicians who, through no fault of their own, are absorbed in their own arts and crafts?

How can U.S. production management be helped to cope with the rising pressures of new markets, more rapid product changes, new technologies, larger and riskier equipment decisions, and the swarm of problems we face in industry today? Let us look at some answers.

BETTER DECISION MAKING

The answers I would like to suggest are not panaceas, nor are they intended to be comprehensive. Indeed, no one can answer all the questions and problems described with one nice formula or point of view. But surely we can improve on the notion that production systems need only be "productive and efficient." Top management can manage manufacturing if it will engage in the making of manufacturing policy, rather than considering it a kind of fifth, independent estate beyond the pale of control.

The place to start, I believe, is with the acceptance of a theory of manufacturing which begins with the concept that in any system design there are significant trade-offs (as shown in *Exhibit I*) which must be explicitly decided on.

Determining Policy

Executives will also find it helpful to think of manufacturing policy determination as an orderly process or sequence of steps. *Exhibit 2* is a schematic portrayal of such a process. It shows that manufacturing policy must stem from corporate

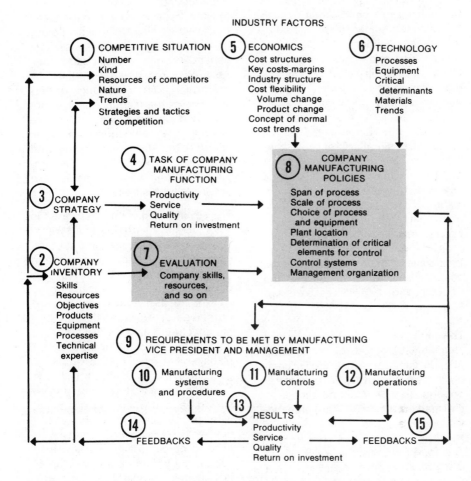

INDUSTRY FACTORS

① COMPETITIVE SITUATION
Number
Kind
Resources of competitors
Nature
Trends
Strategies and tactics
of competition

⑤ ECONOMICS
Cost structures
Key costs-margins
Industry structure
Cost flexibility
Volume change
Product change
Concept of normal
cost trends

⑥ TECHNOLOGY
Processes
Equipment
Critical
determinants
Materials
Trends

④ TASK OF COMPANY MANUFACTURING FUNCTION
Productivity
Service
Quality
Return on investment

⑧ COMPANY MANUFACTURING POLICIES
Span of process
Scale of process
Choice of process
and equipment
Plant location
Determination of critical
elements for control
Control systems
Management organization

③ COMPANY STRATEGY

② COMPANY INVENTORY
Skills
Resources
Objectives
Products
Equipment
Processes
Technical
expertise

⑦ EVALUATION
Company skills,
resources,
and so on

⑨ REQUIREMENTS TO BE MET BY MANUFACTURING VICE PRESIDENT AND MANAGEMENT

⑩ Manufacturing systems and procedures

⑪ Manufacturing controls

⑫ Manufacturing operations

⑬ RESULTS
Productivity
Service
Quality
Return on investment

⑭ FEEDBACKS

⑮ FEEDBACKS

Key

1. What the others are doing

2. What we have got or can get to compete with

3. How we can compete

4. What we must accomplish in manufacturing in order to compete

5. Economic constraints and opportunities common to the industry

6. Constraints and opportunities common to the technology

7. Our resources evaluated

8. How we should set ourselves up to match resources, economics, and technology to meet the tasks required by our competitive strategy

9. The implementation requirements of our manufacturing policies

10. Basic systems in manufacturing (e.g., production planning, use of inventories, use of standards, and wage systems)

11. Controls of cost, quality, flows, inventory, and time

12. Selection of operations or ingredients critical to success (e.g., labor skills, equipment utilization, and yields)

13. How we are performing

14. Changes in what we have got, effects on competitive situation, and review of strategy

15. Analysis and review of manufacturing operations and policies

EXHIBIT 2: The Process of Manufacturing Policy Determination.

strategy, and that the process of determining this policy is the means by which top management can actually manage production. Use of this process can end manufacturing isolation and tie top management and manufacturing together. The sequence is simple but vital:

It begins with an analysis of the competitive situation, of how rival companies are competing in terms of product, markets, policies, and channels of distribution. Management examines the number and kind of competitors and the opportunities open to its company.

Next comes a critical appraisal of the company's skills and resources and of its present facilities and approaches.

The third step is the formulation of company strategy: How is the company to compete successfully, combine its strengths with market opportunities, and define niches in the markets where it can gain advantages?

The fourth step is the point where many top executives cut off their thinking. It is important for them to define the implications or "so-what" effects of company strategy in terms of specific manufacturing tasks. For example, they should ask: "If we are to compete with an X product of Y price for Z customers using certain distribution channels and forms of advertising, what will be demanded of manufacturing in terms of costs, deliveries, lead times, quality levels, and reliability?" These demands should be precisely defined.

The fifth and sixth steps are to study the constraints or limitations imposed by the economics and the technology of the industry. These factors are generally common to all competitors. An explicit recognition of them is a prerequisite to a genuine understanding of the manufacturing problems and opportunities. These are facts that a nontechnical manager can develop, study, understand, and put to work. *Exhibit 3* contains sample lists of topics for the manager to use in doing his homework.

The seventh and eighth steps are the key ones for integrating and synthesizing all the prior ones into a broad manufacturing policy. The question for management is: "Given the facts of the economics and the technology of the industry, how do we set ourselves up to meet the specific manufacturing tasks posed by our particular competitive strategy?" Management must decide what it is going to make and what it will buy; how many plants to have, how big they should be, and where to place them; what processes and equipment to buy; what the key elements are which need to be controlled and how they can be controlled; and what kind of management organization would be most appropriate.

Next come the steps of working out programs of implementation, controls, performance measures, and review procedures (see Steps 9–15 in *Exhibit II*).

CONCLUSION

The process just described is, in my observation, quite different from the usual process of manufacturing management. Conventionally, manufacturing has been managed from the bottom up. The classical process of the age of mass production is to select an operation, break it down into its elements, analyze and improve each element, and put it back together. This approach was contributed years ago by Frederick W. Taylor and other industrial engineers who followed in his footsteps.

What I am suggesting is an entirely different approach, one adapted far better to the current era of more products, shorter runs, vastly accelerated product changes, and increased marketing competition. I am suggesting a kind of "top-down" manufacturing. This approach starts with the company and its competitive strategy; its goal is to define manufacturing policy. Its presumption is that only when basic manufacturing policies are defined can the technical experts, industrial and manufacturing engineers, labor relations specialists, and computer experts have the necessary guidance to do their work.

A. ECONOMICS OF THE INDUSTRY

Labor, burden, material, depreciation costs
Flexibility of production to meet changes in volume
Return on investment, prices, margins
Number and location of plants
Critical control variables
Critical functions (e.g., maintenance, production, and personnel)
Typical financial structures
Typical costs and cost relationships
Typical operating problems
Barriers to entry
Pricing practices
"Maturity" of industry products, markets, production practices, and so on
Importance of economies of scale
Importance of integrated capacities of corporations
Importance of having a certain balance of different types of equipment
Ideal balances of equipment capacities
Nature and type of production control
Government influences

B. TECHNOLOGY OF THE INDUSTRY

Rate of technological change
Scale of processes
Span of processes
Degree of mechanization
Technological sophistication
Time requirements for making changes

EXHIBIT 3: Illustrative constraints or limitations which should be studied.

With its focus on corporate strategy and the manufacturing task, the top-down approach can give top management both its entrée to manufacturing and the concepts it needs to take the initiative and truly manage this function. When this is done, executives previously unfamiliar with manufacturing are likely to find it an exciting activity. The company will have an important addition to its arsenal of competitive weapons.

6

Financial Analysis:

process and techniques

Financial Analysis:

process and techniques

This chapter consists of three major sections. The first discusses the C_3 finance decision variables from a top or general management viewpoint, as is done with marketing variables in Chapter 4 and production/operations variables in Chapter 5. This is followed by a list of the C_4 finance decision variables. The second section deals with the role of financial analysis in policy cases. The final section presents a brief discussion of break-even analysis, its uses and limitations. Throughout the chapter, emphasis is placed on the functional inter-dependence of certain finance decisions and relationships.

The finance manager has three major concerns:

1. Determining the total amount of funds to be used by an enterprise.
2. Determining what specific assets the firm should acquire, or allocating the funds among various assets in an efficient manner.
3. Determining how the needed funds should be financed, or obtaining the best mix of financing with relation to the overall valuation of the firm.

According to one author, these concerns manifest themselves in the form of three major decisions:

1. *Investment decision*—deals with capital budgeting, reallocation of capital, management of existing assets, and mergers and acquisitions.
2. *Financing decision*—involves the determination of the best financing mix or capital structure for the firm.
3. *Dividend decision*—concerns the percentage of the firm's earnings paid to stockholders in cash dividends.[55]

---

[55] J.C. Van Horne, *Financial Management and Policy,* 2d ed. (Englewood Cliffs, N.J.: Prentice-Hall, 1971), Chapter 1.

The financing decision and a portion of the investment decision are considered C_2 decisions within our framework. This was discussed in Chapter 2 and will not be dealt with further.

It should be pointed out that some determinants of a particular decision variable may in turn depend on other C_3 variables and/or their determinants. This leads to the realization that in order to approach optimum finance decisions, one must make or solve these decisions simultaneously. This aspect of finance decisions is beyond the scope of this discussion, but the student should be aware of this situation.

FINANCE DECISION VARIABLES

The following finance decision variables and their determinants are described in this section of the chapter:

Level of working capital = f (uncertainty of cash receipts and disbursements, borrowing capacity, management's utility preference for cash, efficiency of cash management, volume of credit sales, seasonality of sales, credit policies, C_1 and C_2 variables).

Level of dividend payment = f (dividend payment history, the stability of earnings, rate of growth and profit levels, desire for control, liquidity position, ability to borrow, debt contract restrictions, tax position of stockholders, legal constraints, C_1 and C_2 variables).

Level of Working Capital

This decision variable is concerned with the determination of the level of working capital (short-term assets minus short-term liabilities) a firm should maintain. Current assets are usually in the form of (1) cash and marketable securities, (2) accounts receivable, and (3) inventories. Current liabilities are primarily accounts payable.

Management of working capital is significant for several reasons. First, there is a direct relationship between growth in sales and the level of accounts receivable, inventories, and possibly cash balances. Second, current assets represent more than half of the total assets of many firms. Finally, the small firm cannot rely on capital markets as heavily as the larger firms can and therefore must make greater use of trade credit and short-term bank loans—both of which increase current liabilities, which affects net working capital.

Because the last component of working capital, inventories, and its determinants have been described in Chapters 3 and 4, the determinants of only the first two components are discussed here.

Determinants. The determinants of the level of cash and marketable securities, hereafter referred to as cash, are discussed first, followed by an exploration of the determinants of the level of accounts receivable.

The uncertainty with regard to cash receipts and disbursements is a primary determinant of cash level. One approach is to use a cash flow forecast to examine the factors that affect the magnitude and timing of cash flows, such as sales revenues, average collection period of accounts receivable, production schedules, maturity structure of debt, and other expenses. The dispersion or possible deviation of these flows is also of importance in deciding on the level of cash. For instance, if the magnitude of a cash flow is uncertain with a potentially large variance or dispersion, a higher level of working capital or cushion would be needed than if the magnitude of the cash flow is known with relative certainty.

The firm's borrowing capacity to meet emergency needs is another influence on the amount of cash. If a firm has a readily accessible source of funds to carry it through a tight liquidity situation, then the level of working capital could be reduced.

Another determinant is the utility preferences of management with respect to the risk of cash insolvency. A rather risk-averse management obviously would prefer a higher level of cash than a less risk-averse management. This may lead to a loss of income as a result of idle funds, but the risk-averse management is willing to suffer that loss for the security of cash. This type of preference was demonstrated by the actions of Sewell Avery, president of Montgomery Ward, after World War II. Mr. Avery felt the United States would face a depression soon after the war ended. Based on this analysis, the company built up a tremendous cash reserve ($360 million), while its chief competitor, Sears, expanded rapidly. It is only recently that Wards has been able to overcome this mistake and compete effectively with Sears.

A final determinant of the level of cash is the efficiency with which cash is managed. This has to do with reducing the time between when a customer pays his bill and when it becomes usable funds for the firm. As this time is reduced, the level of cash can be lowered. Programs such as concentrated banking and lockbox systems are attempts to achieve this objective. For example, the C.I.T. Finance Corporation has established a cash management system consisting of a banking network with central, regional, and local depository banks, lockboxes, and a computerized financial information system. According to Mr. Alfred DeSalvo, Treasurer and Vice-President of C.I.T.:

Our system is not cumbersome or expensive. More important it works. Indeed, it works so well that the company can borrow from $25 million to $100 million a day for its 925 branches and subsidiaries and at the same time maintain unused cash at an extremely low level. In fact, C.I.T., which uses about $1 billion in short-term funds to run its business, usually concludes a working day with no cash in its banks above the compensating balances needed to maintain credit lines. The remainder of the company's short-term money is at work or en route to work.[56]

---

[56] Alfred DeSalvo, ''Cash Management Converts Dollars into Working Assets,'' *Harvard Business Review* 53,3 (May–June 1972), p. 93.

The accounts receivable level is determined by the volume of credit sales, seasonality of sales, and credit policies. This is an area where the interaction between the marketing and finance functions is quite apparent. Sales personnel do not want to be hindered by a lot of red tape about credit ratings and the like, or to confront a potential customer with embarrassing questions concerning credit worthiness. What might be considered stringent credit terms by the salesperson may eliminate some potential customers and, therefore, sales revenue. Also, annoying or abrasive collection policies may cost the firm some of its existing customers. On the other hand, the finance people feel that it is their function to convert credit sales dollars into usable funds for the firm as quickly and reliably as possible. A popular way to do this is through the use of discounts and discount periods. Of course, the overriding concern is that of bad-debt losses.

In theory, the firm should reduce its quality standards for accounts accepted as long as the profitability of sales generated exceeds the added cost of the receivables.[57] In practice, factors such as the industry's characteristic terms of sale and credit, the firm's financial position, and even the condition of the national economy will affect the level of accounts receivable. For example, if the other companies in the industry give their customers the terms "2/10, net 30," a given firm would be implicitly constrained to these terms.

Level of Dividend Payment

Management must determine first of all whether or not to pay a dividend to stockholders and, if so, at what level. The difference between earnings and dividends is retained earnings. Thus, a conflict can arise: should a firm retain its earnings to finance its growth, return these earnings to the equity investors, or do both to some degree? This decision takes on importance because it affects the valuation of the firm, which can, in turn, affect the firm's cost of capital.

There are two basic viewpoints on this issue. The first is that the stability of dividends is important, and therefore, that the dividend payment level has its rightful claim on the firm's earnings. The second is that investors would prefer the firm to retain and reinvest the earnings, as long as the return on the reinvested earnings exceeds the rate of return that the investor could obtain on other investments of comparable risk. In other words, that the firm should reinvest earnings in opportunities available to it until funds are exhausted or a minimum return is not obtained. The remainer or residual of earnings then could be dispersed as dividends. The latter viewpoint implies that dividends are irrelevant, and that the investor shows no preference for dividends over capital gains.

You will notice that the determinants of dividend policy are oriented more toward external influences on the firm, with little direct influence from the other functional areas.

---

[57] Van Horne, *Financial Management and Policy,* p. 442.

Determinants. The determinants of dividend policy include dividend payment history, stability of earnings, rate of growth and profit levels, desire for control, liquidity position, ability to borrow, debt contract restrictions, tax position of stockholders, and legal constraints.

Maintenance of a stable or target dividend is important for several reasons. First of all, dividends have informational content. They can convey management's view of the firm's future earnings to the investor. Investors may consider a decrease in the dividend payments level as an announcement of a change in the expected future profitability of the firm. This may lead to a reaction in the form of a change in the price of the stock. Some investors live on dividends; for them, dividend stability is a very desirable characteristic. Institutional investors can invest only in firms included on a legal list. One qualification to be placed on this list is dividend stability.

In 1974 Consolidated Edison Company found itself with a liquidity problem. Part of top management's solution was to omit, for the first time in 89 years, its quarterly dividend with the following reactions.

The waves that those decisions generated are battering the stocks and driving down the bond ratings of most other power companies. This week, too, they were pounding the Con Edison management at one of the most boisterous annual meetings on record. There, management faced irate stockholders protesting the loss of their dividends and angry customers furious about steep increases in Con Ed rates.

Most Wall Streeters and power company think that Con Ed Chairman Charles F. Luce had no idea of the furor his decision would produce. Says one analyst: "Luce is a power man, not an investment man. He just didn't realize that big utilities don't cut their dividends." Others, like Cook, believe that Con Ed and some other urban power companies that are under fierce cost pressures must face up to a wholly different future. Says one: "Con Ed lost the institutions long ago, but its dividend allowed it to count on the little old lady in tennis shoes. Now it has lost her, too. And lost her for a lot of other utilities."[58]

Closely related to the stability of dividends is the stability of earnings. A firm that has relatively stable earnings is more likely to pay out a higher percentage in dividends. Conversely, a firm with less stable earnings would pay out a lower percentage to avoid endangering the stability of dividends during periods of low earnings.

The rate of growth and profitability affects the number of investment opportunities available to the firm. A company in a growth industry, such as computers or electronics, would have more investment opportunities available to it than would a company in a mature industry, such as coal or steel, with fewer investment opportunities. The former firm would be more willing to use its earnings to finance these investments. The latter firm would be more prone to pay out a greater portion of its earnings in dividends.

---

[58] "Con Edison: Archetype of an Ailing Utility," *Business Week,* 25 May 1974, p. 102.

A related issue is the timing of investment opportunities. A company may retain earnings for use on a project in the future, but it might be better off if it paid out these earnings in dividends and financed the project using external sources when the time came.

Some managements prefer not to dilute control of a firm by raising capital through the issuance of new stock. Therefore, the firm is financed primarily through retained earnings, leaving little or no funds for dividends. This philosophy could work in reverse if "outsiders" seeking control could convince stockholders that the company was not maximizing shareholder wealth (or some other objectives) and that they, the outsiders, could do a better job. Thus, a company that fears that it may be acquired by such tactics may establish a high dividend to appease stockholders.

Because payment of dividends is a drain on cash, the liquidity position of the firm may act as a constraint. If a firm has the flexibility to borrow funds on rather short notice, this constraint can be offset somewhat. Typically, the age and size of a company will determine the access it has to capital markets. A well-established firm is more likely to have a higher dividend pay-out rate than a new or small firm. This argument correlates highly with the preceding "mature industry" discussion.

The effect of two determinants is illustrated by the situation in which Western Union Corporation recently found itself. This company traditionally has paid a quarterly dividend of $.35. Western Union reported an annual deficit to the Internal Revenue Service, but was able to report a net profit to the stockholders because of a combination of accounting devices. Because the company did not generate enough earnings to pay its traditional dividends, part of the cash came from borrowed funds.

The composition of a firm's stockholders, in terms of their personal income tax brackets, can influence dividend policy. Stockholders in higher tax brackets would prefer capital gains instead of dividends, while stockholders in lower tax brackets generally prefer the opposite. The closeness with which a company is held and the ability of a firm to discern stockholder preference will determine the strength of such an influence in the dividend decision. If a company has a wide diversity of stockholders with regard to income, the impact of this determinant will be minimal. For example, General Motors has well over one million stockholders. In this case, it would be difficult to assess the preferences of all stockholders on this issue.

The last two determinants are somewhat related in that both are constraints on dividend payments. The first deals with contractual constraints that may be written into debt contracts. For instance, payment of dividends may be made contingent upon the amount of net working capital. The second constraint includes legal rules such as state statutes and court decisions concerning corporation dividends. Typical rules include the net profits rule, which says dividends can be paid only from past and present earnings; the capital impairment rule, which protects shareholders and creditors by forbidding payment of dividends from capital; and the insolvency rule, which prohibits a firm from paying dividends while insolvent.

FUNCTIONALLY INDEPENDENT FINANCE VARIABLES

A number of finance decisions are usually not significantly influenced by factors in other segments of the organization:

1. Call features of debt instruments
2. Conversion features of debt instruments
3. Maturity/yield trade-off
4. Method of project proposal evaluation
5. Priority of payment of debt instruments
6. Redemption features of debt instruments
7. Rights of preferred stockholders
8. Rights of lenders when payments missed
9. Risk yield trade-off in financial investments
10. Security offered with debt instruments
11. Time to maturity of debt instruments

In accordance with the framework developed in Chapter 1, these C_4 decision variables do not usually require detailed knowledge on the part of the general manager, and so they are not emphasized in this book

FINANCIAL ANALYSIS IN BUSINESS POLICY CASES

This section demonstrates how financial analysis can be useful in the three major phases of case study: analysis of the situation, problem identification, and development of plans of action to eliminate the problems. In many ways, financial analysis is analogous to a doctor's initial assessment of a patient's health in terms of body temperature, pulse rate, and blood pressure. These indicators are used by the doctor to determine treatment or to identify the additional tests needed for further diagnosis. The student should be warned that this type of analysis may or may not indicate "the problems" in a case. Although financial analysis cuts across traditional functional boundaries, there is a wide variety of problems that this analysis will not reveal. But the relative ease with which it can be carried out and the number of policy problems it can identify make financial analysis an excellent starting point for case studies.

Analysis of the Situation

An analysis of the situation is the first general step in the problem-solving process. This stage involves the collection of facts that are relevant for an assessment of the firm's external effectiveness, internal efficiency, and major strengths and weaknesses. Information gathered here also should relate to the consideration of difficulties that exist in various areas of the firm.

It is hard to indicate the precise information that should be gathered in each and every case. This is partially because of the situational nature of case analysis and also because all the desired information is frequently unavailable. Consequently, the following discussion delineates the *maximum* amount of information that should be gathered to assess the firm's basic financial position.

Basic Financial Statements

At the outset, the student should have the historical income statements and balance sheets at hand. These two basic statements provide the data necessary for most of the financial analyses discussed here. The student should be aware of several precautions concerning the use of these statements in financial analysis. The balance sheet figures refer to *one instance in time,* while the income statement figures refer to events *over a period of time.* Therefore, the income statement figure is best compared to the historical average of the balance sheet figures.[59] While conducting the financial analysis, the student also should be aware of seasonality, window dressing,[60] and adjustments described in footnotes to either of these statements.

Evidence of Financial Objectives

The student should attempt to determine the profitability, growth, and survival objectives of the firm. These objectives may or may not be explicitly stated in the case.

Evidence of External Effectiveness

At this stage, the major financial indicators of the external effectiveness of the firm can be computed for subsequent analysis of their meaning and significance. The most important indicators are usually in ratio form and are discussed below. A summary of these and other financial ratios is provided in Figure 6-1.

Profitability Indicators. Evidence of the firm's profitability should be analyzed to determine the extent to which objectives are being accomplished and to illuminate the current well-being of the firm. There are two types of profitability ratios: (1) those showing profitability in relation to sales and (2) those showing profitability in relation to investment. Gross profit margin (sales minus cost of goods sold divided by sales) and net profit margin (net profit after taxes divided by sales) are examples of the first type. Rate of return on common stock equity (net profit after taxes minus preferred stock dividend divided by net worth minus par value of preferred stock) and return on assets (net profit after taxes divided by total tangible assets) are examples of the second type. Incidentally, return

---

[59] This raises the question of whether one should use a simple average or a weighted average. From a practical standpoint, it probably will depend on the amount and type of information the student has with regard to the balance sheet data.

[60] Companies have been known to take deliberate steps to "clean up" their balance sheets. For instance, loans may be paid off just before the end of one year, which increases the current ratio, and then money is borrowed again early in the next year.

PROFITABILITY RATIOS

Gross profit margin	$$\dfrac{\text{Sales} - \text{Cost of goods sold}}{\text{Sales}}$$
Net profit margin	$$\dfrac{\text{Net profit after taxes}}{\text{Sales}}$$
Rate of return or common stock equity	$$\dfrac{\text{Net profit after tax} - \text{Preferred stock dividend}}{\text{Net worth} - \text{Par value of preferred stock}}$$
Return on assets	$$\dfrac{\text{Net profit after taxes}}{\text{Total tangible assets}}$$ or Net profit margin x Turnover ratio*
Return on capital (equity)	$$\dfrac{\text{Net profit after taxes}}{\text{Net worth}}$$
Earnings per share (common stock)	$$\dfrac{\text{Net profit after taxes} - \text{Preferred dividends}}{\text{Number shares common stock outstanding}}$$

*Sales ÷ Total tangible assets

LIQUIDITY RATIOS

Current	$$\dfrac{\text{Current assets}}{\text{Current liabilities}}$$
Acid-test (or quick)	$$\dfrac{\text{Current assets} - \text{Inventories}}{\text{Current liabilities}}$$
Cash	$$\dfrac{\text{Cash and equivalent}}{\text{Current liabilities}}$$
Inventory to net working capital	$$\dfrac{\text{Inventory}}{\text{Current assets} - \text{Current liabilities}}$$

LEVERAGE RATIOS

Debt	$$\dfrac{\text{Total debt}}{\text{Total assets}}$$
Debt to equity Total debt	$$\dfrac{\text{Total debt}}{\text{Net worth}}$$

FIGURE 6-1: Summary of financial ratio analysis.

Long-term debt	$$\dfrac{\text{Long-term debt}}{\text{Net worth}}$$
Assets to equity	$$\dfrac{\text{Total assets}}{\text{Net worth}}$$
Fixed charge coverage* (number of times interest earned) Before tax	$$\dfrac{\text{Earnings before interest and taxes}}{\text{Fixed charges}}$$
After tax	$$\dfrac{\text{Net profit after taxes + Fixed charges}}{\text{Fixed charges}}$$

**Such as bond interest, lease payments

ACTIVITY RATIOS

Inventory turnover	$$\dfrac{\text{Sales}}{\text{Inventory}}$$
Fixed assets turnover	$$\dfrac{\text{Sales}}{\text{Fixed assets}}$$
Total assets turnover	$$\dfrac{\text{Sales}}{\text{Total assets}}$$
Average collection period	$$\dfrac{\text{Accounts receivable} \times 365}{\text{Annual credit sales}}$$
Accounts receivable turnover	$$\dfrac{\text{Credit sales}}{\text{Accounts receivable}}$$
Operating asset turnover	$$\dfrac{\text{Sales}}{\text{Operating assets}}$$

OTHER RATIOS

Dividend (current) yield on common stock	$$\dfrac{\text{Annual dividends per share}}{\text{Current market price per share}}$$
Earnings yield on common stock	$$\dfrac{\text{Earnings per share of common}}{\text{Market price per share}}$$
Price-earnings ratio	$$\dfrac{\text{Market price per share}}{\text{Earnings per share}}$$

FIGURE 6-1: (continued)

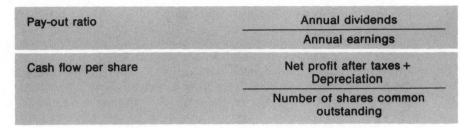

Pay-out ratio	Annual dividends
	Annual earnings
Cash flow per share	Net profit after taxes + Depreciation
	Number of shares common outstanding

FIGURE 6-1:   (continued)

on assets is also the product of the net profit margin (net profit after taxes divided by sales) and the turnover ratio (sales divided by total tangible assets), which might be useful in later stages of the analysis. Ultimately, these ratios indicate how effectively the firm is being managed. It should be recognized, however, that the ratios themselves give no answers as to *why* a firm is or is not profitable.

Liquidity indicators. Computation of liquidity ratios enables determination of the firm's ability (1) to react to unforeseen opportunities in the environment and (2) to meet its maturing financial obligations. Two common indicators of liquidity are the current ratio (current assets divided by current liabilities) and the acid-test or quick ratio (current assets minus inventories divided by current liabilities). The fact that inventories are the least liquid of current assets, and are also the assets on which losses are most likely to occur in the event of liquidation, makes the acid-test extremely important.

Leverage indicators. These ratios serve to indicate the firm's basic position with respect to creditors and its propensity to assume risk. With respect to the former, decisions as to the use of leverage (the extent to which financing is provided by creditors rather than by owners) greatly affect future borrowing power. Furthermore, they always involve a trade-off between higher expected returns and increased risk. In keeping with these considerations, the debt ratio (total debt divided by total assets) measures the extent to which borrowed funds are utilized, and hence the probable reactions of creditors to future requests for funds. The times-interest-earned ratio (profit before taxes plus interest charges divided by interest charges) and the fixed-charge coverage ratio (gross income divided by fixed charges) serve to measure the risk of debt by concentrating on the ability of the firm to meet its fixed charges. Long-term debt divided by total capitalization (long-term debt plus net worth) tells the relative importance of long-term debt in the capital structure.

Overall ability to obtain funds. Some of the ratios noted above give an indication of the firm's ability to acquire funds, but additional information on creditor relations, amount of working capital on hand, and utilization of retained earnings will further illuminate the firm's basic financial position in this regard.

Evidence of Internal Efficiency

Basic indicators of the efficiency with which management has employed its resources may be obtained by calculating the following: inventory turnover ratio (sales divided by inventory), fixed-assets turnover ratio (sales divided by fixed assets), average collection period (accounts receivable times 365 divided by annual credit sales), and aging of accounts—both receivables and payables.

Further Analysis of Financial Indicators

Once the various ratios have been calculated, the meaning of these ratios must be ascertained. For instance, what does a current ratio of 1.75 mean? Or, an inventory turnover ratio of 6? To give the data greater significance, two further analyses can be performed: First, compare a present ratio with past and expected future ratios for the same company—that is, develop trends. Second, compare ratios of one firm with those of similar firms or with industry averages at the same point in time. Avoid using rules of thumb indiscriminately for all industries.

In trend analysis, first examine the composition of the change and determine if there has been an improvement or a deterioration in the financial condition and performance of the firm over a period of time. Do not simply look at one ratio and draw unwarranted conclusions! It is necessary to look at related ratios and possibly at the raw data before a proper interpretation can be made.

A major difficulty in making this type of comparison is the change in the dollar-measuring criterion. Over a period of time there are changes in the value of the dollar, changes in price levels, and, because assets are stated as unexpired historical dollar costs, this causes particular difficulty with ratios calculated from such amounts.

Comparison with industry averages does not imply that all firms in the industry must be the same, but one should be suspicious of deviations and find out if they are justified. A particular firm may have encountered unreasonably good or bad fortune that was not shared by the industry. Comparison of a firm and industry ratio over time also may indicate whether the deviation is caused by an internal or an external condition.

There are several sources for obtaining comparison ratios and/or financial data. These include *Modern Industry,* published by Dun & Bradstreet; *Statement Studies,* by R. Morris Associates; Moody's *Manual of Investments;* Standard and Poor's *Corporation Records;* and quarterly data on manufacturing companies, published by the Federal Trade Commission and the Securities and Exchange Commission. Also, some trade associations and public accountants publish ratios for specific industries. Figure 6-2 presents a list of selected Dun & Bradstreet ratios by line of business, for odd-numbered years, from 1965 through 1973.

These two analyses, trends and industry comparisons, give indications as to whether or not the firm is improving or deteriorating over the years and what its position is relative to other firms in the same industry. They also permit

Line of Business	Year	Current Assets to Current Debt (Times)	Net Profit on Net Sales (Percent)	Net Profit to Tangible Net Worth (Percent)	Net Sales to Tangible Net Worth (Times)	Collection Period (Days)	Net Sales to Inventory (Times)	Fixed Asset to Tangible Net Worth (Percent)	Total Debt to Tangible Net Worth (Percent)	Inventory to Net Working Capital (Percent)
Agricultural Chemicals	65	1.80	1.34	4.36	3.37	45	7.5	57.8	132.9	83.1
	67	1.88	2.17	6.90	3.08	56	6.9	53.2	115.9	74.4
	69	1.86	1.45	5.30	2.78	57	6.6	43.8	123.3	76.5
	71	2.06	2.08	7.11	2.84	57	8.5	41.7	139.4	59.8
	73	1.98	3.65	16.15	3.39	50	9.9	36.2	100.4	55.1
Airplane Parts & Accessories	65	2.15	3.78	10.03	2.90	48	6.8	46.8	74.5	84.7
	67	1.78	4.44	16.67	3.23	39	5.9	55.1	93.5	103.7
	69	2.16	3.04	9.06	2.92	59	5.2	53.6	72.4	86.6
	71	2.47	1.63	3.60	2.24	58	4.9	57.5	107.2	82.0
	73	2.24	3.94	12.70	2.81	52	4.7	50.1	120.6	88.2
Bakery Products	65	1.89	1.52	8.40	4.49	17	27.2	80.2	67.7	54.3
	67	1.84	2.37	10.21	4.15	18	30.4	78.8	57.3	61.7
	69	1.88	2.54	8.70	4.08	22	28.9	80.8	49.6	57.9
	71	2.07	1.77	6.58	4.18	21	27.5	79.5	55.8	51.5
	73	1.90	1.37	6.45	4.25	26	22.7	74.9	77.7	62.5
Blast Furnaces, Steel Works & Rolling Mills	65	*	*	*	*	*	*	*	*	*
	67	2.58	4.07	8.01	1.90	35	4.9	61.4	50.8	92.4
	69	2.56	3.66	8.66	1.98	43	5.4	58.5	55.9	81.1
	71	2.90	2.70	6.37	2.15	39	4.8	80.5	69.9	95.7
	73	2.13	4.31	10.11	2.72	41	6.7	69.9	74.5	91.4
Book Publishing & Printing	65	2.97	7.36	14.74	2.12	71	3.8	31.3	66.0	67.3
	67	2.63	5.20	10.44	2.32	58	4.1	28.8	77.2	71.4
	69	2.52	4.70	8.04	2.13	61	4.4	34.8	52.3	72.0
	71	2.59	4.71	8.15	1.94	68	4.1	36.0	57.8	65.6
	73	2.49	4.76	10.14	1.98	64	4.2	35.4	83.1	62.5

(continued)

NOTE: Median values taken from *Dun's Reviews*.
*Data not available or not applicable

FIGURE 6-2: Selected Dun & Bradstreet Ratios of Manufacturing.

Source: Reprinted with the special permission of *Dun's Review*, November, 1965, 1967, 1969, 1971, 1973. Copyright, 1965, 1967, 1969, 1971, 1973, Dun & Bradstreet Publications Corporation.

Line of Business	Year	Current Assets to Current Debt (Times)	Net Profit on Net Sales (Percent)	Net Profit to Tangible Net Worth (Percent)	Net Sales to Tangible Worth (Times)	Collection Period (Days)	Net Sales to Inventory (Times)	Fixed Asset to Tangible Net Worth (Percent)	Total Debt to Tangible Net Worth (Percent)	Inventory to Net Working Capital (Percent)
Bottled & Canned Soft Drinks	65	1.95	5.04	13.60	2.78	21	19.9	82.9	74.8	56.8
	67	1.78	4.17	10.48	2.82	22	14.4	84.1	91.8	76.5
	69	1.70	3.91	11.94	3.20	21	17.0	83.9	83.9	83.5
	71	2.25	4.46	12.01	2.97	21	16.3	70.6	49.1	62.0
	73	2.32	3.71	11.57	3.27	22	15.3	71.2	55.4	61.0
Broad Woven Fabrics, Cotton	65	2.98	4.87	10.97	1.99	46	5.7	49.0	42.3	72.5
	67	3.00	3.96	7.34	1.82	53	5.7	54.9	34.5	78.8
	69	3.10	2.42	4.88	1.92	56	5.1	57.0	45.9	69.0
	71	3.65	2.75	5.70	1.96	54	5.8	53.8	60.7	62.8
	73	3.32	3.37	8.18	2.38	57	6.3	52.8	85.2	61.6
Canned & Preserved Fruits, Vegetables & Sea Foods	65	1.68	2.51	10.13	3.56	21	4.5	53.9	95.4	171.7
	67	1.63	2.80	11.25	3.13	24	5.1	51.9	121.7	148.5
	69	1.56	1.93	5.79	3.17	24	4.5	50.2	119.7	181.9
	71	2.03	2.66	7.64	3.20	26	4.4	56.0	106.0	124.3
	73	1.93	2.77	11.83	4.11	25	5.2	66.1	118.6	121.0
Children's & Infants' Outerwear	65	1.73	1.11	7.12	7.93	31	7.1	13.6	178.0	112.4
	67	1.73	1.06	8.21	7.92	40	7.5	11.3	116.3	119.0
	69	1.56	1.12	8.96	10.20	42	8.7	16.0	203.5	110.4
	71	1.83	1.52	11.63	6.63	39	8.9	16.8	120.4	89.6
	73	1.60	2.18	11.86	6.96	51	6.7	11.1	295.8	112.7
Commercial Printing (except Lithography)	65	2.14	3.43	9.37	2.94	43	*	62.0	81.5	*
	67	2.37	3.17	9.70	2.98	42	*	55.2	64.2	*
	69	2.33	2.35	7.72	2.98	46	*	61.3	89.4	*
	71	2.32	1.74	5.67	2.94	44	*	59.0	84.9	*
	73	2.05	2.95	8.91	3.02	49	10.8	55.6	72.6	62.5
Communication Equipment	65	2.23	4.24	10.65	2.71	58	5.2	37.0	93.6	76.4
	67	2.22	3.66	11.65	3.32	58	5.1	38.7	78.1	84.0
	69	2.44	3.78	10.34	2.70	61	5.0	37.2	64.3	75.0
	71	2.77	1.99	4.56	2.37	73	4.9	45.2	76.3	69.7
	73	2.44	4.48	11.95	3.07	68	4.5	45.2	121.0	76.3

(continued)

Line of Business	Year	Current Assets to Current Debt (Times)	Net Profit on Net Sales (Percent)	Net Profit to Tangible Net Worth (Percent)	Net Sales to Tangible Worth (Times)	Collection Period (Days)	Net Sales to Inventory (Times)	Fixed Asset to Tangible Net Worth (Percent)	Total Debt to Tangible Net Worth (Percent)	Inventory to Net Working Capital (Percent)
Concrete, Gypsum & Plaster Products	65	2.35	4.06	9.12	2.35	52	9.8	65.6	62.1	52.9
	67	2.46	3.63	7.22	2.10	53	8.8	54.3	46.2	52.9
	69	2.35	3.69	7.28	1.99	54	11.5	61.6	58.8	48.9
	71	2.42	3.88	8.24	2.33	53	11.3	64.9	73.5	48.8
	73	2.34	3.91	10.27	2.57	48	11.3	71.2	88.0	55.1
Confectionary & Related Products	65	2.69	2.92	12.34	3.07	22	8.5	45.9	55.2	76.4
	67	2.68	1.98	6.66	3.50	22	7.9	44.0	67.4	105.8
	69	2.60	2.17	7.52	3.24	20	7.9	44.0	70.2	84.2
	71	2.55	1.46	5.25	3.48	21	7.6	53.6	65.1	85.1
	73	2.52	3.13	6.65	3.55	22	6.4	52.9	55.9	84.9
Construction & Mining: Handling Machinery & Equipment	65	2.58	4.41	13.58	2.83	52	4.4	33.6	73.8	86.7
	67	2.62	3.86	10.77	2.61	47	4.8	32.4	81.1	79.8
	69	2.60	4.02	10.32	2.30	55	4.6	34.9	67.2	80.5
	71	2.96	2.74	7.00	2.36	58	3.8	33.9	85.2	78.9
	73	2.46	3.70	11.72	3.13	55	4.4	36.2	111.0	83.2
Converted Paper & Paper Board Products	65	2.68	4.16	9.69	2.68	38	7.4	43.3	57.4	72.4
	67	2.68	3.31	11.56	2.76	38	6.8	52.2	67.8	74.0
	69	2.45	3.01	9.36	2.90	42	6.8	63.1	81.4	88.9
	71	2.94	2.20	7.46	2.95	41	7.5	54.9	72.6	71.3
	73	2.82	2.92	11.35	3.21	46	6.9	46.8	72.9	76.1
Cutlery, Hand Tools & General Hardware	65	2.95	5.22	12.04	2.01	42	4.0	38.3	60.2	80.4
	67	3.16	4.10	9.51	2.26	39	4.5	34.4	57.1	80.7
	69	3.35	4.12	10.05	2.43	45	4.6	40.0	46.7	79.3
	71	3.87	4.27	8.42	2.27	46	4.4	37.3	71.9	73.2
	73	3.19	4.64	11.62	2.57	49	5.0	36.2	70.3	77.8
Dairy Products	65	1.80	1.58	8.12	4.98	23	31.1	62.8	67.1	53.0
	67	1.59	0.89	5.52	5.00	24	30.0	66.9	75.8	71.1
	69	1.54	1.30	7.02	5.49	24	31.5	62.7	73.4	62.8
	71	1.60	1.39	8.71	6.02	26	28.0	63.4	81.7	59.9
	73	1.52	1.21	7.26	6.15	28	23.8	72.3	97.5	82.0

(continued)

Line of Business	Year	Current Assets to Current Debt (Times)	Net Profit on Net Sales (Percent)	Net Profit to Tangible Net Worth (Percent)	Net Sales to Tangible Worth (Times)	Collection Period (Days)	Net Sales to Inventory (Times)	Fixed Asset to Tangible Net Worth (Percent)	Total Debt to Tangible Net Worth (Percent)	Inventory to Net Working Capital (Percent)
Drugs	65	2.94	5.93	12.47	2.14	44	6.5	37.7	54.6	67.0
	67	2.69	5.87	10.38	2.06	48	6.0	35.7	42.8	69.4
	69	2.24	4.76	12.95	2.12	55	6.0	40.1	54.9	78.9
	71	2.90	5.53	11.02	1.97	56	5.6	49.0	68.2	65.8
	73	2.75	6.05	13.40	2.13	59	5.2	44.6	71.8	68.8
Electric Lighting & Wiring Equipment	65	2.77	3.87	13.91	3.11	40	5.4	36.0	104.5	82.4
	67	3.03	3.07	9.60	2.87	42	5.5	37.5	74.9	83.1
	69	2.85	2.82	9.22	2.78	47	5.0	38.0	76.6	77.7
	71	3.07	2.21	8.47	2.71	45	5.1	48.4	55.6	74.8
	73	3.05	4.08	11.78	2.61	48	5.2	42.2	63.8	79.9
Electric Transmission & Distributor Equipment	65	2.45	4.33	13.56	2.94	53	4.6	31.8	78.9	93.1
	67	2.28	4.55	13.49	3.17	49	4.7	37.1	84.9	92.2
	69	2.70	2.96	8.92	2.87	59	4.1	38.5	93.9	85.6
	71	2.93	2.58	7.15	2.59	62	4.2	41.9	81.8	77.4
	73	2.55	3.69	11.31	2.70	61	4.1	43.0	79.5	84.0
Electrical Industrial Apparatus	65	2.62	4.44	14.43	2.71	46	5.1	43.3	66.1	87.3
	67	2.60	4.32	15.40	2.63	48	5.1	40.9	77.2	89.2
	69	2.56	2.91	7.71	2.71	54	4.6	46.8	83.5	83.9
	71	2.85	2.01	6.08	2.72	60	4.7	42.8	84.1	70.9
	73	2.51	4.47	11.89	3.15	64	5.0	42.2	90.3	78.0
Electrical Work	65	2.06	2.25	11.75	5.27	*	*	22.3	119.4	*
	67	2.21	2.42	12.74	5.05	*	*	18.4	95.4	*
	69	2.06	2.36	10.30	4.74	*	*	19.9	103.2	*
	71	2.15	1.50	9.48	5.03	*	*	20.2	120.6	*
	73	2.02	2.27	10.04	5.03	*	*	22.7	133.7	*
Electronic Components & Accessories	65	2.42	4.13	12.80	3.46	58	5.4	47.1	102.9	80.3
	67	2.75	4.23	14.83	3.27	51	5.3	39.0	100.2	87.3
	69	2.36	3.05	8.46	3.03	55	4.7	40.8	97.4	83.1
	71	2.55	1.83	5.04	2.45	59	4.6	55.1	86.7	79.3
	73	2.32	4.13	14.28	2.93	63	4.7	53.0	94.5	78.4

(continued)

Line of Business	Year	Current Assets to Current Debt (Times)	Net Profit on Net Sales (Percent)	Net Profit to Tangible Net Worth (Percent)	Net Sales to Tangible Worth (Times)	Collection Period (Days)	Net Sales to Inventory (Times)	Fixed Asset to Tangible Net Worth (Percent)	Total Debt to Tangible Net Worth (Percent)	Inventory to Net Working Capital (Percent)
Engineering, Laboratory & Scientific Instruments	65	2.90	4.40	9.84	2.87	54	4.9	33.3	65.9	71.8
	67	2.83	5.91	14.75	2.60	61	4.4	30.9	76.6	68.5
	69	2.96	4.08	9.76	2.20	75	3.7	37.7	76.1	69.0
	71	3.41	3.10	5.76	1.96	66	3.9	35.4	74.8	63.9
	73	3.21	3.83	11.54	2.48	71	4.0	34.9	95.9	74.3
Fabricated Structural Metal Products	65	2.17	3.44	10.54	3.32	52	6.1	37.8	91.2	74.7
	67	2.51	3.09	9.65	3.20	53	6.4	38.7	82.1	66.4
	69	2.69	2.23	7.40	3.13	54	6.1	38.6	93.0	73.6
	71	2.30	2.55	7.79	3.04	51	6.0	40.1	87.5	74.4
	73	2.30	3.03	11.38	3.51	51	6.6	42.0	94.2	75.3
Farm Machinery Equipment	65	2.35	3.97	14.30	3.09	43	4.0	36.3	80.8	105.9
	67	2.40	3.48	12.05	3.32	43	3.8	35.2	97.2	102.6
	69	2.79	2.42	8.95	2.45	43	3.9	38.4	77.2	85.7
	71	2.64	2.49	7.69	2.75	46	3.7	38.4	86.9	95.1
	73	2.49	3.60	13.87	3.16	43	4.0	35.8	94.3	97.7
Footwear	65	2.19	2.00	9.85	4.12	48	5.6	20.1	108.9	96.7
	67	2.24	2.17	8.94	4.17	48	5.8	21.0	105.6	84.8
	69	2.41	2.04	8.89	4.26	51	5.5	25.0	107.9	91.7
	71	2.68	1.73	7.38	3.78	51	5.6	23.7	108.4	83.8
	73	2.34	1.66	6.36	4.02	59	5.3	27.9	122.0	93.3
Fur Goods	65	1.89	0.75	4.93	6.11	44	7.2	3.6	*	89.4
	67	1.79	0.60	5.86	7.12	43	7.3	3.9	*	87.6
	69	1.83	0.54	2.75	5.80	48	5.3	2.9	205.9	100.3
	71	1.70	0.64	2.69	6.10	62	5.6	4.0	*	82.2
	73	*	*	*	*	*	*	*	*	*
General Building Contractors	65	1.51	1.42	9.69	7.18	*	*	20.7	196.0	*
	67	1.52	1.35	9.89	7.82	*	*	22.9	162.9	*
	69	1.45	1.23	9.66	8.45	*	*	25.7	206.3	*
	71	1.54	1.53	12.73	8.99	*	*	24.8	202.8	*
	73	1.42	1.07	10.79	8.81	*	*	24.7	195.0	*

(continued)

Line of Business	Year	Current Assets to Current Debt (Times)	Net Profit on Net Sales (Percent)	Net Profit to Tangible Net Worth (Percent)	Net Sales to Tangible Worth (Times)	Collection Period (Days)	Net Sales to Inventory (Times)	Fixed Asset to Tangible Net Worth (Percent)	Total Debt to Tangible Net Worth (Percent)	Inventory to Net Working Capital (Percent)
General Industrial Machinery & Equipment	65	2.48	5.75	14.16	2.34	51	4.9	40.4	77.3	78.6
	67	2.66	5.37	13.93	2.63	52	5.0	40.9	73.3	76.4
	69	2.49	3.75	10.49	2.76	55	4.9	41.8	72.7	87.9
	71	3.02	2.13	6.08	2.41	54	5.0	42.1	74.9	72.3
	73	2.52	3.84	11.95	2.86	58	4.6	43.8	92.2	81.2
Grain Mill Products	65	2.48	1.74	8.38	4.20	28	11.9	55.3	72.2	65.5
	67	2.26	1.37	7.04	4.26	28	11.4	55.2	66.2	86.7
	69	2.24	2.28	9.85	4.35	27	11.3	50.2	58.0	77.6
	71	2.16	1.75	8.30	5.06	30	10.7	63.4	97.8	74.8
	73	1.99	1.60	12.73	5.49	33	11.2	57.4	128.6	87.0
Heating Apparatus & Plumbing Fixtures	65	2.55	3.58	11.34	3.46	45	5.3	38.8	100.6	95.7
	67	3.08	2.36	8.41	2.97	43	4.8	36.9	71.6	86.0
	69	2.44	2.28	7.25	2.83	48	5.2	42.9	90.5	85.9
	71	3.12	2.42	7.59	2.97	54	5.3	43.4	93.1	83.6
	73	2.92	3.34	11.00	2.89	50	4.3	43.7	74.4	90.0
Heavy Construction (except Highway & Street)	65	1.67	3.24	11.51	3.66	*	*	50.3	109.3	*
	67	1.72	2.75	11.09	3.55	*	*	57.4	108.9	*
	69	1.87	2.67	9.77	3.74	*	*	60.0	88.2	*
	71	1.90	2.09	8.61	4.12	*	*	52.0	101.7	*
	73	1.77	2.27	9.50	3.69	*	*	53.2	100.1	*
Hosiery	65	2.42	2.58	6.38	2.39	35	4.0	43.0	59.9	90.0
	67	2.44	3.18	6.75	2.71	42	5.6	44.6	84.3	91.6
	69	2.39	2.39	7.92	3.10	45	5.5	52.8	81.9	96.0
	71	2.60	1.87	6.23	3.12	42	7.0	46.5	69.6	85.5
	73	2.56	1.05	2.81	2.85	48	4.9	45.1	98.7	83.5
Household Appliances	65	2.67	3.77	10.70	2.91	50	4.6	34.3	87.1	85.8
	67	2.40	2.81	8.62	3.14	44	5.6	34.6	94.3	90.3
	69	2.37	3.16	9.89	2.98	43	4.6	34.7	77.8	91.4
	71	2.65	3.31	10.29	3.23	48	4.9	36.1	97.4	86.3
	73	2.47	3.74	12.52	3.18	52	4.3	38.9	95.4	90.6

(continued)

Line of Business	Year	Current Assets to Current Debt (Times)	Net Profit on Net Sales (Percent)	Net Profit to Tangible Net Worth (Percent)	Net Sales to Tangible Worth (Times)	Collection Period (Days)	Net Sales to Inventory (Times)	Fixed Asset to Tangible Net Worth (Percent)	Total Debt to Tangible Net Worth (Percent)	Inventory to Net Working Capital (Percent)
Industrial Chemicals	65	2.09	6.08	11.39	2.02	44	7.3	67.2	64.6	73.4
	67	2.01	4.28	9.79	1.90	51	6.8	56.1	56.9	87.2
	69	1.93	4.35	9.68	2.07	51	7.1	62.8	57.6	88.3
	71	2.70	3.67	7.69	2.12	57	6.2	73.6	75.5	76.4
	73	2.45	5.25	12.34	2.21	61	7.7	79.6	98.7	69.0
Iron & Steel Foundaries	65	2.17	3.44	10.54	3.32	52	6.1	37.8	91.2	74.7
	67	2.62	4.17	9.23	2.66	37	9.5	60.9	58.4	60.0
	69	2.42	2.87	7.53	2.62	46	11.0	59.2	57.1	68.5
	71	2.89	2.60	6.35	2.27	40	11.0	57.7	55.2	53.2
	73	2.53	3.56	8.95	2.59	51	8.8	63.2	59.9	64.7
Knitted Outerwear Mills	65	1.77	1.60	13.07	5.76	38	6.3	23.3	126.6	122.8
	67	2.04	0.91	6.29	4.88	46	6.3	21.1	99.7	103.4
	69	1.93	1.93	8.86	4.31	40	6.0	24.9	95.5	108.2
	71	1.98	2.00	8.76	4.37	46	7.0	29.5	91.9	89.3
	73	1.98	2.35	10.70	3.75	49	6.3	28.8	86.6	100.6
Malt Liquors	65	2.29	3.17	8.21	2.25	18	12.6	67.6	45.8	51.2
	67	2.04	3.59	7.48	2.26	18	16.4	64.8	75.1	58.9
	69	2.07	3.74	9.53	2.65	16	18.8	67.9	44.7	54.9
	71	2.12	1.91	6.83	2.61	14	16.4	75.6	59.5	59.1
	73	2.33	2.44	8.21	2.80	16	13.7	80.1	56.7	68.5
Mattresses & Bed Springs	65	2.56	2.12	8.74	3.11	42	7.5	29.2	43.6	70.0
	67	2.88	1.43	6.59	3.05	44	8.5	22.5	67.9	58.1
	69	2.35	1.96	5.52	3.31	49	9.2	23.4	89.4	67.6
	71	2.15	2.30	5.22	3.50	51	7.2	26.6	93.0	73.5
	73	2.21	1.44	8.86	4.00	48	8.1	35.6	109.7	83.8
Measuring & Controlling Instruments	65	*	*	*	*	*	*	*	*	*
	67	*	4.89	12.68	2.74	55	4.4	41.8	66.9	74.8
	69	2.83	4.42	12.07	2.65	57	4.2	36.8	82.7	70.3
	71	3.63	4.08	8.81	2.22	63	4.0	35.0	80.6	66.7
	73	2.40	3.62	8.37	2.39	71	3.6	43.3	83.6	86.9

(continued)

Line of Business	Year	Current Assets to Current Debt (Times)	Net Profit on Net Sales (Percent)	Net Profit to Tangible Net Worth (Percent)	Net Sales to Tangible Net Worth (Times)	Collection Period (Days)	Net Sales to Inventory (Times)	Fixed Asset to Tangible Net Worth (Percent)	Total Debt to Tangible Net Worth (Percent)	Inventory to Net Working Capital (Percent)
Meat Packing Plants	65	2.56	0.83	8.52	8.62	12	31.1	51.3	73.8	66.4
	67	2.51	0.99	8.04	9.06	13	29.9	51.1	83.6	62.5
	69	2.06	0.91	8.50	9.33	15	30.5	58.4	71.2	68.3
	71	2.11	0.87	10.14	9.74	14	33.1	63.5	91.9	68.5
	73	1.97	0.64	9.85	11.68	14	28.5	65.2	96.7	88.2
Men's & Boys' Shirts, Underwear & Nightwear	65	1.76	1.89	12.25	5.64	48	4.5	7.3	152.7	137.3
	67	1.88	1.67	6.94	5.35	51	5.3	9.0	164.9	102.5
	69	1.03	1.60	7.83	4.64	54	5.0	12.4	112.4	107.2
	71	1.96	2.34	9.04	4.44	51	4.6	13.5	114.0	96.9
	73	1.99	1.96	8.44	4.70	50	4.1	14.3	106.8	105.2
Men's & Boys' Suits, Coats & Overcoats	65	1.90	1.15	7.13	4.35	53	5.0	7.0	134.7	103.3
	67	2.05	1.55	6.73	4.46	57	5.7	7.0	105.7	90.7
	69	2.07	1.39	8.17	4.59	56	5.0	10.0	131.0	105.0
	71	2.19	0.94	4.69	4.55	51	5.7	8.8	138.8	94.9
	73	2.29	1.82	8.06	4.49	58	4.5	9.1	140.9	91.1
Men's & Boys' Trousers	65	2.12	1.13	5.11	4.01	52	4.3	7.9	112.8	99.5
	67	2.08	1.43	6.77	4.44	45	6.1	6.1	89.4	89.7
	69	1.83	1.64	7.37	5.07	61	4.9	7.2	168.7	93.3
	71	2.07	1.32	9.20	4.78	54	5.6	9.1	135.3	78.9
	73	2.15	1.37	6.91	4.44	48	6.8	9.3	111.3	72.6
Metal Stampings	65	2.29	4.12	13.79	3.09	37	7.7	49.7	74.2	80.8
	67	2.53	3.53	10.90	3.04	35	9.2	47.6	83.8	67.2
	69	2.32	2.63	7.03	3.07	36	8.6	50.0	76.4	75.7
	71	2.51	2.26	5.53	2.84	39	7.7	54.2	81.0	77.1
	73	2.11	2.82	10.91	3.48	43	7.8	54.0	99.0	93.2
Metal Making Machinery & Equipment	65	2.42	5.06	12.60	2.51	49	6.7	43.2	77.2	69.5
	67	2.49	4.48	11.65	2.49	44	6.0	43.7	67.7	75.2
	69	2.29	3.87	9.79	2.29	54	5.5	47.8	72.9	88.5
	71	2.81	1.46	2.69	1.95	55	5.5	50.6	70.9	72.7
	73	2.51	4.10	10.27	2.41	58	5.6	46.6	75.8	80.6

(continued)

Line of Business	Year	Current Assets to Current Debt (Times)	Net Profit on Net Sales (Percent)	Net Profit to Tangible Net Worth (Percent)	Net Sales to Tangible Worth (Times)	Collection Period (Days)	Net Sales to Inventory (Times)	Fixed Asset to Tangible Net Worth (Percent)	Total Debt to Tangible Net Worth (Percent)	Inventory to Net Working Capital (Percent)
Millwork	65	2.71	1.96	5.21	3.55	53	7.7	28.2	77.1	70.3
	67	2.67	2.15	7.41	2.90	55	7.0	45.1	152.7	80.8
	69	2.60	2.06	7.78	4.01	46	6.8	40.3	98.8	74.0
	71	2.65	2.47	7.53	3.73	42	6.9	38.3	91.9	67.4
	73	2.38	2.82	12.27	3.82	37	6.3	39.9	104.2	87.5
Miscellaneous Machinery (except Electrical)	65	*	*	*	*	*	*	*	*	*
	67	2.50	4.90	12.84	3.04	40	10.7	47.5	69.2	60.3
	69	2.72	3.40	10.02	2.46	45	10.9	43.6	73.7	56.0
	71	2.95	2.67	7.28	2.52	45	9.1	52.3	59.8	63.5
	73	2.39	3.61	10.10	2.79	46	9.0	47.8	89.3	61.3
Motor Vehicle Parts & Accessories	65	2.52	4.55	14.07	3.05	40	5.8	38.2	64.7	87.7
	67	2.78	3.78	11.05	2.74	43	5.6	40.6	59.0	77.3
	69	2.70	3.99	12.35	2.80	42	6.2	43.4	78.5	82.7
	71	2.79	3.29	8.81	2.59	45	5.3	46.0	83.9	78.0
	73	2.45	4.03	12.91	3.04	46	5.2	50.5	82.8	89.0
Nonferrous Foundries	65	2.59	3.48	10.72	2.82	37	13.5	51.4	58.0	46.7
	67	2.22	4.27	12.70	2.97	36	13.9	54.8	65.2	59.6
	69	2.30	2.98	7.72	3.07	40	12.5	46.4	65.8	54.7
	71	2.87	2.17	4.61	2.36	39	13.9	45.0	53.2	45.8
	73	2.44	4.49	11.94	3.37	46	9.7	48.1	83.5	66.3
Office & Store Fixtures	65	1.98	1.26	6.88	4.32	49	7.8	27.7	85.8	81.1
	67	2.23	2.44	9.56	3.96	47	10.2	35.8	103.6	66.2
	69	2.08	3.07	10.80	3.91	59	8.6	32.7	123.0	65.7
	71	2.27	2.44	8.35	3.79	54	6.8	35.8	125.3	64.8
	73	2.17	2.85	9.35	3.53	57	6.7	33.6	130.3	89.5
Paints, Varnishes, Lacquers & Enamels	65	3.26	3.74	11.02	2.75	40	6.4	32.9	54.5	65.9
	67	3.48	2.40	6.40	2.84	40	6.9	33.3	47.8	70.8
	69	3.14	2.48	7.32	2.85	41	6.6	34.3	64.4	71.3
	71	3.04	2.26	7.00	3.13	42	6.6	40.3	66.3	70.5
	73	2.93	2.61	8.49	3.18	42	6.3	36.6	70.2	76.4

(continued)

Line of Business	Year	Current Assets to Current Debt (Times)	Net Profit on Net Sales (Percent)	Net Profit to Tangible Net Worth (Percent)	Net Sales to Tangible Worth (Times)	Collection Period (Days)	Net Sales to Inventory (Times)	Fixed Asset to Tangible Net Worth (Percent)	Total Debt to Tangible Net Worth (Percent)	Inventory to Net Working Capital (Percent)
Paper Board Containers & Boxes	65	2.22	3.33	10.44	3.43	37	8.7	61.4	96.1	84.8
	67	2.38	3.71	11.84	3.24	32	9.8	65.7	79.4	61.7
	69	2.43	3.36	9.37	3.00	38	11.6	45.8	83.4	61.9
	71	2.55	2.60	6.72	3.06	34	8.5	67.2	70.4	74.5
	73	2.43	3.57	11.21	3.37	36	7.8	59.7	89.1	78.3
Paper Mills (except Building Paper)	65	2.64	4.63	8.69	1.92	35	8.4	83.4	57.9	70.5
	67	2.83	4.20	8.50	1.78	34	7.4	77.4	43.8	67.7
	69	2.57	4.34	8.19	1.73	40	7.3	70.9	48.8	62.7
	71	2.94	2.72	5.94	1.91	41	6.5	80.8	69.3	65.8
	73	2.40	4.11	10.81	2.20	40	7.7	94.8	85.8	65.7
Passenger Car, Truck & Bus Bodies	65	2.15	3.00	8.20	3.62	42	6.3	38.5	94.9	83.0
	67	2.36	1.93	7.72	3.36	48	6.5	29.7	90.3	90.1
	69	2.12	1.82	7.32	4.12	48	6.4	38.6	100.3	83.0
	71	2.63	1.85	8.29	3.54	49	6.6	41.8	90.1	80.3
	73	1.89	2.59	8.91	4.16	46	4.8	38.7	111.8	125.9
Petroleum Refineries	65	1.43	5.31	8.60	1.37	40	14.1	31.9	25.0	79.6
	67	1.20	5.05	8.88	1.72	33	10.0	35.8	30.5	78.9
	69	1.14	3.76	6.84	1.78	30	13.0	41.1	23.6	117.8
	71	1.72	4.87	8.73	1.91	49	10.5	101.5	69.1	76.8
	73	1.70	7.03	14.37	2.08	59	12.1	99.2	66.0	66.7
Plastics, Materials & Synthetics	65	2.07	3.74	11.08	3.24	49	9.6	45.5	82.5	89.9
	67	1.98	3.24	9.30	3.12	44	8.7	55.4	77.1	84.9
	69	1.88	2.75	8.30	2.63	53	8.0	61.0	60.0	79.0
	71	2.25	2.60	7.64	2.84	55	7.7	57.1	61.2	70.6
	73	2.24	3.80	11.89	2.83	57	7.9	67.7	96.4	72.4
Plumbing, Heating & Air Conditioning	65	1.83	1.71	9.04	5.78	*	*	18.9	156.1	*
	67	1.72	1.97	11.96	6.48	*	*	20.4	124.1	*
	69	1.74	1.71	11.79	6.07	*	*	21.8	114.3	*
	71	1.91	1.30	9.03	6.63	*	*	24.5	142.5	*
	73	1.71	1.29	9.16	6.62	*	*	21.7	171.4	*

(continued)

Line of Business	Year	Current Assets to Current Debt (Times)	Net Profit on Net Sales (Percent)	Net Profit to Tangible Net Worth (Percent)	Net Sales to Tangible Worth (Times)	Collection Period (Days)	Net Sales to Inventory (Times)	Fixed Asset to Tangible Net Worth (Percent)	Total Debt to Tangible Net Worth (Percent)	Inventory to Net Working Capital (Percent)
Saw Mills & Planing Mills	65	*	*	*	*	*	*	*	*	*
	67	2.31	3.50	7.88	2.05	35	6.6	51.7	58.0	81.5
	69	2.27	4.04	10.75	2.46	31	7.3	58.9	69.8	84.8
	71	2.43	3.68	9.85	2.49	33	6.7	58.0	59.3	75.5
	73	2.34	7.23	20.61	2.55	30	9.5	46.7	63.7	64.5
Screw Machine Products	65	2.48	4.43	14.15	2.55	35	5.7	49.9	70.2	81.4
	67	2.67	4.61	13.62	2.64	32	7.7	51.0	65.6	87.1
	69	2.53	4.37	11.12	2.59	37	7.9	52.0	54.3	76.8
	71	2.89	2.54	4.47	2.21	39	5.7	48.4	59.9	70.9
	73	2.35	4.85	14.60	2.73	41	6.9	48.2	78.4	79.6
Soap, Detergents, Perfumes & Cosmetics	65	2.61	4.09	12.39	3.20	37	8.5	32.3	63.2	61.9
	67	2.95	3.39	10.91	3.03	47	7.5	33.0	59.5	62.6
	69	2.27	3.95	12.36	3.22	54	7.8	33.4	57.5	70.9
	71	2.66	3.83	12.74	2.88	51	7.6	29.1	62.3	59.2
	73	2.37	4.04	11.61	3.16	52	7.1	38.7	68.9	65.7
Special Industry Machinery	65	2.85	5.61	12.20	2.35	58	5.1	35.2	86.9	69.7
	67	2.72	3.54	9.83	2.44	52	5.3	36.5	76.7	74.9
	69	2.62	3.78	8.86	2.37	66	4.3	38.3	81.6	82.5
	71	3.16	2.08	4.35	2.03	59	4.7	35.2	62.0	68.2
	73	2.59	3.69	9.89	2.50	61	4.5	36.3	89.7	80.7
Surgical, Medical & Dental Instruments	65	2.85	6.16	12.45	2.74	47	5.7	24.5	67.0	72.5
	67	3.70	4.95	12.23	2.40	49	5.4	22.1	70.9	64.0
	69	3.66	4.90	11.65	2.50	56	4.3	24.6	52.4	68.0
	71	4.37	3.40	8.77	2.30	55	4.9	23.8	53.0	61.0
	73	2.98	4.79	11.51	2.25	62	4.7	31.3	66.1	67.0
Toys, Amusements & Sporting Goods	65	2.09	2.39	7.84	3.41	52	5.2	28.7	103.4	86.9
	67	2.02	2.74	10.97	3.43	47	5.6	31.1	104.0	90.8
	69	1.97	2.55	9.22	3.87	55	5.0	38.3	129.9	116.5
	71	2.37	2.52	8.68	3.43	59	4.9	27.1	111.8	86.8
	73	2.40	3.89	11.90	3.17	56	4.6	39.4	107.4	85.7

(continued)

Line of Business	Year	Current Assets to Current Debt (Times)	Net Profit on Net Sales (Percent)	Net Profit to Tangible Net Worth (Percent)	Net Sales to Tangible Worth (Times)	Collection Period (Days)	Net Sales to Inventory (Times)	Fixed Asset to Tangible Net Worth (Percent)	Total Debt to Tangible Net Worth (Percent)	Inventory to Net Working Capital (Percent)
Women's & Children's Underwear & Nightwear	65	1.76	0.93	6.17	6.20	42	7.7	10.3	156.7	120.9
	67	1.87	1.40	9.18	6.54	40	7.7	12.2	124.0	106.8
	69	2.01	1.62	10.22	5.67	45	6.2	16.0	137.4	115.2
	71	2.19	1.25	6.92	5.96	42	6.0	14.1	89.4	94.3
	73	2.09	1.38	7.46	5.32	46	6.4	12.0	114.6	92.9
Women's & Misses' Blouses & Tops	65	1.70	0.92	13.08	9.77	39	14.1	10.0	149.9	77.8
	67	1.73	0.69	7.86	8.58	36	13.0	7.2	175.3	86.0
	69	1.67	1.34	12.35	9.33	46	12.1	8.3	144.3	88.7
	71	1.51	1.20	13.27	9.93	45	11.6	10.3	161.9	102.6
	73	1.62	1.60	16.04	10.02	40	10.3	6.2	324.0	103.8
Women's & Misses' Suits & Coats	65	1.85	1.27	10.55	7.87	44	9.5	5.1	138.5	78.5
	67	1.90	1.30	8.15	7.75	48	11.6	5.0	184.3	64.3
	69	1.87	0.94	7.16	7.47	48	9.6	6.0	191.7	80.8
	71	1.89	0.80	5.08	6.94	40	8.5	6.4	199.1	68.5
	73	1.95	1.47	11.82	6.55	45	11.0	6.5	242.7	78.9
Women's, Misses', & Juniors' Dresses	65	1.58	0.79	10.44	10.07	41	13.2	10.3	147.2	95.8
	67	1.61	1.12	10.79	10.24	42	15.5	8.7	163.8	80.3
	69	1.58	1.17	10.60	9.30	49	13.4	7.4	179.6	83.3
	71	1.67	1.16	10.42	7.75	51	11.8	7.1	151.5	77.2
	73	1.73	1.19	8.27	6.77	53	8.9	10.8	168.1	86.4
Wooden & Upholstered Household Furniture	65	2.62	2.73	11.74	3.25	44	7.1	35.2	66.3	75.5
	67	2.85	2.41	7.87	3.11	43	6.9	36.0	64.3	79.2
	69	3.02	3.30	9.99	2.90	42	6.4	33.4	55.7	75.7
	71	2.88	2.69	9.57	3.13	47	7.1	35.2	60.2	71.3
	73	2.92	3.18	11.32	3.17	44	6.2	39.2	69.4	82.7
Work Clothing Men's and Boys'	65	2.71	2.33	9.83	3.38	50	3.6	16.3	122.0	89.3
	67	3.06	2.78	5.80	3.21	50	4.0	18.3	91.0	82.7
	69	2.86	2.23	6.80	3.14	46	3.8	15.4	89.8	82.1
	71	2.68	2.63	8.48	3.25	55	4.2	19.5	99.1	89.3
	73	3.19	2.60	8.44	3.29	53	4.6	17.2	89.1	84.9

a comparison of financial objectives with actual results over a period of time and in relation to performance of competitors.

Break-even analysis is another tool that may prove useful during financial analysis. This subject is reviewed in the last section of this chapter.

DIAGNOSIS OF PROBLEMS

The information gathered in the "analysis of situation" phase provides a fairly complete assessment of the firm's financial strengths and weaknesses. This information, in conjunction with data on other aspects of the external and internal situation (for example, organization, marketing, production), provides the base from which problem identification and analysis can begin. For instance, why is the firm's profit margin on sales 2 per cent below the industry average? Is it because prices are too low or because costs are too high? What marketing information in the case indicates that prices may be too low? In this case, a particular financial indicator of external effectiveness ultimately may lead to diagnosis of a problem in the firm's marketing strategy. On the other hand, information may exist to show that costs are too high because of an inefficient plant layout. Here, the profit margin indicator would have led to problem diagnosis in the area of programming the physical resources necessary to implement the master production plan.

In a similar fashion, the student can use the other financial indicators to work back through the many factors that have a bearing on a particular problem. Thus, a low fixed asset turnover relative to other firms in the industry may indicate that the firm is not producing at a high enough percentage of capacity. This, in turn, indicates that the firm either made too large an investment in fixed assets or that sales have not, for some reason, met previous expectations. If the former situation is the case, then the problem possibly may be traced further to an outdated, completely intuitive process of capital budgeting. If sales have not achieved forecasted levels, the problem may be traced either to unforeseeable environmental changes or to some problem in market planning and/or implementation such as market definition, pricing, or the distribution system.

The above examples are suggestive of the nature and use of most financial information in a business policy case as a starting point for problem identification. Financial data can indicate only *symptoms* of problems, leading to consideration of more basic factors which better serve to explain *why* financial growth, profit, liquidity, or efficiency is below industry averages or objectives for the firm. This is not to say, however, that all case problems are indicated by financial trouble symptoms. Rather, only that financial difficulties never, upon identification, constitute an end to the problem-solving process.

In connection with the process of problem identification, the student should be familiar with the interrelationships of the financial data and ratios discussed earlier. An understanding of two different kinds of interrelationships is important here. First, how internal efficiency and external effectiveness indicators interact to determine the profitability of the firm's assets. A basic tool for gaining an appreciation of this interaction is the Du Pont system of financial control shown in Figure 6-3. This system provides a ready-made schematic whereby interactive effects of basic financial ratios may be traced and understood. Second, an appreciation of the implications of shifts in the various ratios and their effects on other ratios. For example, a low fixed charge coverage ratio in conjunction with a high debt ratio may indicate a substantial weakness in the firm from a creditor's perspective. An increase in gross income may raise the fixed charge coverage ratio significantly, however, and therefore offset to some extent the disadvantages of a high debt ratio. The ability to perceive interrelationships between the ratios is a prerequisite for understanding the total financial position, present and projected, of a firm.

Finally, the student should have a basic understanding of the implications of each basic financial indicator in and of itself. For example, just how significant is a high debt ratio to creditors? What other factors may offset this deficiency? Or, to use another example, what are the implications of a low fixed asset turnover for new capital proposals, both present line-oriented and new product-oriented?

DEVELOPMENT OF PLANS OF ACTION

The use of financial analysis in the development of recommended plans of action may be approached from two basic perspectives. First, the student must ascertain the *financial feasibility* of all recommendations, expressed in terms of (1) the effects of plans developed on the basic indicators of financial effectiveness, efficiency, and objectives; (2) the availability of short- or long-term financing, either internally or externally, to implement the recommendations; and (3) the risk-taking propensity of top management. Second, the student must be prepared to compare alternative courses of action in terms of feasibility and risk, which requires a basic understanding of capital investment theory.

With respect to the first line of inquiry, information developed in the "analysis of situation" phase is once again of primary importance. Its *use* is significantly different, however, from what was previously discussed in the "problem identification" phase. In the present phase, the ratios and other indicators must be projected for their *future* implications as to the financial position of the firm, if a given recommendation is implemented. For example, if a recommendation is made to enter a new product market, what would be the effect of the new sales forecast for the firm as a whole on a currently unsatisfactory turnover of fixed assets? Is a heavy investment in fixed assets required to achieve the new sales forecast? If so, how much lead time would be required before sales increased enough in the new product line to offset the short-run inefficiency indicated by an even lower turnover of fixed assets? What will be the impact on creditor relations? How can creditors and stockholders be convinced "to be patient"? These and other similar implications for the financial standing of the firm must be explored to determine the merits of each recommendation. This is not to say, however, that detailed projections of sales and investment requirements must be formulated. Rather, it is more appropriate in a policy

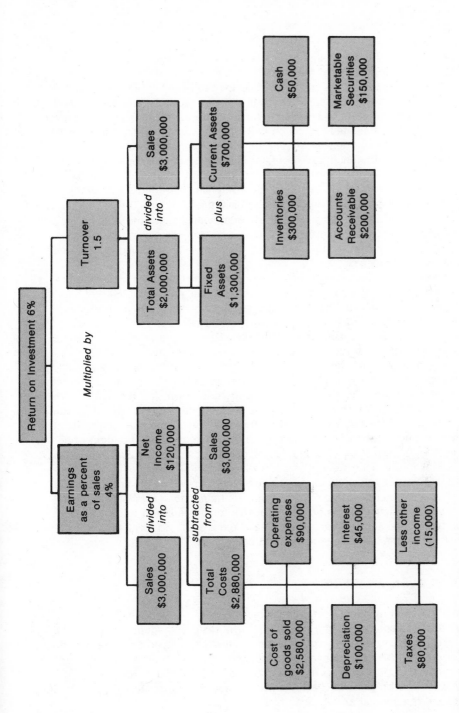

FIGURE 6-3: DuPont system of financial control.

Source: *Essentials of Managerial Finance, 2nd ed.,* by J. Fred Weston and Eugene F. Brigham. Copyright © 1968, 1971 by Holt, Rinehart and Winston, Publishers. Reprinted by permission of The Dryden Press.

case to assess the recommendations in terms of their general implications for the future financial position of the firm.

The student also must be able to prove that adequate resources exist to finance the recommended plans. How will the new plans be financed? What appear to be the trade-offs between external and internal financing? How might the trade-offs be calculated? One should be able to recognize the specific calculations that may be necessary and the trade-offs that actually exist among alternative modes of financing. The major implication of this reasoning is that any recommendation involving deployment of a high volume of financial resources must be qualified by the recognition that alternative modes of financing carry alternative implications for the firm's basic financial structure.

Finally, with respect to feasibility, the student must take into account top management's psychological propensity to assume financial risk. This is a basic aspect of feasibility that is often ignored, but one which is vital in gaining acceptance of proposals.

As noted above, the second major use of financial analysis in developing plans of action requires a familiarity with the techniques of comparison of alternative proposals. The question arises, however, as to what extent the student should be required to rank alternative investment proposals in terms of the appropriate discounted cash flow technique. The body of literature existing in capital investment theory will have been explored in previous finance courses. It appears, however, that detailed evaluation of investment proposals (usually a C_4 variable) through the application of the net present value method, internal rate of return method, or profitability index method is outside the scope of a business policy course. The student should understand how the cost of capital (supply of funds) schedule interacts with projected revenue streams (investment opportunities open to the firm) to determine the optimum capital budget under conditions of uncertainty. This understanding then can be expressed in terms of a qualification of recommendations concerning capital investment until appropriate computations are completed by financial analysts within the firm. It should be emphasized that the foregoing refers only to the *financial* feasibility of investment proposals. Implications of the proposals for present and future strategy, organization, and other matters should have been explored to justify the existence of the recommendations in the first place.

BREAK-EVEN ANALYSIS

The purpose of this final section is to review some of the definitions, mathematical relationships, uses, and limitations of a basic management tool called break-even analysis. This type of analysis is usually displayed on a break-even chart or graph. This chart shows the relationships between profits, fixed costs, variable costs, and volume in a rather compact and visual form. Figure 6-4 presents a typical break-even chart. As you can see, the horizontal axis is volume in units and the vertical axis is in dollars.

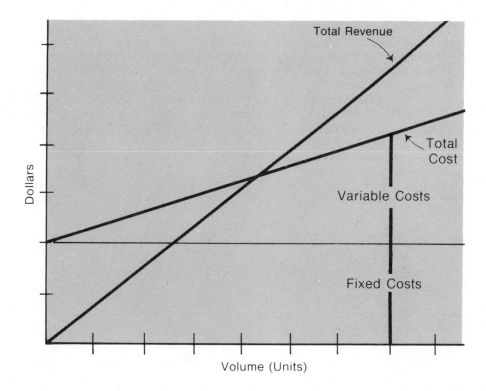

FIGURE 6-4: Typical break-even chart.

One of the first inputs the student must develop is the total cost line. Usually, it is assumed that total cost can be broken into two linear components, fixed and variable costs. Fixed costs are considered to be constant as volume of output changes. Some typical examples of such costs are depreciation on plant and equipment, rentals, interest charges on debt, property taxes, occupancy cost (such as heat and lights), general office expenses, and salaries of supervisory, research, and executive staffs.

Variable costs are assumed to vary directly with the volume produced. The usual components of variable costs include direct labor, direct material, sales commissions, and supplies. One of the problems involved in classifying a cost into one of these categories is the time horizon to which you are referring. Some may argue that all costs are variable, or at least not fixed, in the long run, while others say that in the very short run, all costs are fixed. The conflict is partially resolved when the time period or horizon to be covered by the break-even analysis is determined—this is usually one year.

It may be difficult to classify each cost into either the fixed or variable category over the entire volume range. The semivariable cost has both a fixed and a variable component. Examples of this type of cost are indirect labor, maintenance, and clerical costs.

There are several ways of approximating this cost-volume relationship other than just having the components given in a problem. One way is to locate two points on the break-even chart. The student needs to know the total costs at two different volumes, preferably with some "spread" between them. The straight line that connects these points defines the total cost function. Another method is to plot the historical cost-volume points on the graph and fit a straight line through the resulting scatter diagram. In either case, the fixed cost is where the total cost line intercepts the vertical axis, and the slope of the line is the variable cost/unit.

There are some difficulties involved in using these approaches. First of all, they concentrate on past relationships. By doing this, one implicitly assumes that the conditions which prevailed in the past are still operating, and that may not be the case. Factors other than volume or cost also may have been operating. Then, there are the dangers present in any regression analysis—extrapolating data beyond their boundaries and having too few observations.

The other primary input to break-even analysis is the total revenue line. It is assumed that revenue is derived solely from sales made at a constant price/ unit. Incidentally, it also is assumed that production volume for the year is the same as sales volume—that is, no net change in inventory.

The point at which these two lines cross is called the break-even point. Some say that because of the impreciseness of the inputs (total cost and total revenue) it might be better labeled a "break-even region." Mathematically, the break-even point is where total cost equals total revenue. From this we can easily find an expression for break-even volume. At break-even point

$$TC = TR \qquad (1)$$

where
$$TC = FS + VN$$
$$TR = SN$$
$$F = \text{fixed cost}$$
$$N = \text{volume of output in units}$$
$$V = \text{variable cost/unit}$$
$$S = \text{selling price/unit}$$

Substituting we get

$$F + VN = SN$$
$$VN - SN = -F$$
$$N(S - V) = F$$
$$N = F/(S - V) \qquad (2)$$

Thus, we have a fairly simple equation for break-even volume.

Using the same notation, we can arrive at an expression for profit.

$$\text{Profit } (P) = TR - TC \qquad (3)$$

Substituting the same expressions given above, equation (3) becomes

$$P = SN - (F + VN)$$
$$P = SN - VN - F$$
$$P = N(S - V) - F \qquad (4)$$

Notice that in both equations (2) and (4), the term $(S - V)$ appears. This is called the contribution/unit—that is, this is the amount that covers fixed costs and later profit each time an additional unit is sold. Letting C represent contribution, equations (2) and (4) become

$$N = \frac{F}{C} \qquad (5)$$

$$P = NC - F \qquad (6)$$

respectively.

A brief example might serve to clarify the situation. The Phinque Company has an annual fixed cost of $100,000. The variable cost/unit is $.50 and the product sells for $1.00. The break-even chart and break-even point for this situation is shown in Figure 6-5, but if you have run out of graph paper, you can rely on equation 2.

$$N = \frac{\$100,000}{\$1.00 - \$.50} = 200,000 \text{ units}$$

If you want to find the profit at a particular volume, such as 250,000 units, use equation 4.

$$P = 250,000 \ (\$.50 - \$1.00) - \$100,000$$
$$= \$125,000 - \$100,000$$
$$P = \$25,000$$

Break-even analysis can be used in a variety of ways. One of the more obvious uses is to examine the sensitivity of the break-even point and profit to changes in four factors—selling price, variable costs, fixed costs, and volume. For instance, the greater the ratio of price to variable cost/unit, the greater the absolute sensitivity of profits to volume. By examining equation 2, you can see the cost-price-volume relationship explicitly. If you decrease direct labor by adding an automatic piece of equipment, you may increase fixed costs. How are profits and break-even volume affected? Equations (2) and (4) or the break-even chart can be used to answer this type of question easily.

Analysis of the cost-price-volume structure may lead you to some less obvious conclusions. For example, where there is a great cost variability with volume, cost reduction efforts can be fruitful. On the other hand, if a large percentage of the total cost is fixed, it would be best for a company to focus on sales promotion because, with high fixed costs, the best way to change profits is through increased volume.

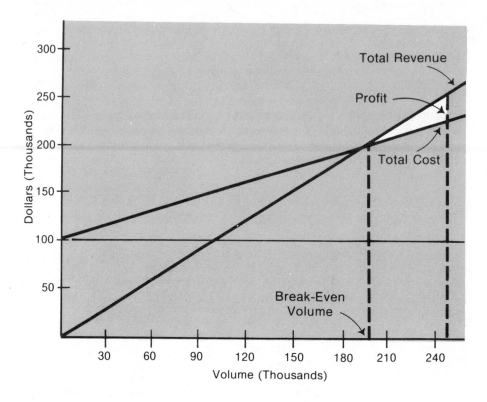

FIGURE 6-5: Break-even chart—Phinque Company.

Given the approximate break-even point, management can compare fluctuations in expected future volume with this point to ascertain stability of profits. This type of information is important to the financial manager in determining the ability of the firm to cover its debt obligations. If there are plans to acquire assets which will increase fixed costs, this knowledge becomes important.

Break-even analysis may be used to evaluate proposals for the expansion or contraction of the firm's operations. For example, the abandonment of, or addition to, a company's facilities can have a far-reaching effect on its financial equilibrium, and break-even analysis can provide management with a fairly accurate estimate of this change. Break-even analysis may be beneficial when examining technological changes, new product decisions, a modernization or automation program, or whenever a horizontal or vertical merger is contemplated. For example, when faced with a decision as to whether or not to purchase another company, one line of analysis is to look at the composite break-even chart. It may reveal that the fixed charges are so high that the break-even point is raised dangerously high, and consequently this purchase would not be desirable.

Another use for break-even analysis is in plant-location analysis. The economic effects of changing production volumes on the operating costs and profits that exist in alternative plant sites can be analyzed using break-even analysis. In this case, one assumes that sales revenue is not affected by the location decision. Break-even analysis allows the manager to consider the relative economic feasibility of alternative sites at different operating volumes. The manager must then decide what the future operating volume will be before a decision can be reached.

Unfortunately, there are several limitations to break-even analysis. These are usually associated with the assumptions that are made. For instance, it is assumed that the selling price and variable cost/unit are constant over the entire volume range. Thus, the end results are linear relationships. The additional assumption is made that each of the factors is independent of the other. As one learns in economics, however, volume may influence the market price. Also, costs may increase as full capacity is approached because of the use of marginal labor and/or costly overtime help. Setup costs and learning prevent labor costs from following a straight line. Quantity discounts make material costs nonlinear.

One way to get around these problems is to develop relationships between total sales and volume, and total cost and volume. This would lead to nonlinear relationships that would correspond more closely to reality but would also make analysis a bit more complicated.

Break-even analysis is best suited for a one-product firm. If it is assumed that the product mix does not change, break-even analysis can be used for multiple products. When the product mix changes, one is faced with the problem of allocating expenses that are common to all product lines. Also, the horizontal axis of the break-even chart must be expressed in some aggregate measure.

Informational inputs for break-even analysis are usually based upon historical relationships. However, it is the future that is usually of interest and these historical relationships may not be stable over time. The short-time horizon used in break-even analysis is a limitation for long-range planning. The benefits of certain expenditures, such as capital expenditures and research and development outlays, are not likely to be realized during the period of time encompassed by most break-even analyses.

Break-even analysis implicitly assumes that changes in the four factors are not accompanied by changes in the amount of capital used. If a decrease in variable cost arises, because of the purchase of a new machine, for example, the effect on return on investment is not given by break-even analysis.

Finally, as in financial analysis, break-even analysis does not take intangible factors into account, such as the reactions of customers and employees and the reactions of competitors. But even with all of these limitations and more, break-even analysis is still a valuable management tool.

SUMMARY

After a brief review of the finance function, the first section of this chapter discussed two functionally dependent decision variables—level of working capital and level of dividend payment—together with the factors that influence each of the decision variables. The section concluded with a listing of functionally independent finance decision variables.

The second section concentrated on the use of financial analysis in the three phases of case analysis: analysis of the situation, problem identification, and development of plans of action to eliminate the problems. Because financial ratios were used to perform much of the financial analysis, this section included a review of selected ratios and an explanation of how these ratios act as symptoms that can aid in identifying problem areas. It also showed how alternative courses of actions may be evaluated through the use of this type of financial analysis.

The final section of the chapter contained a brief discussion of break-even analysis and its uses and limitations for policy cases.

7

Organizational Structure:

a general management perspective

Organizational Structure:

a general management perspective

In order to design an organizational structure to achieve a given strategy the organization must be viewed as a set of interdependent and interacting units. In this way, the overall structure establishes the framework or pattern that links the various organizational parts in an effort to attain corporate objectives. To accomplish this, the development of structure requires "dividing activities, delegating authority for the performance of activities, fixing responsibility for the quality of performance, and coordinating the work of all."[61]

The first chapter of this book established a clear relationship between the strategy of the firm and the top management perspective necessary to develop that strategy. Policies must be designed to attain a balance between the opportunities and constraints of the corporate environment and the strengths and weaknesses of corporate resources. Because the organizational structure supplies the framework for operationalizing the strategic plan, the successful implementation of strategy requires that the chief executive officer shape the formal organizational structure of the firm to the peculiar needs of this strategy. Once the C_1 (strategic) variables have been determined and the overall constraints on organizational activities defined, decisions involving C_2 (coordinative) variables, including the structural variables, can be formulated and implemented. Thus, in a very important sense, strategy and structure are *interdependent* variables. Decisions on organizational structure must be made in terms of the particular strategic posture developed for the firm, because implementation of strategy would be futile without an organizational structure designed to meet strategic needs and constraints.

Most authors propose that strategy influences structure with some degree of time lag. Outside market opportunities and competitive pressures influence strategic plans, which in turn cause changes in organizational structure that facilitate implementation of those plans. The company's past organizational structure can also play a critical role in influencing emerging corporate strategy.[62] Recognition of this two-way interaction between strategy and structure

---

[61] William B. Cornell, *Organization and Management in Industry* (New York: Ronald Press Company, 1947), p. 17.

[62] Larry E. Greiner, "Evolution and Revolution as Organizations Grow," *Harvard Business Review* 53,4 (July–August 1972) p. 38.

is crucial for a complete understanding of the criteria which underlie structural designs. It becomes obvious that a top management perspective in structural design is necessary when one understands that such a design is a result of overall strategy, and that the success of the strategy is also dependent on that same design. The reading at the end of this chapter discusses the interrelationship of structural design and strategy formation, as well as the complexities of interdepartmental coordination, in greater detail.

This chapter describes the major alternative forms of organizational structure, as well as the major forces that determine these different forms. It emphasizes the way in which these variations emerge as the result of changing product/market scope and complexity.

FORCES AFFECTING THE EVOLUTION OF ORGANIZATIONAL STRUCTURE

Before proceeding to a conceptualization of alternative structural forms, it would be beneficial to discuss the forces that cause these different forms to emerge. Key forces include (1) time, or the age of the organization, (2) its size, (3) product/market complexity, and (4) growth rate of the industry.[63] In addition, the interdependent nature of the forces causes complex "hybrid" situations to develop as organizations grow and mature.

Time

All organizations are influenced by a time dimension. As an organization matures, certain changes occur in organizational norms, attitudes, beliefs, values, objectives, policies, and operations. The passage of time also contributes to the institutionalization of managerial attitudes. As a result, employee behavior becomes not only more predictable but also more difficult to change.[64] This institutionalization of attitudes and behavior makes the implementation of structural change all the more difficult and partially accounts for the time lag that occurs between a change in strategy and the necessary change in structure that supports this new strategy.

Size of the Organization

Changes in this dimension take place in various areas—for example, sales volume, number of employees, assets, and cash flow. These changes cause an increase in coordination and communication problems, variations in the distribution of functions and authority, and alterations in reporting relationships. In most cases, the organizational structure must be adjusted to accommodate

---

[63] Adapted from Greiner, "Evolution and Revolution," pp. 38–40.

[64] Ibid., p. 40.

these changes and to provide a more comfortable framework for future operations.

Product/Market Complexity

Increases in the number of products; the number of markets to be served (for example, new markets and further market segmentation); and the number and variety of such channels of distribution as horizontal integration, vertical integration and new contractual channels are key forces that influence the structure of an organization. Implicit in this dimension is the role of technology in the development of new products and new production techniques. Organizational structure evolves in response to the changing technologies and environmental influences that are involved in altering the firm's product/market scope.

Growth Rate of the Industry

The rate at which an industry expands can have a substantial impact on the extent to which an organization adds new employees, increases its assets, and develops new markets. These changes may also require a restructuring of the enterprise itself. In addition, the greater degree of competition that usually exists in a fast-growing industry can affect structures as well. Some authors propose that these competitive pressures may be the most important forces that govern corporate evolution.[65] It appears that under the conditions of increasing competition corporations abandon other forms of organization in favor of the divisional form.[66]

In general, as the forces increase and interact to accelerate the complexity of the organization, structural changes must be made to compensate for whatever new problems or situations arise. For instance, if a corporation's strategy is to increase its market share by adding a new market or a new product, the success of this strategy will depend on the proper functioning of an organizational structure designed to achieve the new strategic goals.

If one assumes that these various forces will gradually increase over a period of time—as the organization grows older, it will become larger, offer a greater variety of products, and experience a spiraling industry growth rate—then organizational structure can be viewed on a continuum with "small" on one end and "divisional" on the other. A functional structure lies somewhere between these two extremes, and, as the four major forces increase in magnitude and complexity, the organization itself will become more complex and will move toward the divisional end of the continuum.

---

[65] Bruce R. Scott, "The Industrial State: Old Myths and New Realities," *Harvard Business Review* 51, 2 (March–April 1973), p. 141.

[66] Scott draws upon extensive research conducted at the Harvard Business School on corporations in the United States and Europe to draw this conclusion. The divisional form is discussed later in this chapter.

ALTERNATIVE STRUCTURAL FORMS

The following discussion focuses on the three basic structural forms depicted in Figure 7-1, and on the variations, or hybrids, derived from them.

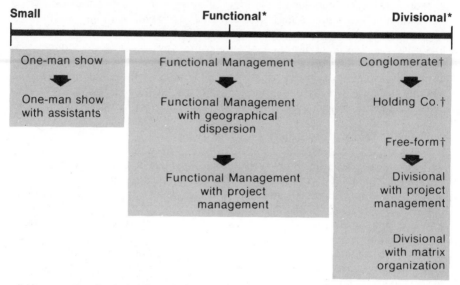

*Also can be divided using dimensions such as products, processes, territories, or customers.

†With project management or matrix organization within divisions.

FIGURE 7-1: Alternative structural forms.

SOURCE: This scheme is basically an adaption of that proposed by Scott. See Bruce R. Scott, "The Industrial State: Old Myths and New Realities," *Harvard Business Review* 51, 2 (March–April 1973) pp. 141.

The "Small" Structure

The small structure refers to an organization that is run by one man, with little or no formal operating procedures or division of labor. For example, in a single proprietorship the owner makes all the strategy decisions and is responsible for their implementation. In this organizational structure there is little confusion between authority and responsibility for the functions and activities of the firm because all of these are guided, or performed, by the same person. If the owner chooses to delegate some authority, this will not affect the firm's "small" status because the owner will usually retain final authority. Individual job descriptions may be less specific in smaller organizations because employees generally have to handle more than one aspect of the firm's activities.

Small firms usually have a single product, or a single line of products, with a single channel of distribution. Therefore, product/market complexity will be very simple too. This feature allows the sole owner to administer all of the firm's activities effectively. In most cases, an increase in the variety of products offered, and/or an increase in the markets served, would be the main force that could cause the organization's structure to evolve into something more complex. And, this force usually would be accompanied by an increase in size to accommodate a more complex product/market dimension. Thus, increases in product/market complexity, sales, and organizational size can all serve as catalysts for the emergence of a more formal organizational structure as one person can no longer make all the management and operational decisions in an efficient manner.

A small organization tends to carry out its activities on an informal basis. For example, research and development, rewards, controls, and other such activities are usually unsystematic and are guided mainly by the manager's "feel" for the situation. However, the lack of a formal system of rewards can be dangerous to the morale of employees, once their number reaches a high point. Also, quality control can be better insured through responsibilities that are established within a formal organizational structure.

There are other disadvantages to the small structure. First, it is very demanding of the owner-manager, who must make a tremendous effort to stay on top of all business operations. Second, as previously discussed, a continuing increase in size will make the structure less efficient—and eventually unworkable. Finally, the small structure generally does not facilitate the development of future managers. This can be a critical problem if the owner-manager is forced to be away from the business, or if the organization is to grow.

The Functional Structure

The functional organizational form lies somewhere in the middle of the continuum shown in Figure 7-1. The basic characteristic of this form is that tasks are identified and classified according to their *function* (for example, production, finance). Then, functions are combined into major groupings that are the basis for the creation of the firm's major departments. This type of structure allows for flexibility in the medium-sized concern, as functions can be regrouped as they are required by changes in strategy. This structure is also characterized by a number of functional managers (for sales, production, engineering, and so on), who are responsible for all operational decisions within their departments. The efficient use of this type of structure is, of course, highly dependent on the competence and commitment of subordinate managers.[67]

---

[67] Robert L. Katz, *Cases and Concepts in Corporate Strategy* (Englewood Cliffs, N.J.: Prentice-Hall, 1970), pp. 503–4.

The establishment of a functional organizational structure usually becomes necessary as a small-structure firm grows and as increases in the complexity of business activities create the need for a more formal, systematized approach to major activities and for an increased delegation of decision making throughout the organization. However, the top management will continue to control decisions that involve strategic and coordinative variables (C_1, C_2). Because overall objectives are defined by top management, the functional units must also be organized from that perspective. A typical pattern of a first-order functional department structure might be: engineering, finance, industrial relations, marketing, production, purchasing, and research and development.[68] An organizational chart depicting this pattern of functional departmentation at the M. W. Kellogg Company is shown in Figure 7-2.

The importance of a functional department is usually indicated by the level occupied by its executive officer in the hierarchy of organizational structure.[69] In most industrial firms production, sales, and finance are classified at the highest level because their activities are considered essential to the company's survival. Purchasing and industrial relations may be lower in the hierarchy, depending on management's attitudes toward their value in the achievement of objectives.

The delegation of authority and responsibilities in a firm with functional departmentation may be best understood by looking at the production department of a manufacturing firm. Although the functional objectives of the department are determined by top management's goals for product quantity and quality, the department management would make all the operational decisions necessary to achieve those objectives. In this case, top management would have overall control of policies, but little control over operational activities.

The Divisional Structure

Further growth may create a strain on the ability of a functionally structured organization to achieve corporate goals efficiently and effectively. At this point, corporate structure must be reorganized to take on the characteristics of a *divisional organization* (the organizational structure on the right side of the continuum shown in Figure 7-1). These characteristics may include product diversification, territorial expansion, changes in customer orientation, and a need for the decentralization of authority so that each operating division can function autonomously under the general direction of top management.[70] Corporate objectives, strategies, and basic policies are generally set by top corporate management for each division. Divisional management then designs its own strategies and operation decisions within these corporate constraints and is

---

[68] Ibid., p. 48.

[69] Ibid., p. 101.

[70] Justin G. Longnecker, *Principles of Management and Organization,* 2d ed. (Columbus, Ohio: Charles E. Merrill Publishing Co., 1969), p. 184.

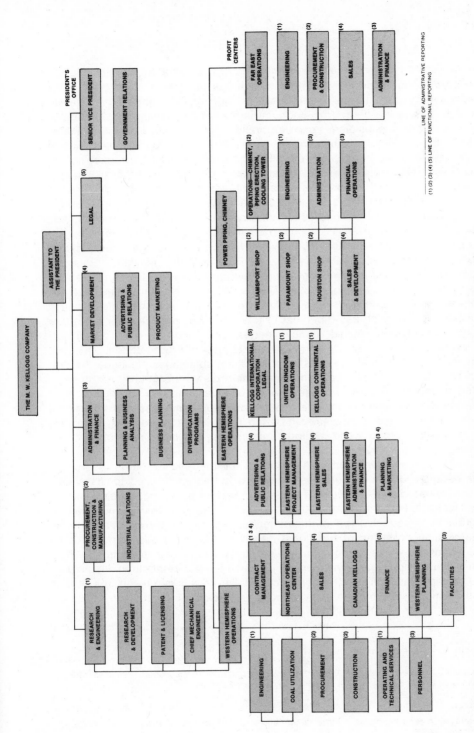

FIGURE 7-2: Functional Departmentation: The M. W. Kellogg Company Organization.

evaluated by its effective achievement of corporate objectives, with little top management direction concerning the methods used to achieve them. The descriptors "conglomerate," "free-form," or "holding company" can be viewed as variations in the degree of autonomy and decision-making capacity given to the divisions or subsidiaries of a corporation. For example, Katz differentiates the free-form from the holding company by the degree of autonomy the individual units have in making strategic decisions concerning product/market scope, competitive emphasis, performance specifications, and resource allocations. According to Katz, the individual units of a holding company exercise greater autonomy in strategic decisions than do the individual units of the free-form.[71]

Because corporate businesses exhibit varying degrees of diversification, they can be classified as three basic types: "dominant," "related," and "unrelated."[72] "Dominant" business companies derive 70 to 95 percent of their sales volume from a single business, as is the case with Schwinn and Maytag. "Related" business companies have no single business that accounts for more than 70 percent of sales (for example, 3M). "Unrelated" business companies have not necessarily related new business ventures to old ones, and no single business accounts for as much as 30 percent of total sales volume. Companies of this nature are generally labeled "conglomerates."

Various hybrids emerge from the divisional form of organizational structure. For example, dominant business companies are sometimes managed through a hybrid structure where top management controls the basic business through a functional structure and manages the rest of the organization through product divisions.[73] A number of additional hybrids can result from crossing the divisional form with the functional form and organizing the divisions by products, territories, or customers. Product and territorial patterns are the most common of these hybrids.

Product departmentation. This form establishes each product or product line as an autonomous business entity and is frequently used to make little organizations out of big ones.[74] As such, each smaller organization has its own functional structure for production, sales, finance, research and development, and personnel. Product departmentation at higher levels can reduce the coordination problems of functional departmentation because each product department operates autonomously with its own functional personnel. Thus, there would be one marketing manager for each product rather than one marketing manager responsible for all products. However, this can result in a serious coordination problem if there is product diversification.

---

[71] Katz, *Cases and Concepts,* pp. 505–7.

[72] Leonard Wrigley, *Divisional Autonomy and Diversification* (unpublished DBA dissertation, Harvard Business School, 1970), cited in Scott, "The Industrial State," p. 138.

[73] Scott, "The Industrial State," pp. 138–39.

[74] Henry H. Albers, *Principles of Organization and Management,* 2d ed. (New York: John Wiley and Sons, 1965), p. 112.

Territorial divisionalization. This form establishes regional offices as autonomous enterprises. The Prudential Insurance Company of America utilizes this pattern (see Figure 7-3). Each regional office has its own set of functional departments and operates under the strategic policies and guidelines established by corporate top management. Geographical location often is "a primary consideration in defining and differentiating executive responsibility."[75] This is usually because there is a major need for knowledge of the local environment, the climate and topography of each region, and the cultural considerations peculiar to each territory.[76]

Basic advantages. The divisional form has several advantages. In a large divisional corporation, especially an "unrelated" business company, each unit can function as an individual enterprise in the open market on a more competitive basis. This structure also simplifies the coordination task of top management, as each division or unit generally is provided with sufficient autonomy to conduct its own business, constrained only by the overall strategic decisions of the firm.

Another advantage of the divisional structure is the ability of top management to capitalize on new developments by creating new divisions. In this way, growth and diversification can be accomplished without distorting the basic organizational structure.[77] When market opportunities arise, a new division, which makes use of the firm's centralized staff and service facilities, can simply be added.

Finally, the ability of top management to draw from a pool of divisional management talent is a major advantage that may be difficult and costly to achieve with other structural forms. In the small structural form, there is relatively little opportunity for management training because of the owner-manager's singular control of all decision making. In the functional form, each manager becomes a specialist in his own area but has little experience with other functional areas. A company that is organized in the divisional form allows for a greater breadth of managerial experience. The talents of one manager can be transferred from one division to another because the manager has undertaken multifunctional responsibilities as the director of a fairly autonomous business entity.

Project Management

Project management was developed by the military as a result of pressure to complete tasks more quickly, in a more efficient manner. "The growth in project activity is due directly to the tremendous pressures on time, cost, and performance resulting from rapidly changing technologies in the environment of international tension."[78] After the project management concept was found

---

[75] Ibid., p. 116.

[76] Ibid., p. 119.

[77] George R. Terry, *Principles of Management,* 4th ed. (Homewood, Ill.: Richard D. Irwin, 1964), p. 428.

[78] Stanley J. Baumgartner, *Project Management* (Homewood, Ill.: Richard D. Irwin, 1963), p. 2.

to be the most effective means available to meet these pressures, whether or not particular firms maintained project management structures became a prime criterion for the awarding of government contracts. As a result, the concept filtered into the defense industry first and then into others. Although the full impact of project organization probably has not yet been felt outside the defense industry sphere, companies that utilize this structure have gained some advantages over competitors. In many cases, they have brought new products to market faster than their competition, completed major expansions on schedule, and met crucial commitments more reliably than ever before.[79]

The project management concept (see Figure 7-4) is actually a substructure, which is utilized primarily for the ad hoc activities that arise within the firm. It is a temporary structure, because the project organization only lasts until the project is completed.

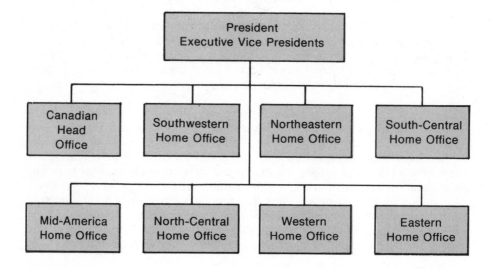

FIGURE 7-3: Territorial Divisionalization:
Prudential Insurance Company of America.

SOURCE: Justin G. Longenecker, *Principles of Management and Organizational Behavior* (Columbus, Ohio: Charles E. Merrill Publishing Co., 1969), p. 188.

Project management is a general management activity encompassing planning, control, supervision, and the engineering or manufacturing involved in producing the end item. It is similar to functional management and administration in that it is basically getting work done through people, with all

[79] John M. Stewart, "Making Project Management Work," *Business Horizons,* Fall 1965, reprinted in David I. Cleland and William P. King, *Systems, Organizations, Analysis, Management: A Book of Readings* (New York: McGraw-Hill, 1969), p. 292.

that implies regarding objectives, incentives, and communications. It differs from general administration, however, in ways which have a far-reaching effect. The project manager has very specific objectives which, when achieved, mean the end of his functions. He usually has no line authority over the organizations producing the items which he must deliver. . . .

Communications must be very clear, prompt, and comprehensive, and frequently cut across intracompany and intercompany lines. . . .[80]

There are certain criteria that indicate the need for a project-type structure. The first is the *scope* of the project in terms of the work force, dollars, time, and organizational units required for its completion. It should be larger than any of the firm's previous projects, and it should have a specified completion date. The second criterion is the organization's *unfamiliarity* with the project. This is based upon the assumption that unique or infrequent projects are coupled with a high degree of uncertainty about the task to be accomplished. This uncertainty requires that people on lower levels be more precisely informed about the specific tasks they must perform. The third criterion involves the *complexity* of the project in terms of the interdependence of the tasks that must be performed. This necessarily involves the degree to which the project is dependent upon several functional areas. Because the integrated effort of these functional areas is necessary for the cost and timing of individual subtasks, project management's emphasis on integrating the diverse activities of these areas will enhance the successful completion of the project.[81] The final criterion is referred to as *stake*. This refers to the adverse effect that failure to complete the job on schedule or within budget might have on the company. This may be in terms of direct out-of-pocket costs or in the form of a lost opportunity caused by delayed production and the consequent loss of sales volume, for example.

Some specific advantages of project management have been proposed for ventures that meet the aforementioned criteria:

Project management provides the concentrated management attention that a complex and unfamiliar undertaking is likely to demand. It greatly improves, at very small cost, chances of on-time, on-budget, completion. And it permits the rest of the organization to proceed normally with routine business while the project is underway.[82]

Project management evolves with the advancement of technology and the increased complexity of development and manufacturing projects. Because an

---

[81] Keith Davis, "The Role of Project Management in Scientific Manufacturing," IEEE Transactions on Engineering Management, 1962, reprinted in Cleland and King, *Systems,* p. 309.

[82] Criterion from Stewart in Cleland and King, *Systems,* pp. 293–95.

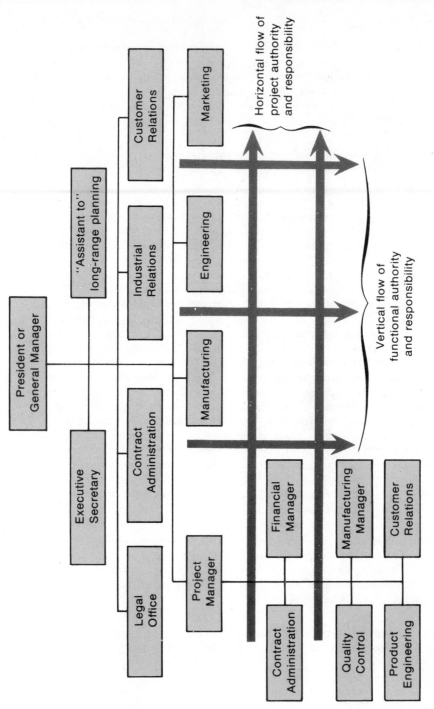

FIGURE 7-4: Project Management Organization.

Source: *Management: A Systems Approach* by David I. Cleland and William R. King. Copyright 1972, McGraw-Hill, Inc. Used with permission of McGraw-Hill Book Company.

integrating effort must be made to manage tasks across functional lines in order to achieve objectives, the establishment of a project-type organization insures an integrative focus. Decisions and actions emanating from a number of different functional areas; involvement of personnel at various levels of the existing structure; the necessity for close lateral relationships; and the necessity to consider time, cost, resources, and human factors requires an integrating effort that traditional functional structures generally do not provide.

The Matrix Organization

The matrix form of organization, depicted in Figure 7-5, represents a merger of the project and functional forms.[83] It provides a framework within which an organization can operate continuously on a project-type basis. Unlike the project management concept, which is temporary and only lasts for the duration of the project, the matrix structure is permanent. People may be assigned to different project groups and project managers may change as new tasks are undertaken, but the basic framework or apparatus within which people function is maintained.[84]

The criteria for determining whether the project-type organization is feasible are also applicable here. The firm, or division of a firm, must be undertaking projects with the scope, unfamiliarity, complexity, and functional interdependence that necessitate a focus on timely completion of the project. *However, in order for a company to warrant a matrix structure, it must be undertaking these projects as an everyday part of its business.* This requires that the firm, or division, be a "job-shop" operation—performing, for example, contract work for government or other industrial organizations. In this situation, the production emphasis is on the completion of action or project objectives instead of on the implementation of production programs to increase product volume.[85]

This does not mean that a firm, or a division, that produces a standardized product, or products, may not occasionally warrant a project-type approach. For example, the design and construction of a new plant, or entry into a completely new product line, may temporarily call for a project team approach. If work performed by an operating division of a company is applied to standardized products or services with high volume, however, there may be no need to consider a matrix organizational design.[86] It can be seen that the essence of a matrix organization is a continuous stream of ad hoc activities superimposed on the traditional functional organization.[87]

---

[83] Cleland and King. *Management,* p. 239.

[84] This situation can be thought of as being analogous to the traditional functional structure. People are swapped and promoted within the structure while the structure itself does not change.

[85] John F. Mee, "Matrix Organization," *Business Horizons,* Summer 1964, reprinted in Cleland and King, *Systems,* p. 24.

[86] Ibid., p. 23.

[87] Cleland and King, *Management,* p. 339.

The matrix structure evolved out of the need to deal with the complex but recurring ad hoc activities that were first recognized in major military and space projects. The large number of different projects that were constantly being started and completed required the design of a flexible and adaptable system of resources and procedures to achieve a series of individual project objectives. In addition, as can be seen in Figure 7-5, there are two dimensions of authority and responsibility in these cases: a vertical flow pertaining to the functional organization and a horizontal flow reflecting the project organization. A coordinating and integrating effort becomes necessary to draw from the various units so that the marketing, financing, and production of the goods can be accom-

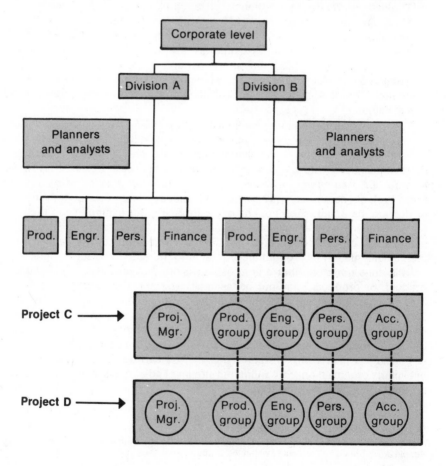

FIGURE 7-5: Matrix organization.

SOURCE: David I. Cleland and William R. King, *Management: A Systems Approach* (New York: McGraw-Hill Book Co., 1972), p. 338.

plished. Because of this, the key to effective functioning of both the matrix organization and the project management system is the sharing of authority and responsibility between project and functional managers.

The structure that is produced by the matrix organization is a network of relationships between the participating individuals and teams in the organization. The teams are oriented toward the completion of project goals in a timely manner. With this major focus on the achievement of project objectives, the matrix structure permits a higher degree of specialized talents to be utilized with maximum efficiency of operations.

A prime example of a company using the matrix organization is TRW Systems. The impetus to utilize the matrix-type structure at TRW is derived from the predominant characteristics of the aerospace industry, within which it operates. The industry is basically job shop-oriented and subject to frequent changes. One writer described the industry as follows:

> Because of rapid changes in technology, in customer requirements, and in competitive practices, product lines in the aerospace industry tend to be transitory. The customers' needs are finite and discrete. . . . Although the aerospace industry as a whole has grown steadily during the last decade, the fluctuations of individual companies underscore the job-shop nature of defense work. Aerospace industry planners must be constantly aware of the possibility of cancellation or prolongation of large programs.[88]

Another major characteristic of the industry is the complexity of its products. Parts are extremely interdependent, because the functioning of a product—for example, a rocket—could be jeopardized by a single part. This means that the groups or divisions that design and manufacture the various parts also are highly interdependent. The traditional functional structure lacks the flexibility to meet changing project requirements, technologies, and environmental influences in order to remain viable in this dynamic environment.

The matrix organization and project management supply another means to create hybrid organizational structures. Some authors imply that the matrix structure is an organizational structure continuum.[89] In other words, that the matrix form is really a substructure that causes the organization to become more complex in a hybrid manner. The matrix form grew out of the traditional functional and project-management forms and exists within the functional form or, more likely, within a division or a subsidiary of the divisional form. It is within the divisional form that the product/market complexities that warrant a matrix organization usually exist.

---

[88] T. C. Miller, Jr., and L. P. Kane, "Strategies for Survival in the Aerospace Industry," *Industrial Management Review,* Fall 1965, pp. 22–23. Cited in Gene W. Dalton, Paul R. Lawrence, and Larry E. Greiner, *Organizational Change and Development* (Homewood, Ill.: Richard D. Irwin, 1970), pp. 107–8.

[89] Greiner, "Evolution and Revolution," p. 45, and Cleland and King, *Systems,* p. 279.

SUMMARY

Corporate strategy cannot be implemented, nor can its objectives be achieved, without proper organizational structure. This chapter has discussed the factors that affect the evolution of organizational structure and the alternative structural forms. It should be clear from our discussion that these forms are dynamic. They change as an organization passes through its life cycle and changes its product line(s) and market(s) emphases.

The complexities of the formation, implementation, and operation of organizational structures is well illustrated in the following article by Lorsch and Lawrence, "Organizing for Product Innovation." The article also delineates many of the behavioral problems which arise in accomplishing the integration of functional areas.

Structure-related decisions are very difficult to make and to implement as they affect the human element of the organization. The following chapter deals with the problems and dimensions of effective organizational change.

Organizing for Product Innovation

Jay W. Lorsch and Paul R. Lawrence

- How can we get our research people to be more responsive to the needs of the market?
- What can we do to get our salesmen more involved in selling new products and seeking new applications?
- Why are our production people so conservative when it comes to introducing new products?
- How can we get sales, research, and production people to pull in the same direction on product development?

Questions such as these have become of increasing concern to executives in companies operating in the many industries characterized by rapid technological and market change, in which new and improved products are the key to corporate success. Several years ago we were all concerned with obtaining effective research organizations. It was generally believed that if a climate could be developed in which talented scientists and engineers could work creatively, we would be assured of a constant flow of product improve-

ments and new products. As companies have become successful in developing more effective research organizations, however, it has become increasingly apparent that creative, innovative researchers are not enough by themselves. What is needed, as the questions above indicate, is an organization which provides collaboration between scientific innovators and sales and production specialists, so that:

- The skills of the innovators can be directed at market needs and technological problems.
- Sales and production specialists can be actively involved in the commercialization of ideas developed in the laboratory.
- And, as a result, ideas can be transferred smoothly from laboratory prototype to commercial reality.

HOW COMPANIES INNOVATE

We can begin our discussion of the problems of organizing for innovation by briefly examining the essential functions of any organization. Basically, an organization, whether it be the product division of a diversified chemical company or a corner drug store, provides a means by which more than one person can work together to perform a task that one individual could not perform alone. This means each individual or unit of the larger organization will be performing some specialized portion of the organization's task.

The first function of an organization, then, is to divide the total task into specialized pieces. The organization's second function is to provide a means by which units working on different parts of the total task may coordinate their activities to come out with a unified effort. While these processes of specialization and coordination are essential in any organization, they are particularly crucial for companies competing in developing new products.

Perhaps the best way to understand the specialization and coordination required in the innovation process is to describe the steps involved in developing products in the two plastics companies we studied. These were prominent companies in their industry, chosen to show similarities and contrasts in their organizational approach to product innovation. To protect their identities we shall refer to them as the "Rhody" and "Crown" companies. It should be stressed that the two companies sold their products for industrial applications and there was, therefore, a constant demand not only for major new products but also for a flow of modifications in properties and processes that could improve the performance of old products and yield new applications for them. In our description of the innovation process we will be referring

to the steps required for both types of innovation.

Required Collaboration

Exhibit 1 provides a schematic representation of the innovation process as the executives in the two organizations think it should be in order to obtain effective innovation. As we have already indicated, there are three major groups of specialists in each organization. Sales, production, and research specialists are each coping with a different sector of the organization's environment, and each should have a different portion of the total skills and knowledge required to discover a product idea and convert it into a tangible product:

- The sales department in dealing with the market environment should be in a position to extract information about market trends and customer needs.
- The research department in dealing with the scientific environment should be able to provide data about the technical and scientific feasibility of any new product development.
- The production department should have a store of knowledge about the limits of plant processes from the production environment.

Information from the sales department about customer needs and from production about processing limits has to be passed on to the research unit so that this information can be assimilated with the scientific feasibility of developing or modifying a product. Within the limits set by the needs of

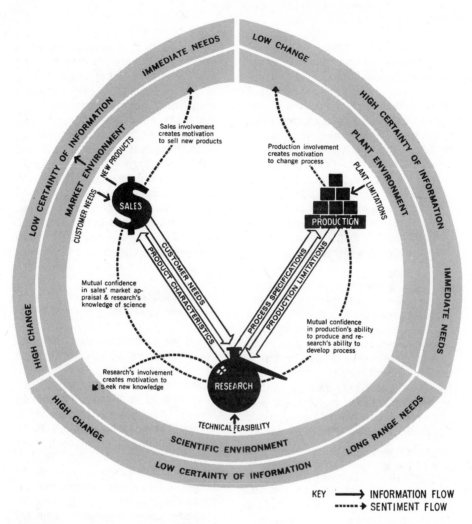

KEY ⟶ INFORMATION FLOW
------▶ SENTIMENT FLOW

EXHIBIT 1: Scientific transfer process—the ideal.

the customer and the capacities of the production process, the research units are then required to come up with a new development. If they succeed, it is then necessary to transfer information back to the sales department about product characteristics and to the production department about process specifications. With this information sales should be in a position to make and implement market plans, and production should

have the data for planning and executing its task of manufacturing the product.

In short, product innovation requires close coordination between research and sales, on the one hand, and between research and production, on the other. This coordination is necessary not only to provide the two-way flow of technical information described earlier, but also to develop mutual trust and confidence between the members of the units which are required to collaborate in product development. Sales personnel must have confidence in research's knowledge of science, while research scientists must have confidence in sales' appraisal of the market. Similarly, there must be mutual confidence between research and production about production's ability to operate the process efficiently according to specifications and about research's capacity to develop a process that can be operated efficiently.

Product innovation, then, requires close collaboration between the sales and research units and the production and research units if the specialists involved are effectively to bring their separate skills to bear on a successful product development. However, the complexity and uncertainty of the factors which must be dealt with (at least in companies developing a multiplicity of new products) make it necessary for this coordination to take place at the *lower* levels of the organization. Executives in both Rhody and Crown indicate that it is difficult for managers at the upper levels of the organization to keep in touch with the multitude of rapidly changing factors which must be considered in the day-to-day process of developing many new products. Only the specialists on the firing line have the detailed knowledge of markets and technologies to make the frequent day-to-day decisions which the innovation process requires.

So far we have presented only a description of what *should* happen in both organizations if innovation is to be successfully accomplished. But our interests are in investigating not only what should happen but also, and more importantly, what *actually* happens in each organization as a result of the processes of specialization and coordination required for product innovation. We want to find out in what ways the groups of specialists working on diverse tasks in the two companies are different in their ways of thinking, in the ground rules they work by, and in terms of the organizational structures in which they work.

DIMENSIONS OF SPECIALIZATION

When we undertook our study, we decided to find out first how groups of specialists actually were differentiated. We expected the differences to be related to the problems of obtaining coordination between units. Exhibit 2 presents our findings about the dimensions along which the departments were different. Departmental differences are classified in terms of four main dimensions: (a) degree of departmental structure, (b) members' orientation toward time, (c) members' orientation toward others, and (d) members' orientation toward the environment.

Each of the differences between departments is seen to be a function of the characteristics of the environmental sector (market, science, or plant) with which a unit is coping in performing its task. Groups, such as production units, which have a very certain environment (as measured by the certainty of information at a given

CHARACTERISTICS OF ENVIRONMENTAL SECTORS
(Market, Science, Plant)

CERTAINTY OF INFORMATION AT A GIVEN TIME
UNCERTAIN ←—→ CERTAIN

RATE OF CHANGE IN ENVIRONMENT
HIGH ←—→ LOW

TIME RANGE OF TASK
LONG ←—→ SHORT

SPECIALIZATION IN TERMS OF:

DEGREE OF DEPARTMENTAL STRUCTURE
LOW ←—→ HIGH

MEMBERS' ORIENTATION TOWARD TIME
LONG ←—→ SHORT

MEMBERS' ORIENTATION TOWARD OTHERS
PERMISSIVE ←—→ DIRECTIVE

MEMBERS' ORIENTATION TOWARD ENVIRONMENT

Differences in departmental organizational structures are important. One department may have very tight rules and procedures, very close spans of supervisory control, many levels in the departmental hierarchy, and frequent and very specific reviews of departmental and individual performance. Such a department is highly structured. In another department just the opposite situation may occur. There may be fewer rules and regulations, very infrequent reviews of a general nature, broader spans of control, and fewer levels in the departmental hierarchy. Most departments, of course, fall in between these two extremes of the continuum.

Organizational units are also different in terms of the members' orientations toward time. Members of a unit tend to have a primary concern with problems of either a long, short, or middle-range character.

Members of different units prefer different ways of dealing with their coworkers. Members of one unit tend to prefer open, permissive interpersonal relationships while those in another prefer directive, authoritarian relationships with their co-workers.

Each department's members have different orientations toward the environment. They are primarily concerned with the specific environmental sector with which they are coping. Scientists can be expected to be more concerned with the development of new technical knowledge, while salesmen are primarily concerned with the customer and the activities of the competition. Production specialists are most concerned with processing problems, material costs, and so forth.

EXHIBIT 2: Relation between departmental specialization and environment.

time, the rate of change in the environment, and the time range of the task) are highly structured. Because they are working with a highly stable environment, they tend to develop explicit routines and highly programmed ways of operating, adopt a directive interpersonal style, and also find a short-range time orientation useful for the performance of their task.

On the other hand, units, such as research, which are coping with less certain environments tend to be less structured, are characterized by a more permissive interpersonal orientation, and have a longer time orientation. These characteristics are consistent with an uncertain, nonroutine task, since effective performance of such a task requires opportunity for open consultation among colleagues in seeking solutions to problems and freedom to consider and attempt different courses of action.

Principal Patterns

How do the differences in orientation and structure characterize the departments in Rhody and Crown? Exhibit 3 summarizes our findings on this question. The data presented here are representative of the *general* pattern which exists in both organizations; some minor variations between the two organizations are not depicted. We see that:

Members of each department tend primarily to be oriented toward the sector of the environment with which their task involves them. Research people tend to be more oriented toward discovering new scientific knowledge, while sales people are more concerned with customer problems and market conditions, and production personnel indicate a primary concern with production costs and processing problems.

In time orientation, the research scientists tend to be more concerned with long-range matters which will not have an impact on company profits for several years in the future. Sales and production specialists are primarily concerned with the more immediate problems which affect the company's performance within the current year.

	Departmental Structure	Orientation Toward Time	Orientation Toward Others	Orientation Toward Environment
Research	Low	Long	Permissive	Science
Sales	Medium	Short	Permissive	Market
Production	High	Short	Directive	Plant

EXHIBIT 3: Patterns of specialization.

The interpersonal orientations of the members of the units in both companies are also different. Research and sales personnel tend to prefer more permissive interpersonal relationships, while production specialists indicate a preference for a more directive manner of working with their colleagues.

As for the degree of departmental structure, the research units have the lowest amount and the production units have the highest. The sales units, which seem to be performing a task of medium certainty, have a structure which falls between the extremes represented by research and production.

What we find in both companies, then, are units which are quite different from each other both in terms of members' orientations and the structure in which the members work. These differences in ways of thinking about the job and in ground rules and operating procedures mean that each of these groups tends to view the task of innovation somewhat differently.

Impact on Ability

While we next want to examine the influence of these differences on the process of obtaining coordination, we should first emphasize a point which too often has been overlooked: The differences have a *positive* effect on the ability of each individual unit to perform its particular task. The common orientations and ground rules within a unit and a departmental structure which facilitate task performance direct the efforts of people in the unit to their segment of the orga-

nizational task and enhance their ability to carry out their mission. Because the units are performing different tasks, we have to expect that they will develop different departmental structures and that their members will be oriented differently. If attempts were made to standardize the structures of all units and to have all members of the organization oriented in the same direction, we would lose the benefits of specialization.

The two companies in our study recognize this fact to differing degrees. At Rhody the differences along the four dimensions tend to be greater than at Crown. Each department at Rhody not only has a structure conducive to the performance of its task, but also tends to be more highly concerned with a single task dimension or with a particular period of time than does the same unit at Crown. While in both organizations the specialization of units enables them to address their separate tasks, the units at Rhody, by virtue of their higher degree of specialization, often seem to be better able to perform their individual tasks.

ORGANIZATIONAL PARADOX

While specialized orientations and structures facilitate a unit's task performance, we would expect the patterns to be closely related to the problems of coordination in both firms. Because members of a given department hold common attitudes about what is important in their work and about dealing with each other, they are able to work effectively with each other. But to the extent that the ground rules and orientations held by members of one department are different from those held by members of another, we would expect the departments to have increased difficulty achieving the high degree of coordination required for effective innovation.

The data we collected through a questionnaire about the effectiveness of coordination between departments at Rhody and Crown confirm this expectation. When two units are similar in departmental structure and in the orientations of their members, we find that they have few problems in obtaining effective collaboration *with each other*. But when units tend to be on opposite poles along the four dimensions, we find that there are more problems in integrating their efforts. Within each organization there is clear evidence that the greater the differences in orientation and structure between any pair of units, the greater the problems of obtaining effective coordination.

Although this relationship holds within each company, we find an interesting paradox when the two organizations are compared. As already indicated, there is a higher degree of specialization and differentiation at Rhody than at Crown. Pairs of units which are required to collaborate at Rhody tend to be less similar than the comparable pairs of units at Crown. Since units at Crown are more similar, this *should* mean that Crown encounters fewer problems of coordination. However, this does *not* turn out to be the case. Rhody appears to be achieving better integration than Crown, even though it also has a higher degree of differentiation. In

short, within each organization there is a relationship between the effectiveness of coordination and the degree of differentiation, but the organization which has the highest degree of specialization also has the most effective collaboration.

The significance of this paradox grows if we recall that specialization is a two-sided coin. Specialization is useful because it is necessary for the performance of individual departments; on the other hand, it can have negative consequences in that it is at the root of the problems of achieving the coordination required for innovation. At Rhody we have a situation in which one organization is able to have its cake (in the form of specialization) and to eat it too (in the form of coordination).

Contrasting Methods

Does the explanation reside in the methods used by the two organizations to facilitate coordination between units? We believe it does.

Attempts at devising methods to improve coordination between the specialized departments involved in product innovation are certainly not novel. New-product departments, or coordinating departments with other appelations, have been established in many organizations with the primary function of coordinating the activities of research, sales, and production specialists in the development of new products. Similarly, many firms have appointed liaison individuals who are responsible for linking two or more groups of functional specialists. Another frequent device has been to develop short-term project teams with representatives from the several functional departments to work on a new product. Finally, many companies have relied on permanent cross-functional coordinating teams to deal with the continuing problems of innovation around a given group of products.

Both Rhody and Crown have developed the same types of devices:

1. In each company there is a coordinating department which has the primary task of coordinating or integrating the innovation activities of the research, production, and sales units.
2. Each company is making use of permanent cross-functional coordinating committees which have representatives from each of the basic departments and the coordinating department. The primary function of these committees is to serve as a setting in which coordination can take place.

Since both organizations are utilizing the same devices to achieve coordination, it is pertinent to ask whether there are differences in the functioning and effectiveness of these devices. The answer provided by our investigation is an emphatic *yes*.

We now turn to an examination of these differences, looking first at the coordinating departments, then at the committees.

COORDINATING DEPARTMENTS

In addition to seeking teamwork among research, production, and sales, the coordinating departments at Rhody and Crown perform certain other tasks. At Crown the department is also involved in market planning and the coordination of sales efforts. At Rhody the coordinating department is also involved in technical service and market-development activities. As might be expected, both departments have developed orientations and structural characteristics somewhat different from those of the other units in the companies.

Key to Coordination

While various similarities exist between the two coordinating groups, there is also, as our measurements reveal, a major distinction:

At Rhody the coordinating department falls in a middle position on each of the four dimensions we have considered. That is, if we compare the department's degree of structure and its members' orientations with those of the sales, production, and research departments, it always has an intermediate value, never an extreme one. For instance, members of the coordinating department have a balanced orientation along the time dimension. They are equally concerned with the short-range problems of sales and production and the long-range matters with which research wrestles. Similarly, coordinating personnel have a balanced concern with production, scientific, and market environments. The degree of departmental structure and the interpersonal orientation of coordinating members also fall between the extremes of the other departments.

At Crown the coordinating department is in the middle along the structure and interpersonal dimensions but tends to be highly oriented toward short-range time concerns and toward the market environment. Personnel indicate a high concern with immediate sales problems, and less concern with longer-range matters or with research or production environments. On both the time and the environment dimensions, therefore, the coordinating department is not intermediate between the departments it is supposed to be linking.

The foregoing difference, which is shown schematically in Exhibit 4, appears to be related to differences in the effectiveness of the two units. Our questionnaires and interviews indicate that the coordinating department at Rhody is generally perceived by members of that organization to be doing an effective job of linking the basic departments. On the other hand, the coordinating department at Crown is not perceived to be as effective as most members of the Crown organization think it should be.

Observations by Executives

The reactions of executives in the two companies pretty well explain for us why the intermediate position of the Rhody coordinating department is associated with effective coordination, while the imbalance in certain orientations of the Crown unit inhibits its performance. The following are a few typical comments from Rhody managers:

> The most important thing is that we have the coordinating department with its contacts with the customers and its technically trained people who are in contact with research. They are the kingpins. They have a good feel for research's ability, and they know the needs of the market. They will work back and forth with research and the other units.

> Generally speaking, the feeling of close cooperation between the coordinating unit and sales is echoed in the field. The top salesmen all get along well with the coordinating guys. You take a good coordinating fellow and a good salesman and that makes a powerful team. In our business the boys upstairs in the coordinating unit are top notch. They know what the lab can do, and they know the salesman's problems.

But at Crown the comments of executives have a different tone:

> My biggest criticism of our situation is that the coordinating department isn't a good enough mechanism to link the research activities to the customer. We need a better marketing strategy on certain products and some long-term plans. The lack of planning in the coordinating department is deplorable. One of our troubles is that the coordinating people are so tied up in day-to-day detail that they can't look to the future. They are still concerned with 1964 materials when they should be concerned with 1965 markets.

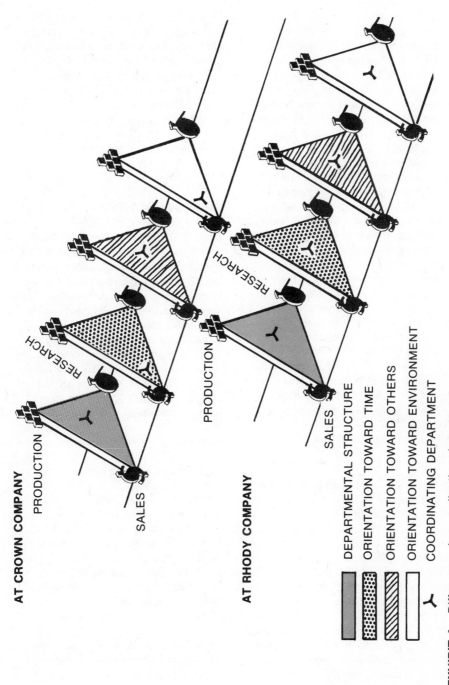

AT CROWN COMPANY

PRODUCTION

RESEARCH

SALES

AT RHODY COMPANY

PRODUCTION

RESEARCH

SALES

DEPARTMENTAL STRUCTURE
ORIENTATION TOWARD TIME
ORIENTATION TOWARD OTHERS
ORIENTATION TOWARD ENVIRONMENT
COORDINATING DEPARTMENT

EXHIBIT 4: Differences in coordinating departments.

Our problem is we can't clearly define the technical problems the customer is having. Theoretically the coordinating men should be able to handle this for research because they know the customer best. But they are so involved in present business that it takes all their time. They have a budget they have to live up to, and the best way to make money is to sell existing products. They know that selling existing products is more profitable than selling new products, so they keep on selling existing products to live up to the expectations of the budget.

In other words, we have a marked difference in reaction. What managers at Rhody are stressing is that the coordinating unit in their organization is effective because it has a familiarity with the problems, orientations, and ways of operating of the basic units it connects. At Crown the primary complaints about that organization's less-effective coordinating unit are that its members tend to be too oriented toward immediate sales matters.

The situation in these two organizations seems to indicate that for a coordinating department to be effective in linking the several specialized departments, it must be intermediate between any two along each of the several dimensions of orientation and structure. When a coordinating department is in this position, its members have more in common with members of the other units. Coordinating personnel tend to think and act in ways which are more understandable and agreeable to members of the other departments—and this facilitates collaboration. If members of the coordinating department have orientations and ground rules which are more suited to one specialized unit, as is the situation at Crown, their ways of thinking will necessarily be different from the other departments —and this situation will impair their effectiveness as coordinators.

CROSS-FUNCTIONAL GROUPS

Even in an organization like Rhody, where the coordinating unit is doing an effective job of facilitating cooperation between the specialized units, certain disagreements between the various specialist units seem to be inevitable. Management's problem is to provide a setting in which attempts at resolving these disagreements can be made effectively. Both organizations in this study have turned to permanent cross-functional coordinating committees as devices for providing a setting in which to work at achieving coordination between units.

In investigating the functioning of these committees in the two organizations, we again want to obtain an assessment of their effectiveness as well as some understanding of the factors which might be related to their performance. If we listen to some of the comments made by members of both organizations, the differences between the devices in the two companies become apparent.

At the Rhody company, managers make comments such as these about the cross-functional teams:

Our problems get thrashed out in committee. We work them over until everybody agrees this is the best effort you can make. We may decide this isn't good enough; then we may decide to ask for more people, more plant, and so forth. We all sometimes have to take a modification and be realistic and say this is the best we can do.

I may want us to do some work on a particular new product. The coordinating guy may say, "Let's get the customer to change his process instead." A research guy may say we need both. It is the way we do it that becomes argumentative and rightfully so. These things take several meetings to work out, but we are never really stalemated. We have decided in our committee that we won't stalemate. There is more than one way to our ends. If I don't agree with the others, then I abdicate my position—sometimes gracefully and sometimes not.

We had a disagreement about releasing confidential information to a customer and had quite a discussion about it. This was only the second time we had gotten so formal as to have a vote. I was out-voted three to one, but that afternoon I was the one who had to call the customer and give him the information as we had decided.

Since we have had these committees, we are working more closely with other groups. It is really working out. In the past, production was reluctant to give us information, and they wanted to keep the prerogative of making process changes. Since this committee has been operating, there has been a greater exchange of information. . . .

At Crown the executives speak differently about their experiences with cross-functional committees:

Unfortunately, the committees are not decision-making groups as much as I would like. Generally there is a reporting session. We don't have time going over all these things to make some of the decisions which need to be made. I would like to see more hashing out of the problems and making of decisions. Of course we do make decisions every day between us.

If I want something very badly and I am confronted by a roadblock, I go to top management to get the decision made. If the research managers are willing to go ahead, there is no problem. If there is a conflict, then I would go to their boss.

I think these meetings only intensify the arguments. I haven't learned much that I didn't know already before I got to the meeting. It used to be that we had some knock-'em down, drag-out fights, but then we would get things settled. But this doesn't take place anymore, so there isn't any place for us to resolve our difficulties.

These and similar comments indicate that members of the Rhody organization find the cross-functional committees an important aid in achieving collaboration, while members of the Crown organization do not. They also indicate, as do our observations of meetings of these committees in both organizations, that there are at least two important differences between the functioning of these committees in the two organizations. Before going into these contrasts, however, we must first point to an important distinction in the organizational structures of the two companies.

The Crown organization tends to have a higher degree of structure (tighter spans of control, more specific rules and procedures, and so forth) in *all* its parts than does the Rhody organization. (One important aspect of this difference is that the level at which decisions about product innovation are supposed to be made is much lower in the organizational hierarchy at Rhody than at Crown.)

Decision Authority

The significance of this distinction becomes apparent if we turn to look at the teams at Rhody. In this organization team members are in most cases first-line supervisors who (being right down at the working level) have the detailed market and technical knowledge required to make decisions. They are the only persons who attend the meetings, and they usually have the formal authority to make decisions.

Our observation of meetings at Rhody, along with comments made by company executives, indicate that there are ground rules or norms operating in cross-functional committees which sanction the open confrontation of disagreement between members. Members of the committees tend to recognize their differences and seek ways of resolving them within the constraints of the situation with which they are dealing. This working through of disagreements often takes a great deal of emotional and intellectual effort, but members of the committees at Rhody tend to persevere until some resolution is reached. After decisions are made, the members of the committees are highly committed to them. As we learned from one executive, even though a member is not in initial agreement with the decision taken, he is expected to—and he does—carry out the actions worked out in the meetings.

In contrast with the situation at Rhody, we find at Crown (as we would expect from the greater degree of structure throughout this company) that members of the committees are at a higher level than their counterparts at Rhody, but even these managers often do not have the authority to make decisions. Furthermore, because they are at a higher level, they usually do not have either the technical or market knowledge required to make the detailed decisions necessary to develop products.

As a consequence of this situation, members of the Crown committees often bring both their superiors and their subordinates to the meetings with them—the superiors in order to provide someone who has the authority to make decisions, the subordinates so that someone is present who has the detailed technical and market knowledge to draw on for decisions. Bringing in all these participants results in meetings two or three times as large as those at Rhody.

Resolving Conflict

Our observations of meetings at Crown and the comments of executives indicate that there are other shortcomings in the Crown committees. The norms of behavior in these groups sanction withdrawal from disagreement and conflict. Whenever there is a disagreement, the members tend to avoid discussing the matter, hoping it will magically go away. If this doesn't place the problem out of sight, they find another avenue of avoidance by passing it on to their superiors. As a consequence, many decisions which should be made at Crown seem to get dropped. They are not picked up again until they have festered for so long that somebody *has* to deal with them—and it is often too late by that time.

There will always be disagreements between members of departments which have highly different orientations and concerns. The problem facing members of coordinating committees is to learn to fight together constructively so that they can resolve these differences. At Rhody members of the cross-functional teams have developed this ability. They work at resolving conflict at their own level. They do not withdraw from disputes, nor do they try to smooth over their differences or arrive at some easy compromise. Rather, they seem willing to argue the issues involved until some understanding is reached about the optimal solution in a given situation.

In essence, the committees at Rhody have developed the ability to confront their differences openly and search persistently for solutions which will provide effective collaboration. At Crown, on the other hand, the committees avoid fights and forfeit the opportunity to achieve the coordination required for innovation.

CONCLUSION

The foregoing comparisons seem to provide an answer to the paradox of the Rhody organization achieving both greater specialization and more effective coordination than the Crown company does. The effective coordinating unit and cross-functional coordinating committees allow members at Rhody to concentrate on their specialties and still achieve a unity of effort. Sales, research, and production specialists are each able to address their separate departmental tasks and work in a climate which is conducive to good performance. At the same time, the men in the coordinating department, who have a balanced orientation toward the concerns of the three departments of specialists, help the three units to achieve a unity of effort. The cross-functional committees also provide a means by which the specialist groups and the coordinators can work through their differences and arrive at the best common approach.

At Crown, in spite of the fact that the specialist departments are more similar in orientation and structure than are the units at Rhody, there is more difficulty in obtaining unity of effort between them. Since the coordinators are overly concerned with short-term matters and sales problems, they do not effectively perform their function of linking the three groups of specialists. The cross-functional committees do not contribute much to coordination between these departments, either. They do not provide a setting in which problems can be solved, since authority to make decisions often resides in the higher levels of the organization and since norms have developed within the committees which encourage members to avoid conflict and pass it on to their superiors.

But what about the results the two companies have achieved in the market place? We have been asserting that both a high degree of specialization and effective coordination are important in achieving product innovation in this situation, but we have not presented any evidence that Rhody, with its greater specialization and more effective coordination, is in fact doing a better job of product innovation than is Crown. The following figures do show that the Rhody organization *is* achieving a higher level of innovation than Crown:

- At Rhody, new products developed in the last five years have accounted for 59% of sales.

- At Crown, the figure is only 20%, or just about one-third of Rhody's.

Part of this difference may have been due to some variation in market and technical factors confronting the two organizations. However, since these two organizations have been operating in the same industry and have been confronted by similar market conditions and technical problems, and because of the different levels of coordination and specialization achieved in each company, it seems safe to conclude that there is indeed a relationship between innovation performance and the internal organizational factors we have been discussing.

Management Challenge

While this discussion has been based on an examination of two organizations in the plastics industry, there is no question that the requirements for specialization and coordination are just as urgent in other industries confronted with the need for product innovation. It seems safe to generalize that, whatever the field or function, managers interested in improving their record with new products must recognize two essential organizational ingredients of success:

1. Specialists who are clearly oriented toward their individual tasks and who work in organizational structures which are conducive to task performance.
2. Effective means of coordination which permit specialists with diverse knowledge and orientations to work together. (There will be disagreements and conflicts among these specialists, but the organization must provide a means to resolve the conflicts in such a way that the full energy of research, sales, and production people can be brought to bear on innovation.)

Our discussion has focused on two devices to achieve this coordination—*coordinating departments* whose members have a balanced point of view enabling them to work effectively among the several specialist groups, and *cross-functional coordinating committees* in which members have learned to confront their differences and fight over them constructively so they can reach an optimal resolution. But other means of coordination are also available.

The challenge confronting managers responsible for organizing for innovations is to work at developing means of coordination which permit effective specialization *and* effective coordination. This is the combination that is needed to produce the constant flow of innovations necessary for corporate growth in changing markets.

8

Organizational Change:

an integrated approach

Organizational Change:

an integrated approach

As indicated in Chapter 1, the formulation of recommendations for problem solution in a policy case always signals the need for change in one or more parts of the total organization. The purposes of this chapter are (1) to clarify what is meant by the term "organizational change," (2) to delineate the basic elements of the change process, and (3) to present a summary of research findings on the reasons for resistance to change. The material presented should clarify the process of change, as well as point out basic barriers to change as found in various studies.

THE CONCEPT OF ORGANIZATIONAL CHANGE

An organization has been described as *a complex system of mutually dependent parts*. It follows logically that the term "organizational change" refers to *an alteration or modification of one or more parts of the system*. What is needed, however, is an operational scheme of organization parts so that (1) the focus and direction of the change sought may be clearly identified for any given situation and (2) the extended and interactive effects of a change in any one part of the system on the other parts may be anticipated and traced.

As discussed in Chapter 1, it is useful to view any organization within the framework of five interdependent dimensions when classifying the information found in a case. This same basic framework also may be utilized to clarify the notion of organizational change. Figure 8-1 summarizes those dimensions and their component parts. Thus, organizational change occurs when one or more of the parts outlined in Figure 8-1 are altered or modified in some fashion.

Given this background, we now can proceed to a discussion of the *process* of organizational change. The following sections delineate the major elements or phases of that process and indicate the major variables involved. They place emphasis on conceptualizing and categorizing change activities no matter what their genesis—whether they arise as a result of a changed product mix, a merger, the dissatisfaction of workers, declining profitability, or from other sources. However, special attention will be given to the effects of a change in strategy on other parts of the organization.

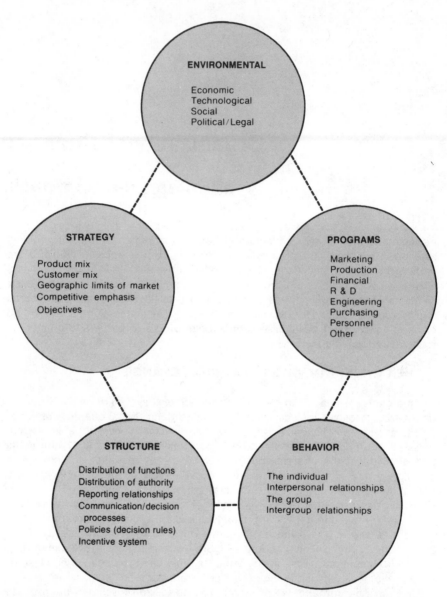

Note: Each of the major organizational parts comprises numerous subparts which are not explicity identified above. For example, the marketing program may be further subdivided into distribution, sales, promotion, and market research. Similarly, numerous subparts of the individual could be listed (for example, his values, sentiments toward work, abilities, desires, overt behavior) to provide a more detailed focus for analytical purposes.

FIGURE 8-1: Summary of the parts of an organization.

THE ORGANIZATIONAL CHANGE PROCESS

Figure 8-2 presents the overall process of organizational change. The following sections examine the major phases of that process and their interrelationships.

Forces Toward Change

Forces toward change are classified as either exogenous or endogenous to the organization. Major exogenous (external) forces that create a need for change are new technology, changing values, and perceived environmental opportunities or constraints (economic, political/legal, and social). These major external forces create the need for internal change, and internal changes can be consciously planned so that the organization will be minimally upset in adjusting to these new external conditions.

Endogenous (internal) conditions that create the need for change may be grouped under the general heading of organizational stress—stress in task activities, interactions, employee sentiments, or performance results. These forces arise internally and are generally associated with inefficiency, morale, or interpersonal problems.

Tension always exists in an organization that is undergoing change. It may be consciously created by management in response to external forces, or it may itself create the need for change in the form of organizational stress of one kind or another. Consequently, recognition of the *source* of the tension makes it easier to predict probable reactions to change by those individuals who will be affected. If internal tension creates the need for change, then those affected should welcome relief. On the other hand, if the response to external forces disturbs comfortable internal situations, then change is more likely to be resisted. Because shifts in the strategy of a firm usually result from changing external conditions, one can expect considerable resistance from individuals whose secure positions might be threatened by the new strategy. As discussed more fully below, changes in overall strategy have far-reaching effects throughout an organization.

Perception of Forces

How is the need for change recognized by the firm? Changes in exogenous forces are generally perceived by long-range planning offices, research and development departments, or market research units, as previously discussed in Chapter 2. In fact, the very reason for the existence of these units is to continually monitor and assess changes in external conditions that may signal the need for adjustments in overall strategy or in other parts of the firm. On the other hand, internal organizational stress is generally perceived by individual employees who became aware of poor morale, inefficiency, bad workmanship, or other difficulties.

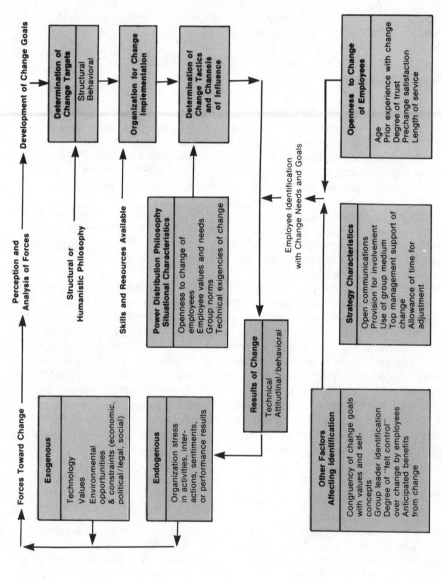

FIGURE 8-2: The organizational change process.

No matter how the need for change is recognized, the next step in the process shown in Figure 8-2 involves *analysis* of the forces toward change. In the case of a new technological development, for example, analysis must be conducted to determine the feasibility of its application to existing facilities. This will determine whether or not the formal change goal "to utilize new process A in the production of product X" should be established, and its implications for any further changes required in organizational structure and worker skills and attitudes. Or, consider the case of newly recognized market opportunities which may be capitalized on by means of alternative methods. The feasibility of merging with another organization may need to be analyzed in depth, as well as the feasibility of growth through internal expansion. The basic reason for the analysis is, of course, to determine what the firm should do in order to respond to changing external conditions. Once this decision is made, change goals then may be developed to guide the adjustments required in the various parts of the organization.

The scheme of organizational parts shown in Figure 8-1 can serve as a useful tool at this stage of analysis. When one is trying to develop some sort of action plan for responding to external or internal forces, the scheme provides a handy reference for systematizing the approach to the problem. A proposed change in the technology of production (for example, utilization of some new equipment or process) may be subjected to an evaluation of its extended consequences for other parts of the organization. What will be the effect of such a change on individual skill requirements and/or attitudes (see Figure 8-1, V, A)? What will be the effect on task interactions (see IV, A)? What will be the effect on production scheduling (see III, B)? What will be the effect on the current piece-rate scheme (IV, F)? In general, what other parts of the total organizational system will be affected by this change in technology? Have the costs and benefits of these *extended effects* of the proposed change been estimated to the maximum extent?

Development of Change Goals

Once the analytical process described above has been completed, the next step (as shown in Figure 8-2) is the development of change goals. Illustrative goals include:

1. *To diversify into additional product/markets*—perhaps as a result of changing market opportunities and/or poor performance results in existing markets.
2. *To merge with another corporation*—perhaps as a result of poor performance caused by the lack of the volume production necessary to achieve economies of scale in existing facilities.
3. *To install specified antipollution devices*—as a result of a new legal constraint requiring such modifications.
4. *To move decision authority downward* — as a result of organizational stress caused by authoritarian decision making at top levels of management.

5. *To eliminate interdepartmental competition and to foster collaboration*—as a result of stress in departmental interactions, perhaps a conflict between the production and marketing departments over levels of finished goods inventory.

6. *To change the structure of the current distribution channels*—because of increased middleman costs, which have contributed to poor performance results.

Although these change goals obviously cover a broad spectrum of change situations, it is possible to classify them in a general fashion consistent with the basic scheme of organizational parts:

1. *Strategic Goals*—are concerned with altering the relationship between the firm and its environment (for example, revised objectives, new product/market scope). Examples of change goals of this type include 1 and 2 above.

2. *Technological Goals*—are directly related to changes in the technology of production, plant and equipment, and the like. An example of this type is goal 3 above.

3. *Structural Goals*—are concerned with alterations in reporting relationships, location of functions and authority, communication/decision processes, spans of control, formal incentive programs, and similar aspects of an organization's "anatomy" fall in this category. An example is goal 4 above. Structural change is elaborated upon below.

4. *Behavioral Goals*—aim initially at changing values, attitudes, beliefs, norms, interpersonal relationships, group behavior, intergroup behavior, and similar "humanistic" phenomena. An example is goal 5 above. Behavioral change is also elaborated upon in the next major section below.

5. *Program Goals*—focus on altering the objectives or structure of the technical implementation plans developed for marketing, production, R & D, and other task areas. An example is goal 6 above.

It should be noted that the various types of goals are *not* mutually exclusive, as two or more may be needed at the same time. Changes in organizational structure and behavior may be pursued in and of themselves, but changes in strategy and technology also will necessitate changes in structure and behavior for their successful accomplishment. For example, the strategic goal of "merger" usually will require some structural changes (for example, consolidation of some administrative functions) and also some behavioral changes (for example, transplanting sole identification with one organization to that of a newly merged concern). On the other hand, structural change may be appropriate given an *unchanged* strategy or technology, in order to increase administrative efficiency or effectiveness. The classifications outlined above should pinpoint just what type of change is necessary in a given situation.

Determination of Change Targets

As noted earlier, the initial adjustment or modification of *any* organizational part in response to external or internal forces creates reverberations throughout the total organization. It was also noted that when any of the types of change goals is acted upon, eventually some subsequent change along the structural and behavioral dimensions will have to take place. Thus, this stage of the change process makes it necessary to determine what must be changed within the organization in order to accomplish the goals established in the preceding step. In the case of a strategic change goal, almost all parts of the organization will require some internal adjustments in order to implement the new or modified strategy. Figure 8-1 provides a means for structuring an evaluation of the effects of the strategic change on other parts of the organization. As discussed above, an attempt should be made to predict the effects of such change *before* actual change goals are established; if this has been done, this stage requires only that the targets of change be evaluated in more detail to determine the specific adjustments that should be made.

Organization for Implementation

Decisions on goals and targets of change usually are made by top managers who may or may not be involved in the actual implementation. This task generally falls to the lower-level managers who have direct responsibility for the tasks and for the people who will be affected by the change. On the other hand, major change efforts may require the help of consultants who possess both the necessary expertise and objectivity. For instance, if the firm is seeking to change authoritarian personalities (a behavioral target) outside consultants with an extensive background in this particular problem area may be hired. If, however, adequate financial resources are not available for such consultants, the persons responsible for the implementation of the change might be the superiors of the authoritarian individuals in question. Two points are especially important at this stage of the change process: First, those responsible for effecting change must be carefully chosen in light of both the target and the resources available. Second, an explicit definition of their responsibilities and authority to implement change is mandatory in order to prevent subsequent conflict with those affected by a particular change.

Determination of Change Tactics and Channels of Influence

Change tactics and channels of influence refer to the methods used to implement change. Major structural tactics now utilized are (1) direct alteration of structural elements and (2) training in new task activities and interactions. Behavioral change tactics are those commonly labeled laboratory training, counseling, or therapy. The major channels of influence generally utilized are formal exercise of authority, personal persuasion, and various types of group decision-making processes. As indicated in Figure 8-2, selection of the appropriate mix of change tactics and channels of influence depends on three major factors: (1) targets of change, (2) one's "power distribution philosophy," and (3) various situational characteristics. The interactive nature of the three is evidenced in the following paragraphs, using merger as a case in point.

In a merger, some direct alteration of structure—for example, centralization of certain administrative functions—usually would be followed by an appropriate mix of techniques designed to effect desired changes in behavior. Although the selection of behavioral change tactics is assumed to follow the direct changing of structure in this example, this does *not* mean that structural change tactics should be applied without consideration for the individual. This depends on one's "power distribution philosophy." Thus, structural change can be accomplished under conditions of mutual goal setting and discussions to better assure acceptance of the change by those most affected. Those individuals being asked to change must feel that they have adequate power or control over their own situations.

Other aspects of a merger require behavioral change target selection as the first priority. Assume that the goal sought is related to gaining support for the proposed merger. Structural change is not called for here. Rather, the basic goal would be to persuade individuals that the benefits which would accrue to them should make all the adjustments worthwhile. Thus, a persuasive strategy may be called for, and the extent of the persuasion required will be a function of the extent to which the benefits are made clear and meaningful to the individuals involved (a prime example of the need to assess situational characteristics).

As indicated in Figure 8-2, many situational characteristics also determine the nature of the tactics and influence channels which should be used. For example, the extent to which employees are inherently flexible or open to change ultimately may determine the success of any change effort. Consequently, some attempt should be made to ascertain employee "states" in this respect so that tactics may be tailored accordingly.[90] Similarly, the extent to which employees identify with group norms will condition the extent to which informal group leaders may be used effectively as channels of influence. Also, a participative approach to change may or may not be appropriate, depending on the values and needs of affected employees. Finally, the technical exigencies of the particular change situation (for example, how fast must we move?) exert a great influence on the nature of the tactics and channels selected.

The foregoing has indicated the dynamic interrelationship among several major elements of the change process. Perhaps the most important point is that the proper selection of tactics and influence channels is a difficult task and depends greatly on the particular situation. Each change situation requires close scrutiny to ascertain the appropriate tactics and channels to be utilized.

---

[90] Factors associated with "openness to change" of employees are discussed more fully in the final section of this chapter.

Results of Change and Intervening Variables

The final direct link in the change process reflects the results of change efforts with respect to productivity, morale, and other indicators of performance. The relationship between performance results and the preceding elements of the scheme is extremely complex, however, and is mediated by many other variables. Figure 8-2 indicates three major groupings of such variables: (1) openness to change, (2) strategy characteristics, and (3) factors influencing identification with change needs and goals.

Strategy characteristics ("good" communications, use of the group medium as a vehicle for effecting change, allowance of sufficient time for adjustment, and top management commitment and support) are utilized to try to counteract any possible negative influences of the openness-to-change indicators on the extent of identification with change goals. The latter is also affected, however, by the extent to which (1) change goals are congruent with broader social values (societal and organizational) and with self-concepts; (2) the group or organization leader identifies with the need for change; (3) the employees feel they have a degree of control over the changes affecting them; and (4) the employees anticipate benefits from the necessary changes. The strategy characteristics operate to try to create these conditions, rather than, as in the case of the openness-to-change indicators, to try to *overcome* or counteract any possible negative influences on acceptance of change. It should be emphasized that the openness-to-change indicators represent *prior* states or conditions, as they reflect the inherent flexibility of affected employees. Thus, in effect they constitute parameters at this stage of the process. On the other hand, the group of "other factors" that influence identification represents variable states that may be *created* by change agents. Therefore, both classes of variables, as well as any of the individual variables within each class, operate to determine the extent of acceptance of change, and their influence on such acceptance may be modified by the strategy characteristics shown in Figure 8-2.

Even though management may be successful in cultivating employee identification with change goals, the ultimate success of any change program is, of course, the extent to which the goals themselves are accomplished. This is frequently very difficult to determine because causal influences other than those consciously designed in the change program may affect the end result.

Additional Remarks

It should be emphasized that the individualistic nature of change situations makes it impossible to specify a normative model which will apply in all cases. The major point is to recognize that mediating influences such as those discussed above do exist and do modify the degree of success that can be achieved with any change program.

One final point should be noted with respect to the interrelation of the major elements of the model. Although a definite sequential pattern of the elements is evident both in the model (Figure 8-2) and in the discussion, an attempt also has been made to indicate the interactions among the major elements. Thus, it was shown that the selection of tactics and influence channels requires a situational assessment of several factors, many of which may involve trade-offs. Similarly, the selection of change goals obviously does not result from a simple sequential process of perception, followed by the analysis of change causes and conditions. A complex process involving the consideration of various alternatives and associated combinations of resources required to adjust to change forces must take place before any final decisions are reached. However, reference to a sequential process will help to identify the basic interrelationships. More detailed interactions then can be developed to guide the implementation of change in any given situation.

RESISTANCE TO CHANGE

Much empirical research has been conducted on factors causing resistance to change. This section summarizes the major findings into three categories: (1) openness to change of employees, (2) method of implementation of change by management, and (3) other factors affecting the extent to which employees will identify with the goals of change.

Openness to Change

The major findings to be discussed here refer to the *flexibility* of employees, relative to their ability to accommodate change. The importance of looking at "individual openness" is indicated by Edgar H. Schein:

> . . . flexibility and capacity to change ultimately rest with the human resources of the organization. If the managers and employees are themselves flexible, the organizational blueprint can be consciously and rationally altered in the face of changing external situations . . . The psychological problem . . . becomes, therefore, how to develop in its personnel the kind of flexibility . . . needed . . . [91]

Three major indicators of openness to change have been identified for this discussion. First, the individual's *prior experience with change* has been found to be related to how well he or she will accept the need for changes. Individuals who have become accustomed to change will be more receptive than those who have worked in very stable and unchanging environments. However, Floyd C. Mann and Franklin W. Neff note that:

---

[91] Edgar H. Schein, *Organizational Psychology* (Englewood Cliffs, N.J.: Prentice-Hall, 1965), p. 16.

Major changes create a climate in which additional change can often be introduced without materially increasing problems. With the unfreezing of an organization, it is often possible to make changes which have been postponed because of the impact that such a single change would have. . . .[92]

Thus, an organizational climate that has been characterized by some unpredictability is generally better suited for the creation of flexibility and openness towards change on the part of employees. It should be noted, however, that prior *negative* experiences with change may contribute to change resistance in the same fashion as no prior experience with change does.

A second major influence on individual openness to change appears to be the *degree of trust* in top management, or in whoever initiates the change. The reputation of top management for fairness and honesty will be a primary factor in determining the response of employees to any plan for change. Based on a detailed analysis of four case histories, Mann and Neff conclude that reactions to organizational change are very much related to trust in management. Moreover, the degree of trust is significantly influenced by (1) the amount of information about the change provided to employees and (2) the amount of participation employees feel they will have concerning the changes to be made.[93] One can generally infer from case materials whether or not top management does have the trust of employees. A decision then can be made as to whether one feels that the proposed recommendations will be feasible and acceptable to lower-level employees.

A third major indicator of the extent to which employees are likely to be receptive to change is the *degree of satisfaction with existing conditions.* Of course employees who are dissatisfied with the situation generally will tend to welcome change. On the other hand, a comfortable and satisfactory condition of equilibrium may exist, which will cause employees to resist disruptive changes. It is possible, however, that a high state of morale or satisfaction with existing conditions also may contribute to *acceptance* of change. The same management responsible for creating those satisfactory conditions may command the respect of employees and thus their willingness to accept changes which promise to make things even better.

Method of Implementation of Change

As discussed earlier in this chapter, the manner in which change techniques are implemented in a given situation is a function of the targets selected, one's "power distribution" philosophy, the results of a situational assessment of employee openness to change, the values and needs of employees, and the tech-

---

[92] Floyd C. Mann and Franklin W. Neff, *Managing Major Change in Organizations* (Ann Arbor, Mich.: Foundation for Research on Human Behavior, 1961), p. 48.

[93] Mann and Neff, *Managing Major Change,* p. 70.

nical exigencies associated with particular change objectives. Certain common denominators related to successful implementation can be identified, however, and are discussed below.

First, the importance of frequent, open, and well-timed *communication of information about change* is well documented. Harriet O. Ronken and Paul R. Lawrence note that open communication is especially important during a period of change because:

> ... the social factors (such as membership in a group, the chances of working with people with complementary frames of reference, the assurance of durable and satisfying relationships, etc.) which would otherwise enhance the individual's ability to give and receive communications accurately are themselves upset during periods of change and uncertainty.[94]

There are two important points here. Management must effectively communicate the reasons for change to affected employees, as well as the benefits that should accrue as a result. Also, management must keep employees informed as to the progress of any change efforts and solicit the advice of the people affected concerning the best ways to make the changes.

Second, means must be provided to allow affected employees to be *involved,* or to *participate,* in both the planning and the implementation of the change process. The implication of all the studies and writing on participation is that greater identification with change needs and goals can be instilled in this way. However, much evidence exists to indicate that a participative approach is not appropriate for all employees and all situations and may, in fact, be resisted by some employees—findings to date again indicate the need for a *situational* approach in the choice of implementation tactics related to participation.[95]

Closely related to the desirability of participation in many situations is the *use of the group* as a vehicle for gaining acceptance for change. The basic rationale here is that the attitudes of individuals are anchored in a "social matrix" of co-workers, family, friends, and reference groups. Thus, the influence of the group as a whole may be used to persuade reluctant individuals. Use of the group mechanism also permits the interchange of ideas and misgivings about change objectives and procedures that might otherwise never be identified.

The fourth requisite for effective implementation of change techniques is related to the timing of change, particularly the *period allowed for adjustment*

---

[94] Harriet O. Ronken and Paul R. Lawrence, *Administering Change* (Boston: Harvard University, Division of Research, 1952), p. 318.

[95] Robert C. Shirley, "Analysis and Theoretical Synthesis of the Arguments Advanced For and Against a Participative Leadership Style" (Unpublished monograph, Northwestern University, 1969). This research report showed that approximately 40 intervening variables related to needs of employees, predispositions of supervisors and exigencies of the situation have been found to be related to the degree to which a participative style will be effective. Thus, such a style is obviously not a panacea for gaining employee acceptance of change and should be used only after an assessment of the situation.

to new structural and behavioral patterns. Usually, too little attention is given to the fact that much time is required to alter behavior patterns and to learn new skills. It is also important to allow time for a gradual accommodation to the idea of change before introducing it.

The final requisite for effective implementation is related to the *commitment and support by top management.* Employees will not support a major change effort if they do not perceive a real commitment to what is being attempted on the part of top management. If such a commitment is not visible, then employees will naturally attach less importance to the change goals.

Effective methods of implementation frequently can overcome any negative influences of those factors discussed earlier under the concept of "openness to change." Other factors can influence the extent of acceptance of change goals, however, and these are discussed in the following paragraphs.

Other Factors Affecting Acceptance of Change

Identification with, or acceptance of, the goals of change is partially a function of the openness to change of employees and of the manner in which change techniques are implemented. Certain other factors can contribute to acceptance of change, as well.

One particularly important influence on the acceptance of change is the *extent of identification by the group leader with the goals of change.* Here, the key implication appears to be the need to instill a "total organization" view in formal or informal group leaders, as distinct from a "subsystem" view. The following observation by Robert H. Guest is particularly appropriate here, and his basic reasoning may be applied to various levels within an organization:

> When an organization is a subordinate unit to a larger organization and when the patterns of internal relationships within the subordinate organization are similar to those linking it to the larger, changes leading to more successful performance within the subordinate organization will take place *after* there has been a change in the patterns of relationships (interactions and sentiments) linking the larger to the subordinate organization.[96]

Thus, it is helpful to convince formal or informal group leaders of the desirability of any proposed change so that other employees will be more receptive.

Another important influence is the *extent to which change goals are congruent with larger social values and with individual self-concepts.* With respect to congruency with social values, two different perspectives may be taken. First, Cyril Sofer has noted the importance of making sure that change goals are congruent with the cultural norms or values of the *organization* as an entity. In the study of changes required in internal operations of three British hospitals after the nationalization of health care delivery, he found that:

---

[96] Robert H. Guest, *Organizational Change: The Effect of Successful Leadership* (Homewood, Ill.: Richard D. Irwin and The Dorsey Press, 1962), pp. 153–54.

A variety of formal rules have been changed without corresponding adjustments occuring in the internal social structure and in the whole "culture" of the hospital. . . . A whole body of informal relationships, traditions, and values remains out of gear with formal arrangements.[97]

Second, the perspective on congruency with social values may take the total *society* as its reference point. Such a perspective is illustrated by Guest's observation that:

The process of successful change in a hierarchical organization will start and continue to the extent that the members perceive the behavior of superiors, peers, and subordinates to be more in keeping with the norms of behavior in the larger culture.[98]

With respect to the need for congruency of change goals with an individual's self-concept, Mann and Neff conclude the following:

A person who has worked in one job for a long time usually has come to see his job performance as consistent with the kind of person he sees himself to be. A major change in the way he is required to perform his job is likely to conflict with his concept of himself. A new adjustment, requiring some modification of his self-image, will have to occur before he will be effective and satisfied.[99]

A third major influence on acceptance of change is *the employee's evaluation of his control over the change situation.* This feeling of control will be influenced by the amount of information an employee has about the change and the amount of participation he or she feels will be permitted.[100] This supports the use of two devices discussed earlier: (1) clear communication of change goals and rationale and, frequently, (2) a participative approach to involve affected employees in planning and implementing change.

Finally, a fourth major class of influences on acceptance of change goals encompasses the *employee's anticipated benefits from the change.* The list of anticipated benefits relevant to change acceptance covers the major dimensions of morale or job satisfaction (pay, duties, working conditions, chances for personal growth and development, and relationship with supervisor). If employees perceive positive effects of change on these various dimensions at the time change plans are made known, then positive attitudes are likely to be expressed about the change goals.

---

[97] Cyril Sofer, "Reactions to Administrative Change," *Human Relations* 8 (1955), p. 313.

[98] Guest, *Organizational Change,* p. 117.

[99] Mann and Neff, *Managing Major Change,* p. 23.

[100] Ibid., p. 70.

SUMMARY

The first part of this chapter outlined the major phases of the organizational change process. Each phase was discussed in some detail to provide some general guides for understanding the numerous complexities of change.

The next part of the chapter examined reasons for resistance to change. It found that a greater ability to adjust to change is usually found in employees who exhibit the following characteristics:

1. They have had frequent and positive experiences with change.
2. They trust the top management personnel or others who initiate major changes.
3. They are dissatisfied with existing conditions (unless a satisfaction with existing conditions is reflected by a high degree of trust in top management).

The chapter also showed that certain characteristics related to the manner in which change techniques are implemented tend to increase the probability of acceptance to change:

1. Open and well-timed communication of information about changes.
2. Provision of means by which employees can participate in both the planning and implementation of change (depending on various situational characteristics).
3. Use of the group as a vehicle for influencing positive attitudes toward change.
4. Allowance of sufficient time for adjustment to required changes.
5. Evidence of commitment and support of proposed changes by top management.

Although these characteristics of the change implementation process may serve to overcome resistance among employees who are not as open to change (for example, those who may have experienced negative effects of major changes in the past), certain other factors also were seen as conditioning the final extent of acceptance to change in any given situation:

1. The extent to which group leaders identify with the need for changes affecting group members.
2. The extent to which change goals are perceived by employees to be congruent with larger social values (both within and outside the organization) and with individual self-concepts.
3. The employee's evaluation of his or her control over the changes.
4. The employee's anticipated benefits from proposed changes.

Index

Aggregate output:
  description of, 150
  determinants of, 150–151
  planning of, 150–151. *See also*
Production/operations function

Brand strategies:
  brand extension, 126–127
  multibrand entries, 126
Break-even analysis, 198–203
  break-even point, 200
  fixed costs, 199
  total revenue, 200
  variable costs, 199
Break-even point, calculation of,
  200

Capability audit. *See* Resource
  audit
Case analysis, 4–20
  framework for, 6–7
  stages of, 6–20
    analysis of data, 11–17
    classification of data, 6–11
    formulation of
      recommendations, 18–19,
      196–198
    identification of problems,
      17–18, 195–196
Competitive advantage, 61–62
Computer simulation, 4–5
Corporate strategy. *See* Strategy
Credit decisions, 109–110. *See also*
  Marketing

Discounts, 106–107
  determinants of, 106–107
  types of, 106. *See also* Marketing
Distribution channel structure,
  104–105. *See also* Marketing
Dividend payment, level of, 174–176
  description of, 174
  determinants of, 175–176
  stability of, 175
  stockholder preferences for, 176.
  See also Financial function
DuPont system of financial control,
  196–197

Environmental forces:
  analysis of, 37–39
  impact on strategy of, 31–39
  types of:
    economic, 31–34
    political/legal, 36
    social, 34–35
    technological, 35–36. *See also*
      Strategy

Facilities layout, 144–147
  determinants of, 145–147
  process layout, 145
  product layout, 145. *See also*
  Production/operations function
Financial analysis, 177–203
  action plans in, 196–198
  diagnosis of problems in,
    195–196
  financial statements in, 178

industry averages in, 182
leverage indicators in, 181
liquidity indicators in, 181
profitability indicators in, 178–181
ratio analysis in:
  Dun & Bradstreet Ratios,
    183–194
  types of ratios, 178–182
trend analysis in, 182
Financial function:
  decision variables in, 172–176
  description of, 171–172

General managers:
  definition of, 4n
  perspective of, for
    problem-solving, 11–16
  tasks of, 3–4, 13, 17, 21–23
Growth strategies, 97–99
  conglomerative, 99
  integrative, 99
  intensive, 98

Innovation, organizing for, 223–239
  collaboration required in, 224–226
  conflict resolution in, 237
  dimensions of specialization of,
    226–229
  factors affecting success of, 230,
    238
  methods of coordination of,
    231–237
Inventory levels, of raw materials
and work-in-process,
  151–152
  description of, 151
  determinants of, 151–152. See
  also Production/operations
  function

Job design and process planning.
See Process planning and job
  design

Manufacturing decisions, 159–168
  alternatives in, 160–163
  design trade-offs in, 159–160
  limitations on, 167
  policy determination of, 164–166
Market research, 38, 102

Market segmentation, 123–124
  examples of, 123
  dangers of, 124
Marketing, 95–133
  definition of, 95–96
  objectives of, 118
  strategies of, 121–133
  types of decisions in, 96–115
    credit, 109–110
    discounts, 106–107
    distribution channels, 104–105
    packaging, 110
    physical distribution, 110–114
    price, 105–106
    product research and
      development, 97–101
    promotion, 107–109
  vision in, 117–121
Marketing information systems, 102
Matrix organization. See
Organizational structure
Mergers and acquisitions, 129–130

Organizational change, 243–257
  concept of, 243–244
  forces causing, 245
  goals of, 247–248
  implementation of, 249–251,
    253–255
  openness to, 252–253, 255–256
  process of, 245–247
  resistance to, 252–256
  targets of, 249
Organizational decisions:
  functionally dependent, 14–16
  functionally independent, 14–16
  multifunctional coordinative, 13–15
  strategic, 13–15
Organizational dimensions, 6–12
  behavioral, 10–11
  environmental, 8
  program, 9
  strategic, 8–9
  structural, 9–10
Organizational structure, 207–222
  factors affecting evolution of,
    208–209
  matrix form of, 219–221
  project management form of,
    215–219

relationship of, to strategy, 207, 209, 211, 214, 219, 221
types of:
divisional, 212–215
functional, 211–212
"small," 210–211

Packaging decisions, 110. *See also* Marketing
Personal values, 64–70
impact on strategy of, 65–69
resolution of conflicts in, 69–70
types of:
culturally derived, 65–67
organizationally derived, 67.
See also Strategy
Physical distribution, 110–114. *See also* Marketing
Plant location and capacity, 140–144
description of, 140–141
determinants of, 141–144
objectives of, 141. *See also*
Production/operations function
Price determination, 105–106
approaches to, 105
determinants of, 105–106
objectives, 105–106. *See also*
Marketing
Process planning and job design, 147–150
description of, 147
determinants of, 147–150
impact of technological change on, 148–150. *See also*
Production/operations function
Product life cycle, 100–101. *See also* Marketing
Product research and development, 97–101
determinants of, 100
reasons for, 99–100. *See also*
Marketing; Product life cycle
Production/operations function:
decision variables in, 138–152
description of, 137–138
types of systems, 139

Production smoothing, 150
Project management. *See*
Organizational structure
Promotion, 107–109
determinants of, 109
objectives of, 107–108
product publicity as form of, 108–109. *See also* Marketing

Raw materials inventory. *See*
Inventory levels
Resistance to change. *See*
Organizational change
Resource audit, 59–61, 72–92

Social responsibility, 34–35. *See also* Environmental forces
Strategic decisions, 8–9, 13–14, 15, 27–30. *See also* Strategy
Strategy:
definition of, 27–31
determinants of, 30
impact of environmental forces, 31–39
impact of personal values, 64–70
impact of, on manufacturing function, 154–168
process of formulation of, 40–55
adaptive mode of, 43–45
entrepreneurial mode of, 40–43
planning mode of, 45–48
strategic decisions identified, 8–9, 13–14, 15, 27–30
Synergy, 62–64

Working capital, level of, 172–174
cash flow forecast of, 173
cash management of, 173
cash preference of management, 173
determinants of, 172–174
impact of credit on, 174. *See also*
Financial function
Work-in-process inventory. *See*
Inventory levels